HEROES AND VILLAIN

BUSHIDO™

THE WAY OF THE WARRIOR

WRITTEN BY:
ROB LEVIN

ART BY:
JESSADA SUTTHI
FOR STUDIO HIVE

PUBLISHED BY TOP COW PRODUCTIONS, INC. LOS ANGELES

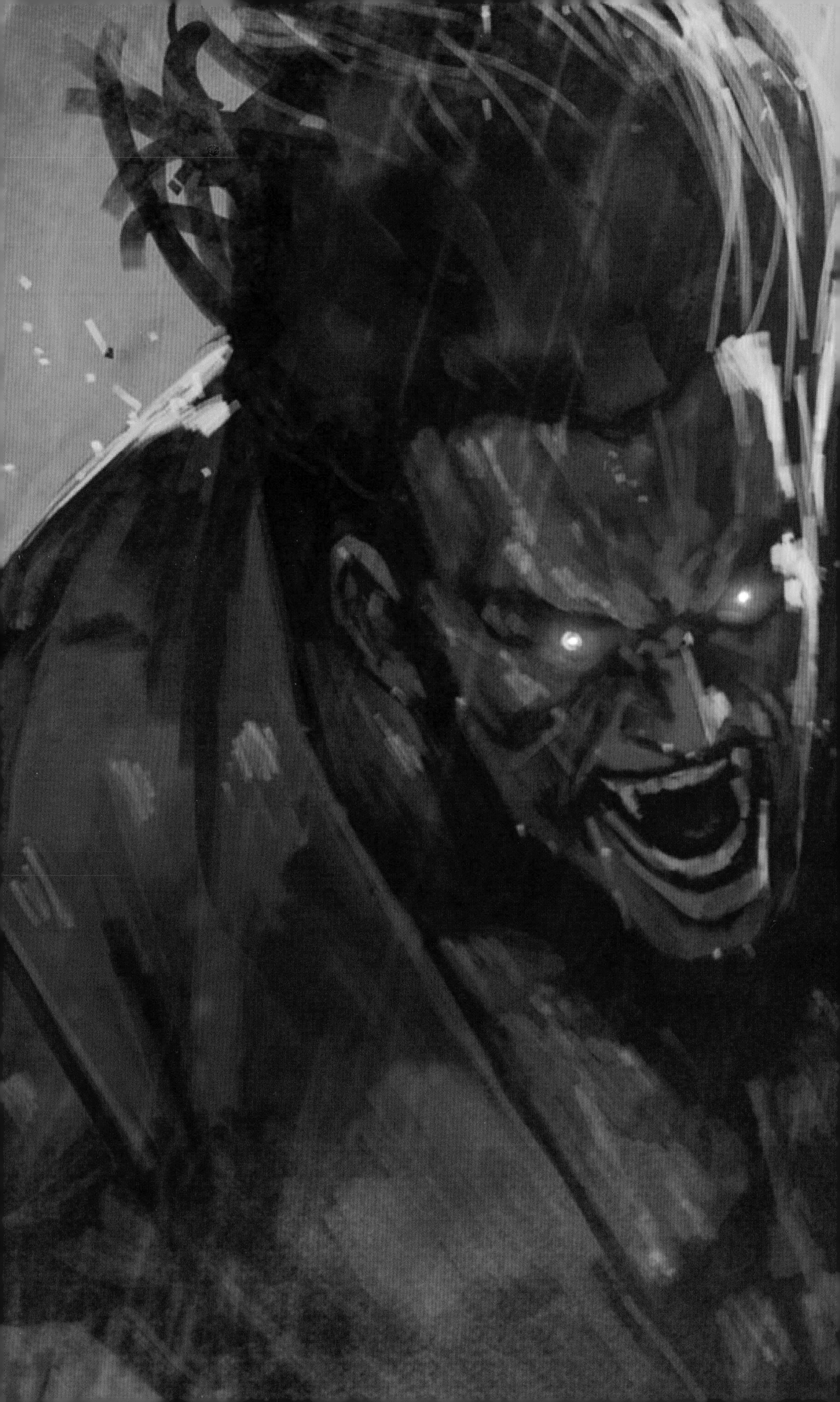

HEROES AND VILLAINS ENTERTAINMENT

BUSHIDO
THE WAY OF THE WARRIOR

WRITTEN BY:
ROB LEVIN

ART BY:
JESSADA SUTTHI
FOR STUDIO HIVE

ART DIRECTOR:
SKAN SRISUWAN

LETTERED BY:
TROY PETERI

BUSHIDO IS INSPIRED BY THE SCREENPLAY *'RISING SUN'* BY SHAHIN CHANDRASOMA

COVER ART BY - STUDIO HIVE

ORIGINAL EDITIONS EDITED BY:
BRYAN ROUNTREE, BETSY GONIA, & MATT HAWKINS

FOR THIS EDITION BOOK DESIGN AND LAYOUT BY: TRICIA RAMOS

FOR TOP COW PRODUCTIONS, INC.
MARC SILVESTRI - CEO
MATT HAWKINS - PRESIDENT & COO
BETSY GONIA - MANAGING EDITOR
ELENA SALCEDO - OPERATIONS MANAGER
RYAN CADY - EDITORIAL ASSISTANT
VINCENT VALENTINE - PRODUCTION ASSISTANT

FOR HEROES AND VILLAINS ENTERTAINMENT
MARKUS GOERG, DICK HILLENBRAND,
MIKHAIL NAYFELD, & ROBERT WATTS
FOR RIGHTS INQUIRIES, CONTACT
HEROES AND VILLAINS ENTERTAINMENT:
323-850-2990
INFO@HEROESANDVILLAINS.COM

To find the comic shop
nearest you, call:
1-888-COMICBOOK

Want more info? Check out:
www.topcow.com
for news & exclusive Top Cow merchandise!

IMAGE COMICS, INC.
Robert Kirkman – Chief Operating Officer
Erik Larsen – Chief Financial Officer
Todd McFarlane – President
Marc Silvestri – Chief Executive Officer
Jim Valentino – Vice-President
Eric Stephenson – Publisher
Ron Richards – Director of Business Development
Jennifer de Guzman – Director of Trade Book Sales
Kat Salazar – Director of PR & Marketing
Corey Murphy – Director of Retail Sales
Jeremy Sullivan – Director of Digital Sales
Emilio Bautista – Sales Assistant
Branwyn Bigglestone – Senior Accounts Manager
Emily Miller – Accounts Manager
Jessica Ambriz – Administrative Assistant
Tyler Shainline – Events Coordinator
David Brothers – Content Manager
Jonathan Chan – Production Manager
Drew Gill – Art Director
Meredith Wallace – Print Manager
Monica Garcia – Senior Production Artist
Addison Duke – Production Artist
Tricia Ramos – Production Assistant
IMAGECOMICS.COM

BUSHIDO VOLUME 1 TRADE PAPERBACK.
DECEMBER 2014. FIRST PRINTING. ISBN: 978-1-63215-022-6. $19.99 U.S.D.

PUBLISHED BY IMAGE COMICS, INC. OFFICE OF PUBLICATION: 2001 CENTER STREET, 6TH FLOOR, BERKELEY, CA 94704. BUSHIDO 2014
HEROES AND VILLAINS ENTERTAINMENT. ALL RIGHTS RESERVED. ORIGINALLY PUBLISHED IN SINGLE ISSUE FORMAT AS BUSHIDO #1-5.
"BUSHIDO," THE BUSHIDO LOGOS, AND THE LIKENESS OF ALL FEATURED CHARACTERS ARE REGISTERED TRADEMARKS OF HEROES AND
VILLAINS ENTERTAINMENT. ANY RESEMBLANCE TO ACTUAL PERSONS (LIVING OR DEAD), EVENT, INSTITUTIONS, OR LOCALES, WITHOUT
SATIRIC INTENT IS COINCIDENTAL. NO PORTION OF THIS PUBLICATION MAY BE REPRODUCED OR TRANSMITTED, IN ANY FORM OR BY
ANY MEANS, WITHOUT THE EXPRESS WRITTEN PERMISSION OF HEROES AND VILLAINS ENTERTAINMENT. PRINTED IN SOUTH KOREA.

Chapter One

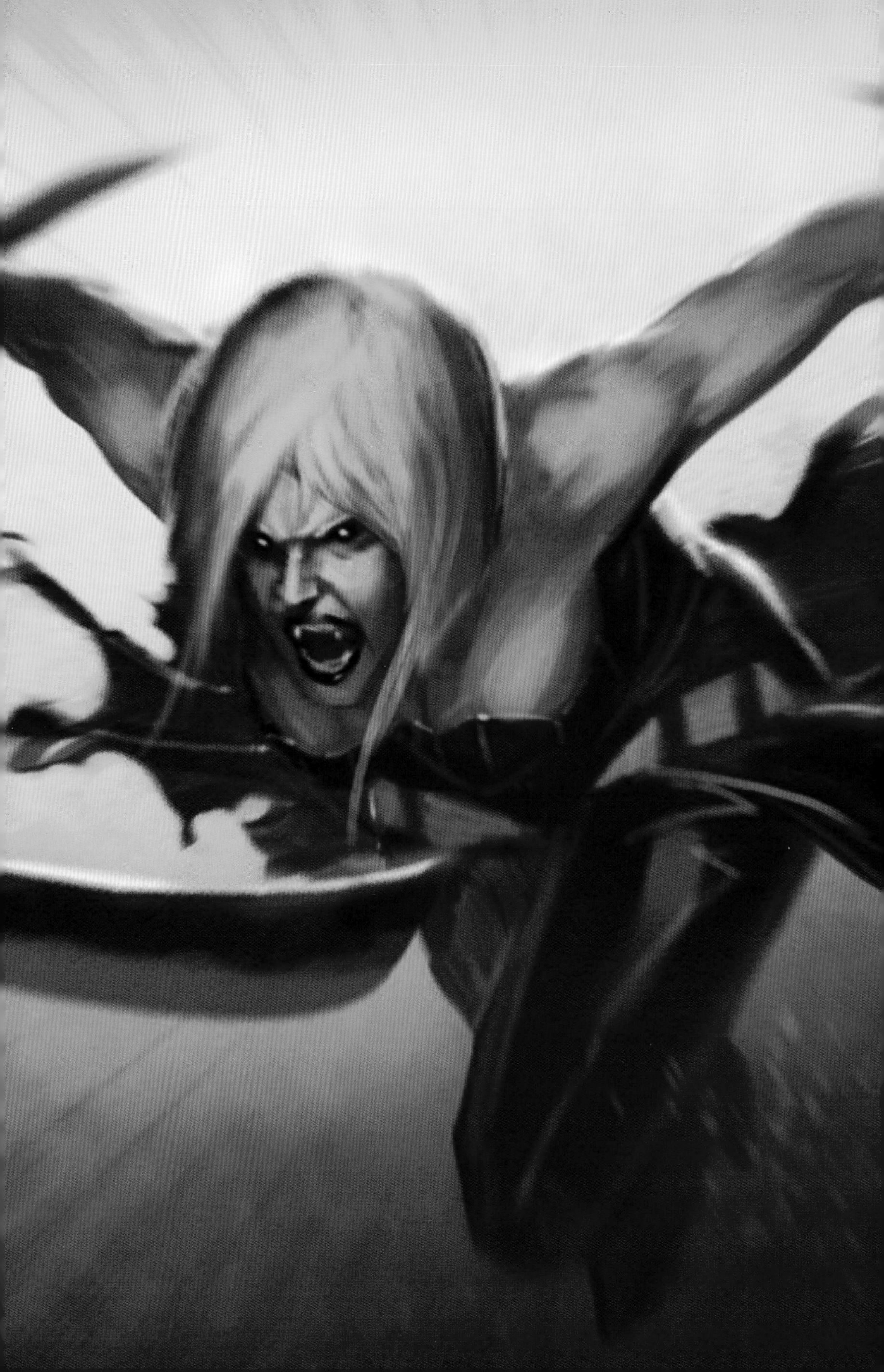

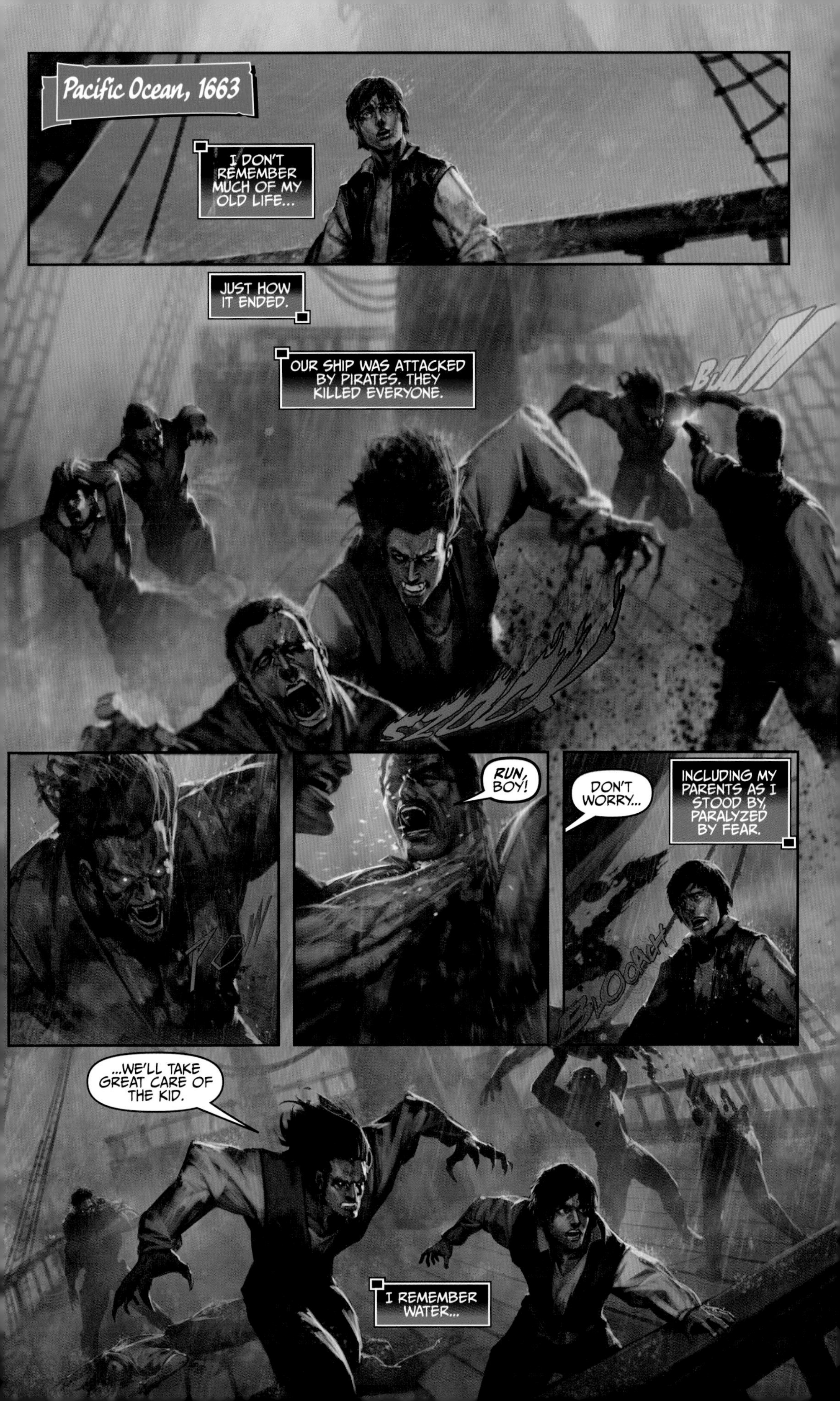
Pacific Ocean, 1663
I DON'T REMEMBER MUCH OF MY OLD LIFE...
JUST HOW IT ENDED.
OUR SHIP WAS ATTACKED BY PIRATES. THEY KILLED EVERYONE.
RUN, BOY!
DON'T WORRY...
INCLUDING MY PARENTS AS I STOOD BY, PARALYZED BY FEAR.
...WE'LL TAKE GREAT CARE OF THE KID.
I REMEMBER WATER...

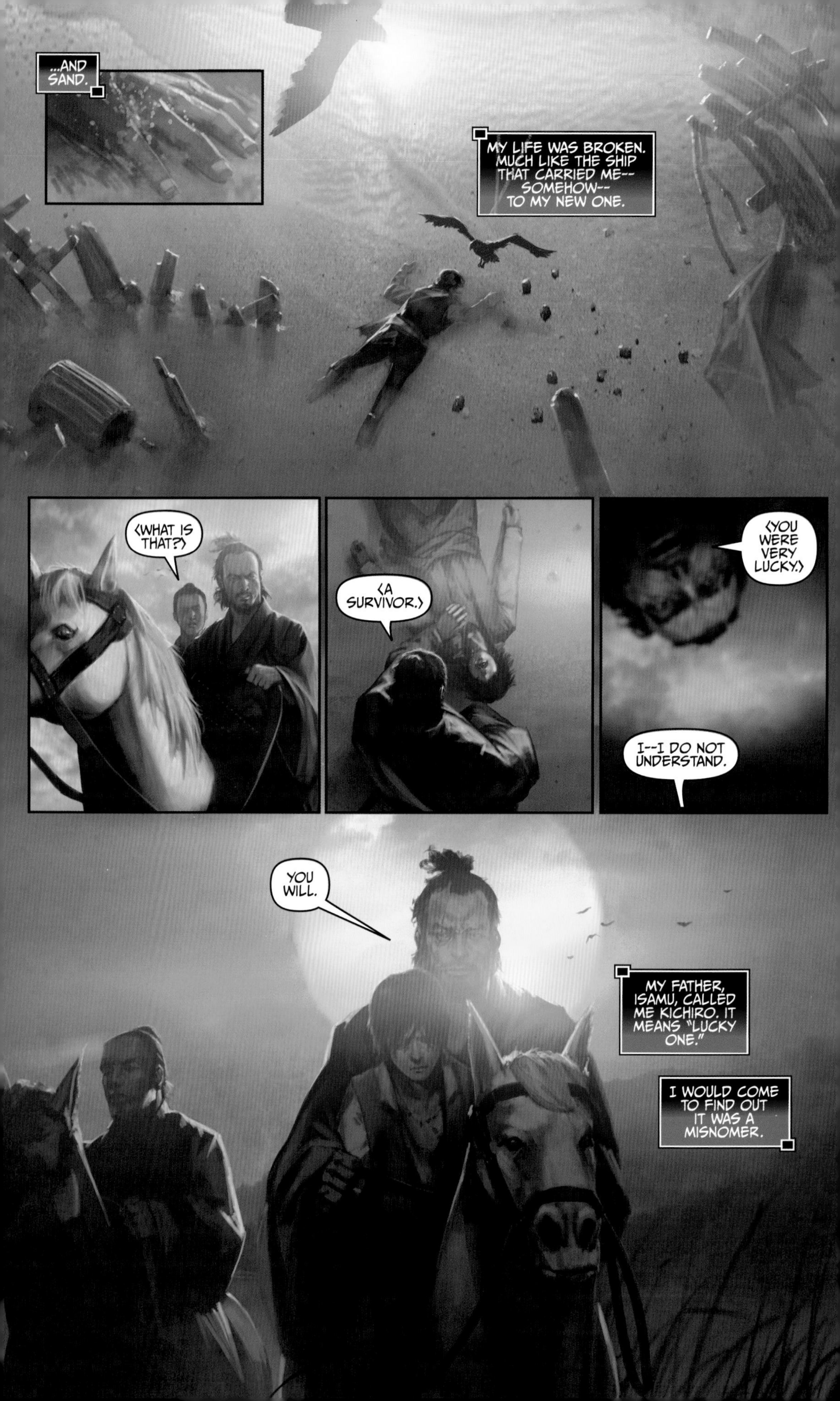
...AND SAND.
MY LIFE WAS BROKEN. MUCH LIKE THE SHIP THAT CARRIED ME-- SOMEHOW-- TO MY NEW ONE.
<WHAT IS THAT?>
<A SURVIVOR.>
<YOU WERE VERY LUCKY.>
I--I DO NOT UNDERSTAND.
YOU WILL.
MY FATHER, ISAMU, CALLED ME KICHIRO. IT MEANS "LUCKY ONE."
I WOULD COME TO FIND OUT IT WAS A MISNOMER.

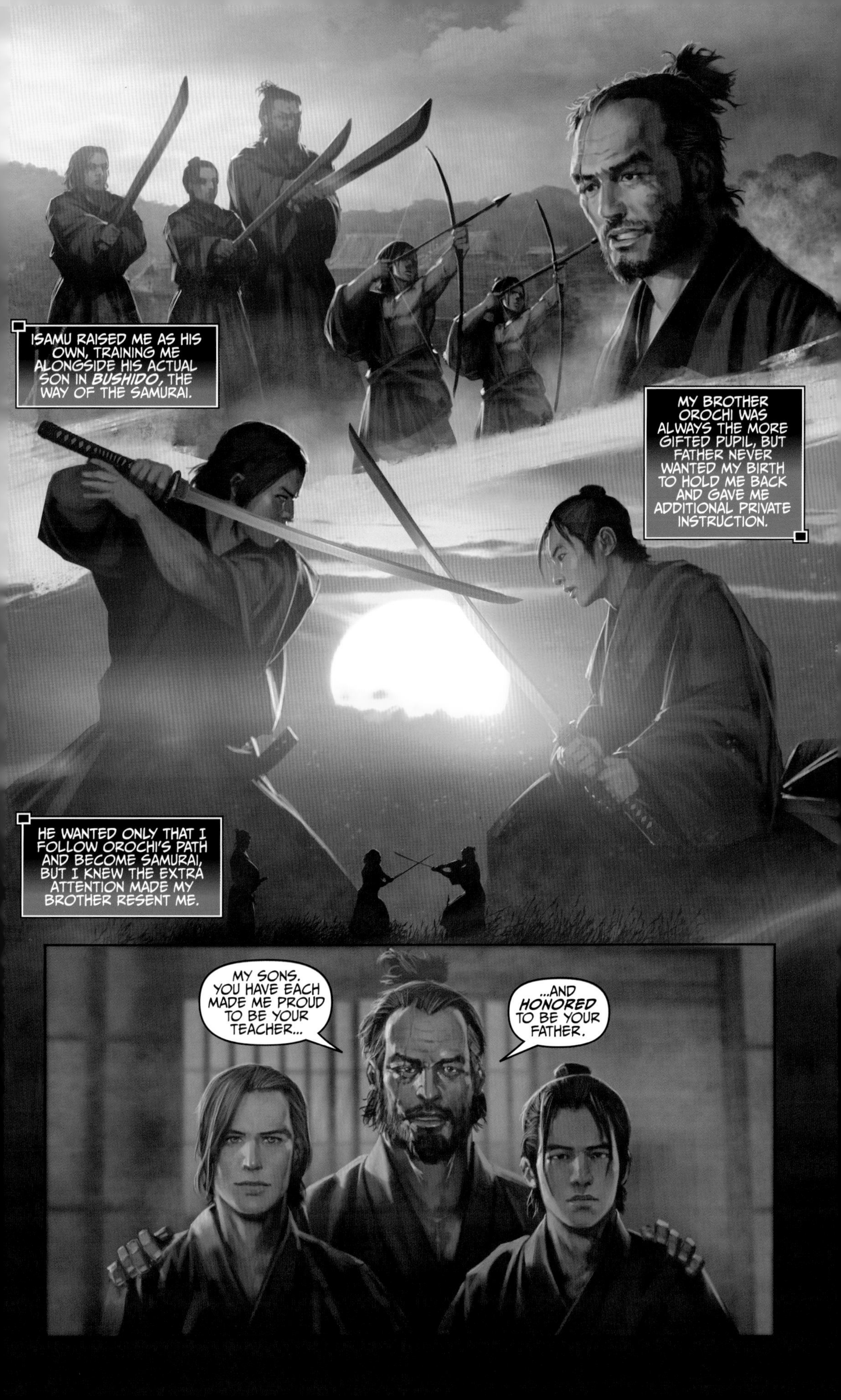
ISAMU RAISED ME AS HIS OWN, TRAINING ME ALONGSIDE HIS ACTUAL SON IN *BUSHIDO*, THE WAY OF THE SAMURAI.
MY BROTHER OROCHI WAS ALWAYS THE MORE GIFTED PUPIL, BUT FATHER NEVER WANTED MY BIRTH TO HOLD ME BACK AND GAVE ME ADDITIONAL PRIVATE INSTRUCTION.
HE WANTED ONLY THAT I FOLLOW OROCHI'S PATH AND BECOME SAMURAI, BUT I KNEW THE EXTRA ATTENTION MADE MY BROTHER RESENT ME.
MY SONS. YOU HAVE EACH MADE ME PROUD TO BE YOUR TEACHER...
...AND *HONORED* TO BE YOUR FATHER.

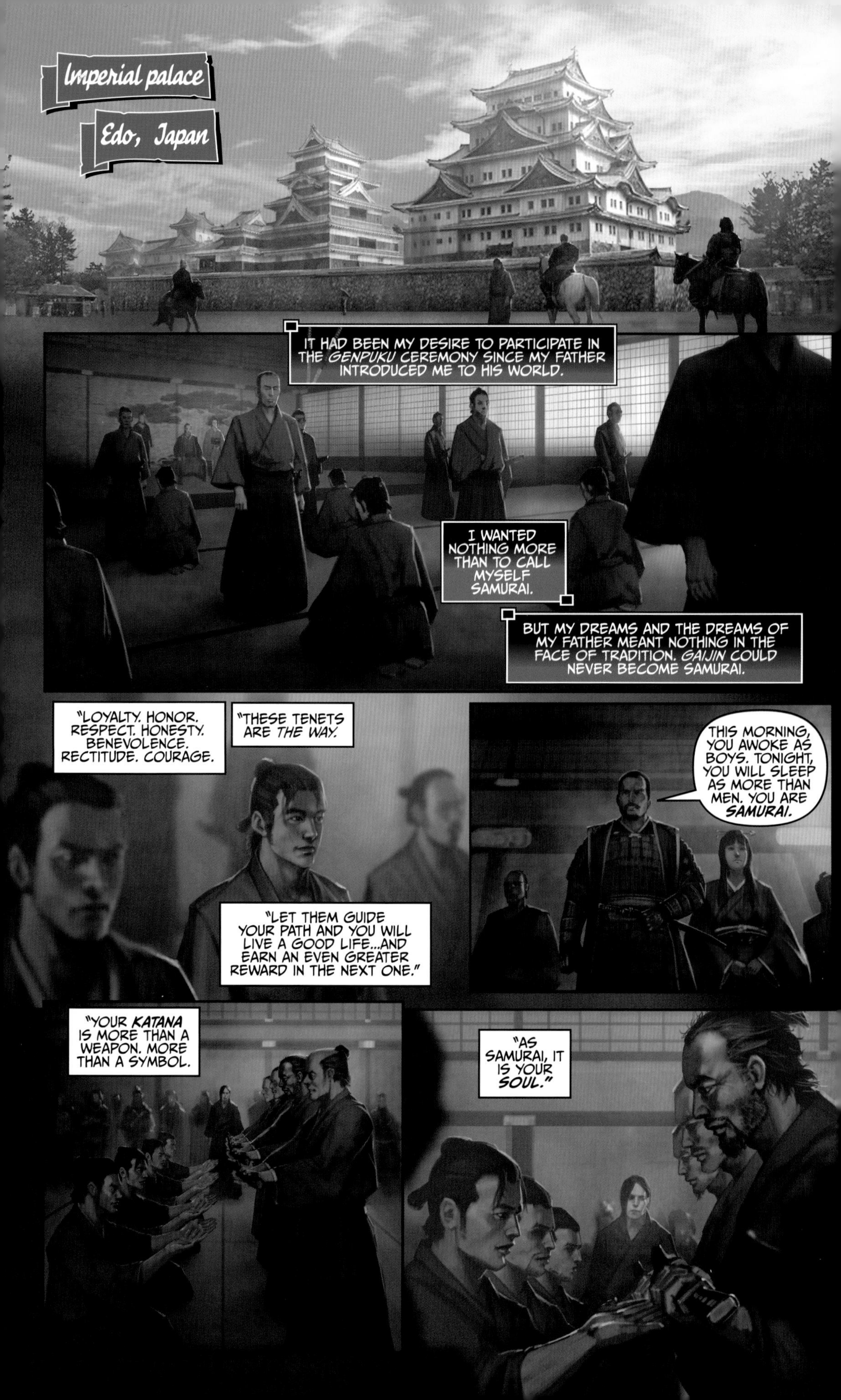
Imperial palace
Edo, Japan
IT HAD BEEN MY DESIRE TO PARTICIPATE IN THE GENPUKU CEREMONY SINCE MY FATHER INTRODUCED ME TO HIS WORLD.
I WANTED NOTHING MORE THAN TO CALL MYSELF SAMURAI.
BUT MY DREAMS AND THE DREAMS OF MY FATHER MEANT NOTHING IN THE FACE OF TRADITION. GAIJIN COULD NEVER BECOME SAMURAI.
"LOYALTY. HONOR. RESPECT. HONESTY. BENEVOLENCE. RECTITUDE. COURAGE.
"THESE TENETS ARE THE WAY.
"LET THEM GUIDE YOUR PATH AND YOU WILL LIVE A GOOD LIFE...AND EARN AN EVEN GREATER REWARD IN THE NEXT ONE."
THIS MORNING, YOU AWOKE AS BOYS. TONIGHT, YOU WILL SLEEP AS MORE THAN MEN. YOU ARE SAMURAI.
"YOUR KATANA IS MORE THAN A WEAPON. MORE THAN A SYMBOL.
"AS SAMURAI, IT IS YOUR SOUL."

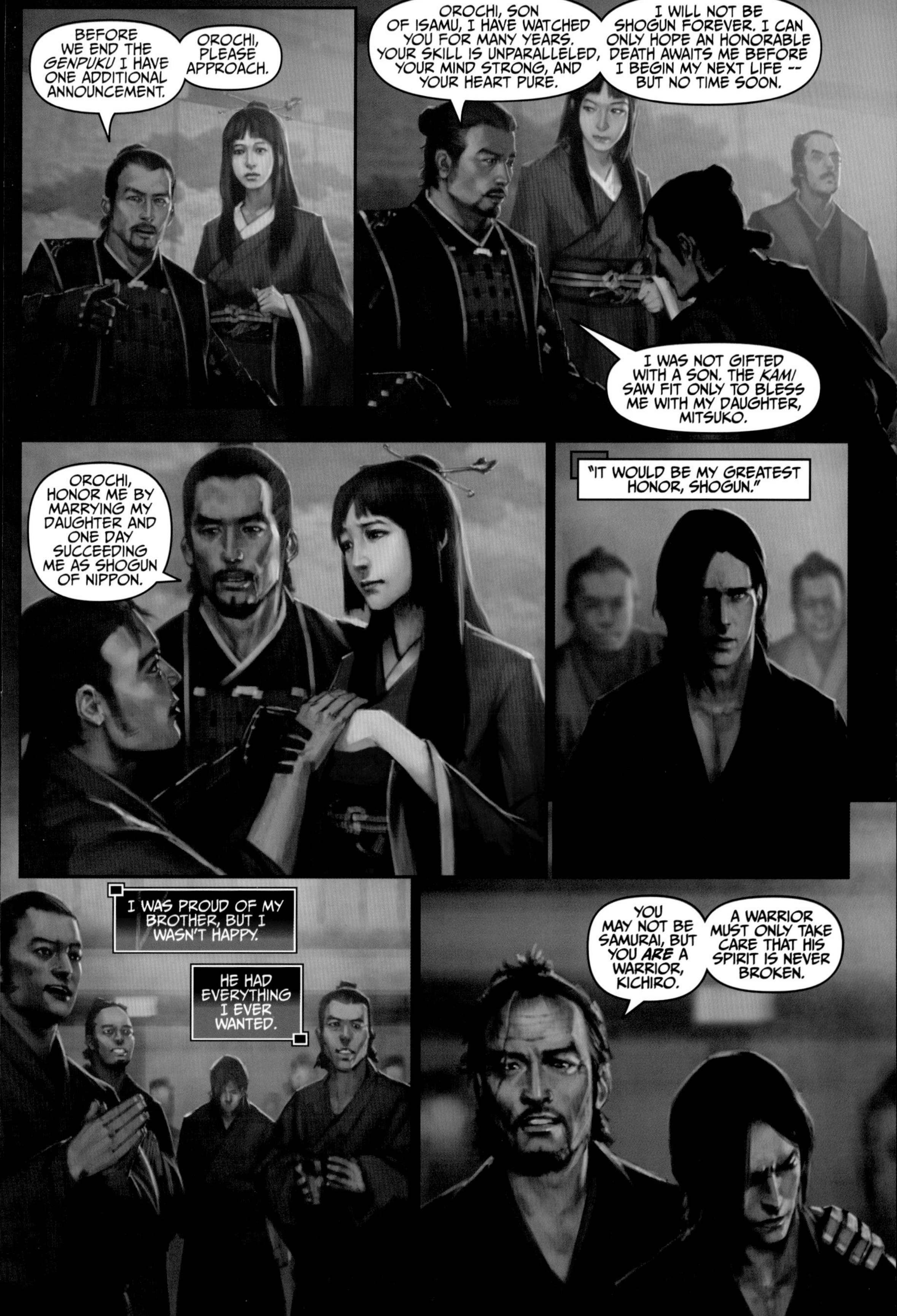
BEFORE WE END THE *GENPUKU* I HAVE ONE ADDITIONAL ANNOUNCEMENT.
OROCHI, PLEASE APPROACH.
OROCHI, SON OF ISAMU, I HAVE WATCHED YOU FOR MANY YEARS. YOUR SKILL IS UNPARALLELED, YOUR MIND STRONG, AND YOUR HEART PURE.
I WILL NOT BE SHOGUN FOREVER. I CAN ONLY HOPE AN HONORABLE DEATH AWAITS ME BEFORE I BEGIN MY NEXT LIFE -- BUT NO TIME SOON.
I WAS NOT GIFTED WITH A SON. THE *KAMI* SAW FIT ONLY TO BLESS ME WITH MY DAUGHTER, MITSUKO.
OROCHI, HONOR ME BY MARRYING MY DAUGHTER AND ONE DAY SUCCEEDING ME AS SHOGUN OF NIPPON.
"IT WOULD BE MY GREATEST HONOR, SHOGUN."
I WAS PROUD OF MY BROTHER, BUT I WASN'T HAPPY.
HE HAD EVERYTHING I EVER WANTED.
YOU MAY NOT BE SAMURAI, BUT YOU ***ARE*** A WARRIOR, KICHIRO.
A WARRIOR MUST ONLY TAKE CARE THAT HIS SPIRIT IS NEVER BROKEN.

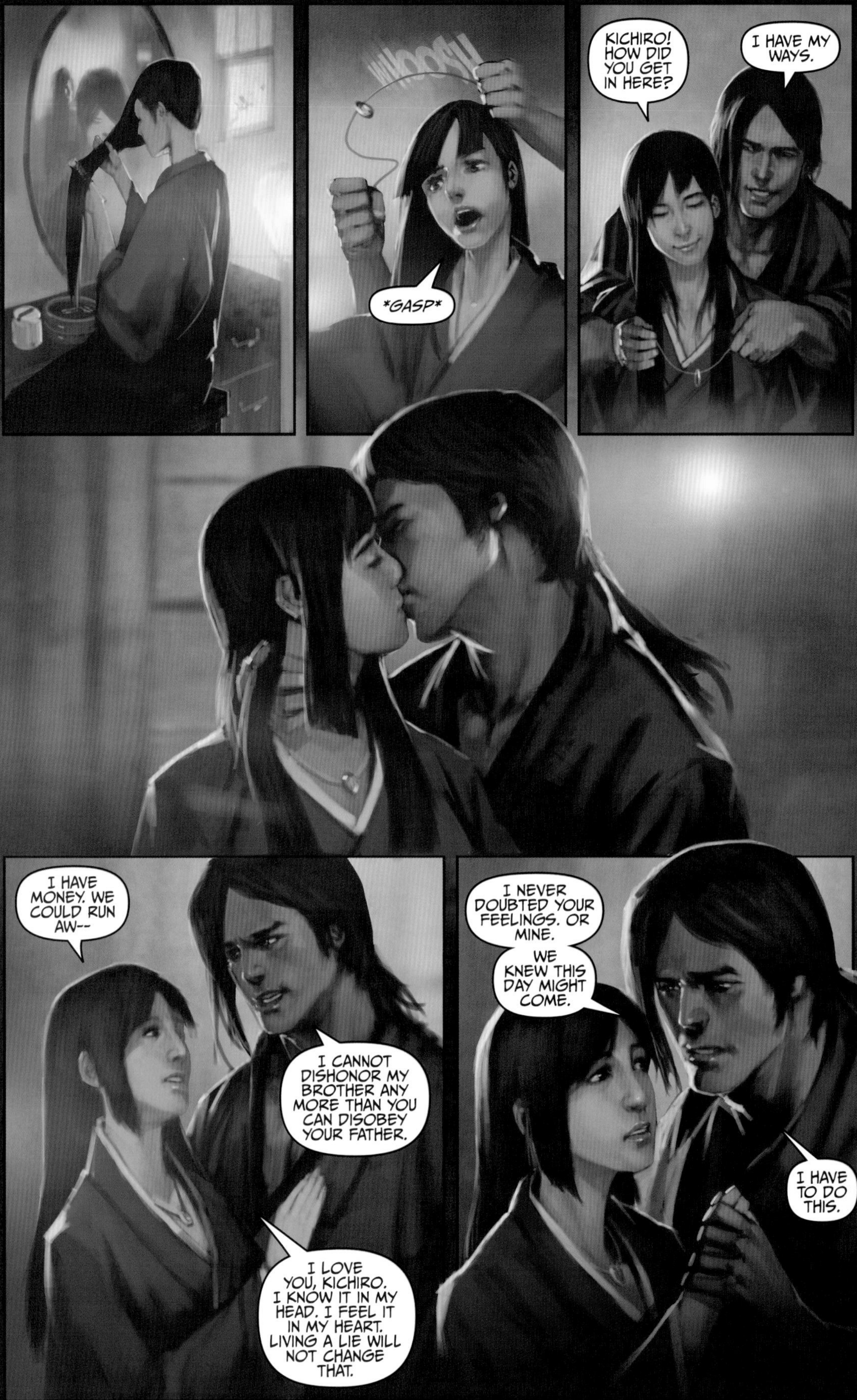
GASP
KICHIRO! HOW DID YOU GET IN HERE?
I HAVE MY WAYS.
I HAVE MONEY. WE COULD RUN AW--
I CANNOT DISHONOR MY BROTHER ANY MORE THAN YOU CAN DISOBEY YOUR FATHER.
I LOVE YOU, KICHIRO. I KNOW IT IN MY HEAD. I FEEL IT IN MY HEART. LIVING A LIE WILL NOT CHANGE THAT.
I NEVER DOUBTED YOUR FEELINGS. OR MINE.
WE KNEW THIS DAY MIGHT COME.
I HAVE TO DO THIS.

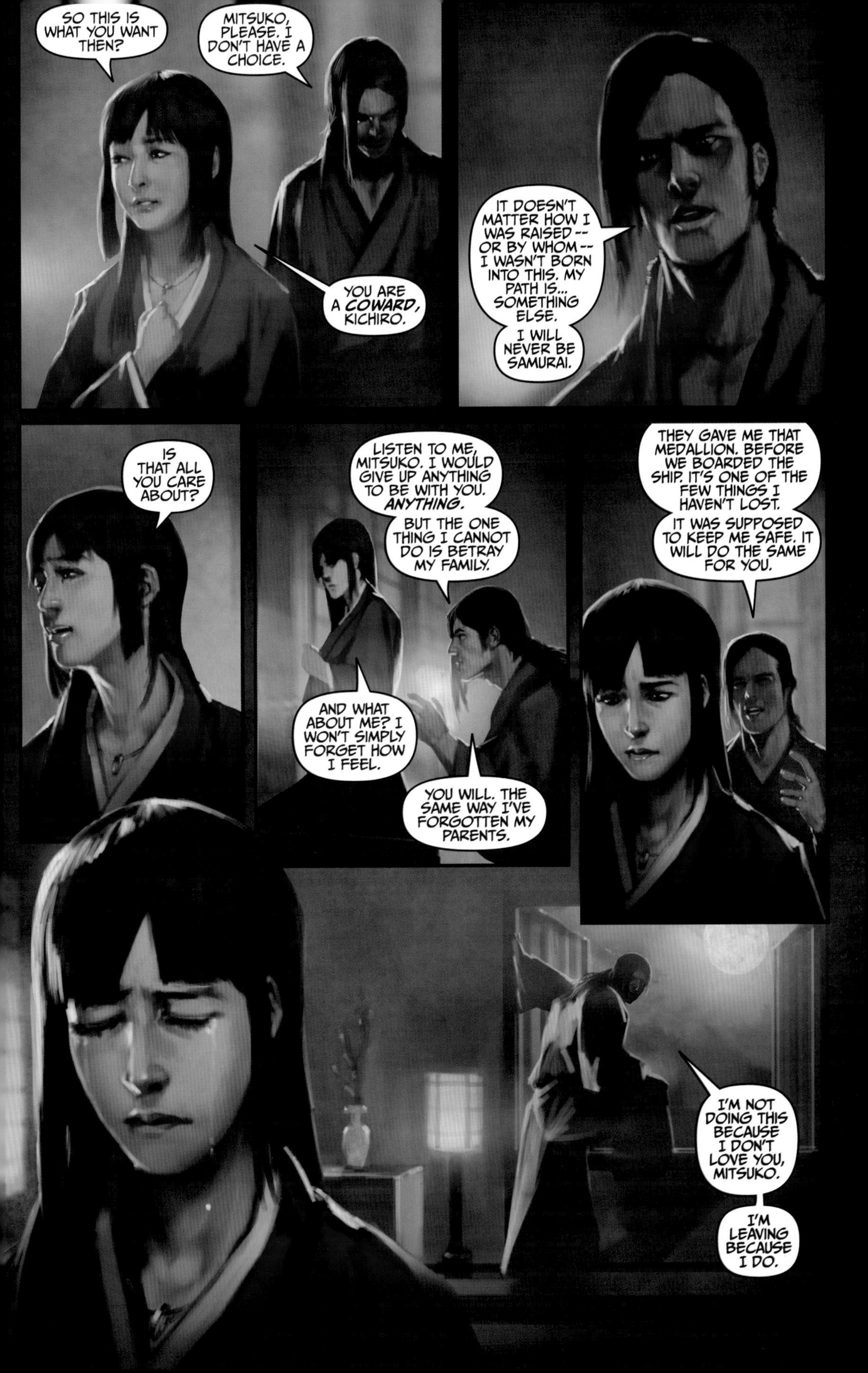
SO THIS IS WHAT YOU WANT THEN?
MITSUKO, PLEASE. I DON'T HAVE A CHOICE.
YOU ARE A *COWARD,* KICHIRO.
IT DOESN'T MATTER HOW I WAS RAISED -- OR BY WHOM -- I WASN'T BORN INTO THIS. MY PATH IS... SOMETHING ELSE.
I WILL NEVER BE SAMURAI.
IS THAT ALL YOU CARE ABOUT?
LISTEN TO ME, MITSUKO. I WOULD GIVE UP ANYTHING TO BE WITH YOU. *ANYTHING.*
BUT THE ONE THING I CANNOT DO IS BETRAY MY FAMILY.
AND WHAT ABOUT ME? I WON'T SIMPLY FORGET HOW I FEEL.
YOU WILL. THE SAME WAY I'VE FORGOTTEN MY PARENTS.
THEY GAVE ME THAT MEDALLION. BEFORE WE BOARDED THE SHIP. IT'S ONE OF THE FEW THINGS I HAVEN'T LOST.
IT WAS SUPPOSED TO KEEP ME SAFE. IT WILL DO THE SAME FOR YOU.
I'M NOT DOING THIS BECAUSE I DON'T LOVE YOU, MITSUKO.
I'M LEAVING BECAUSE I DO.

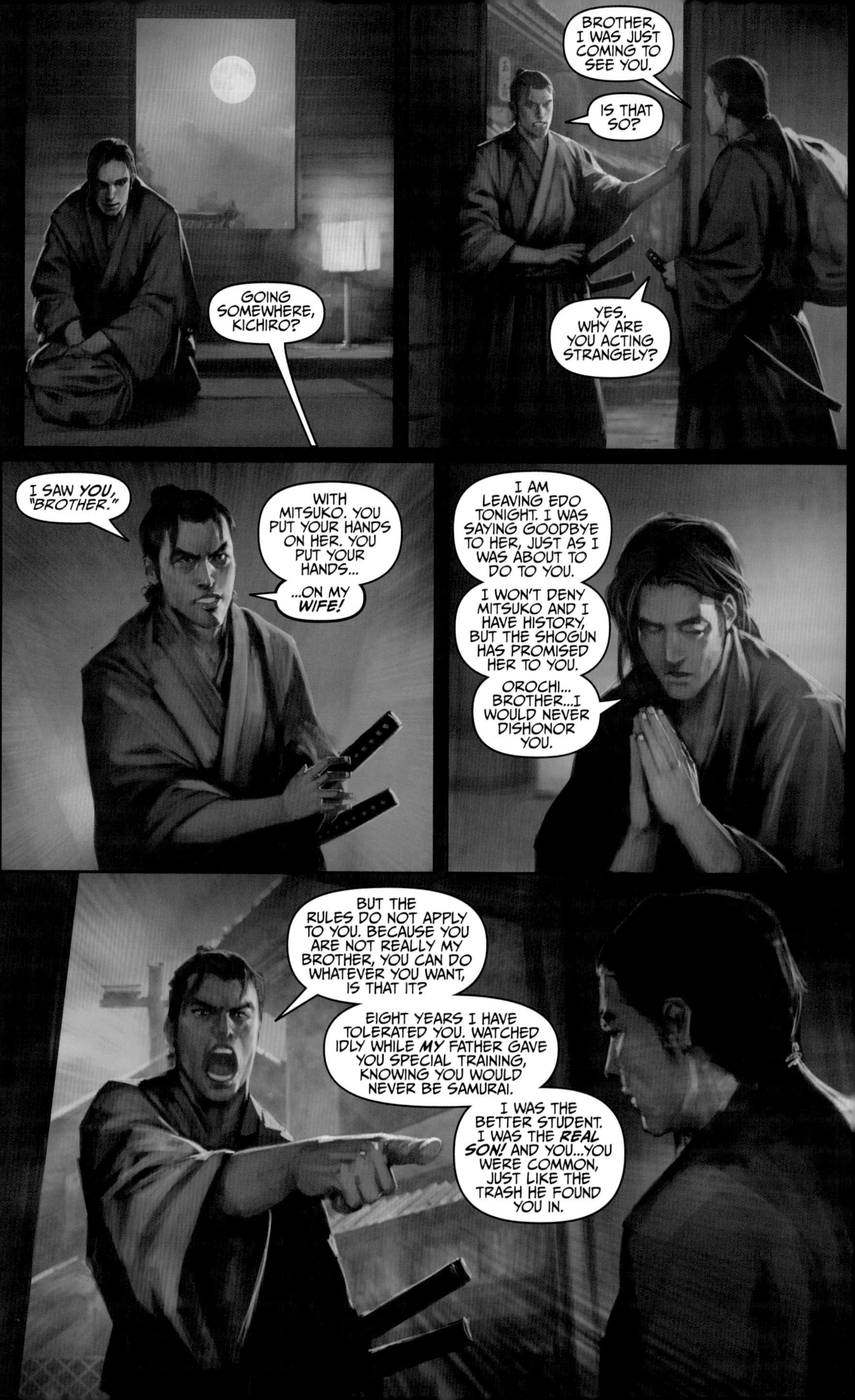
GOING SOMEWHERE, KICHIRO?
BROTHER, I WAS JUST COMING TO SEE YOU.
IS THAT SO?
YES. WHY ARE YOU ACTING STRANGELY?
I SAW *YOU*, "BROTHER."
WITH MITSUKO. YOU PUT YOUR HANDS ON HER. YOU PUT YOUR HANDS...
...ON MY ***WIFE!***
I AM LEAVING EDO TONIGHT. I WAS SAYING GOODBYE TO HER, JUST AS I WAS ABOUT TO DO TO YOU.
I WON'T DENY MITSUKO AND I HAVE HISTORY, BUT THE SHOGUN HAS PROMISED HER TO YOU.
OROCHI... BROTHER...I WOULD NEVER DISHONOR YOU.
BUT THE RULES DO NOT APPLY TO YOU. BECAUSE YOU ARE NOT REALLY MY BROTHER, YOU CAN DO WHATEVER YOU WANT, IS THAT IT?
EIGHT YEARS I HAVE TOLERATED YOU. WATCHED IDLY WHILE *MY* FATHER GAVE YOU SPECIAL TRAINING, KNOWING YOU WOULD NEVER BE SAMURAI.
I WAS THE BETTER STUDENT. I WAS THE ***REAL SON!*** AND YOU...YOU WERE COMMON, JUST LIKE THE TRASH HE FOUND YOU IN.

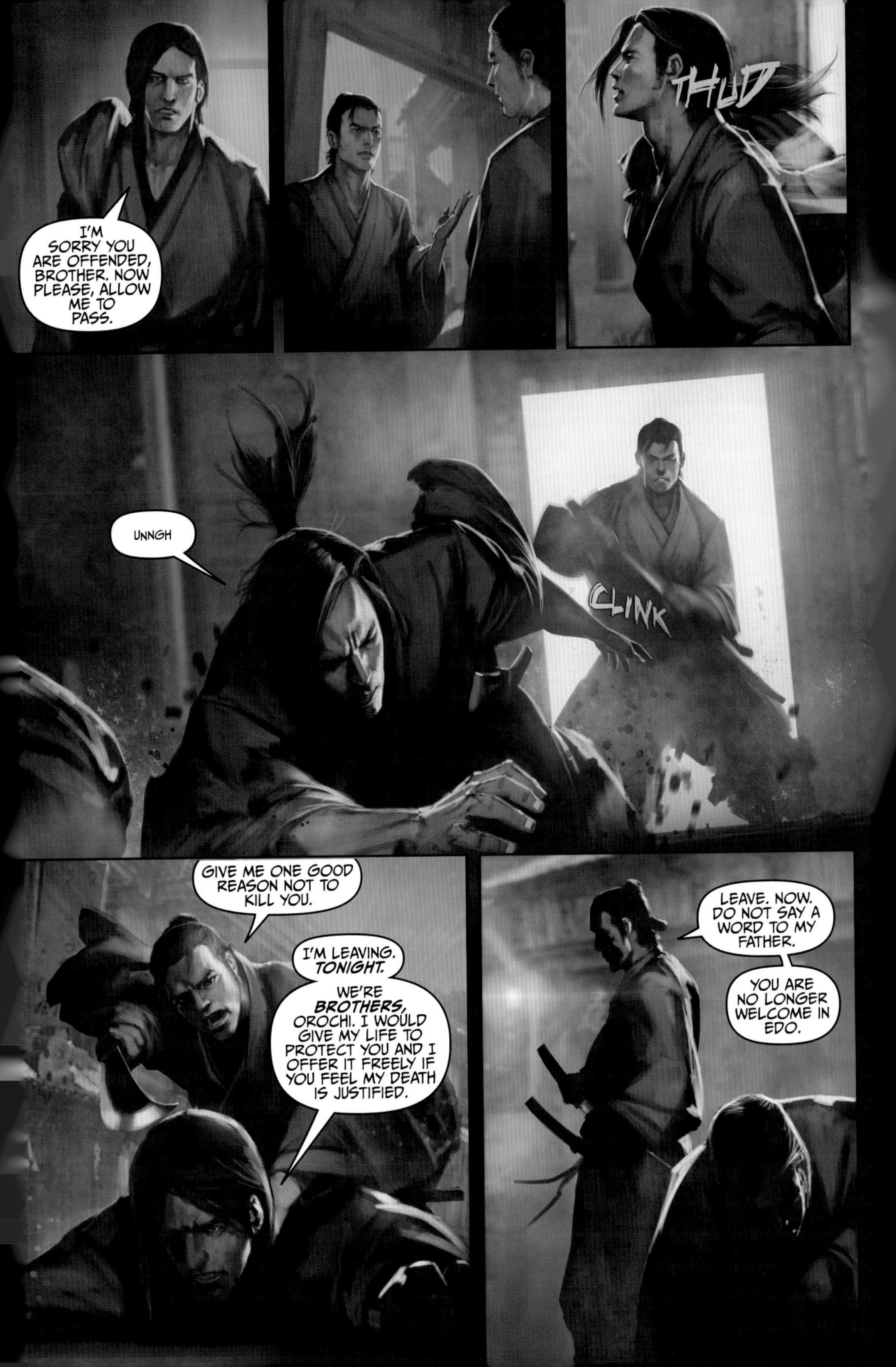
I'M SORRY YOU ARE OFFENDED, BROTHER. NOW PLEASE, ALLOW ME TO PASS.
THUD
UNNGH
CLINK
GIVE ME ONE GOOD REASON NOT TO KILL YOU.
I'M LEAVING. *TONIGHT.*
WE'RE ***BROTHERS,*** OROCHI. I WOULD GIVE MY LIFE TO PROTECT YOU AND I OFFER IT FREELY IF YOU FEEL MY DEATH IS JUSTIFIED.
LEAVE. NOW. DO NOT SAY A WORD TO MY FATHER.
YOU ARE NO LONGER WELCOME IN EDO.

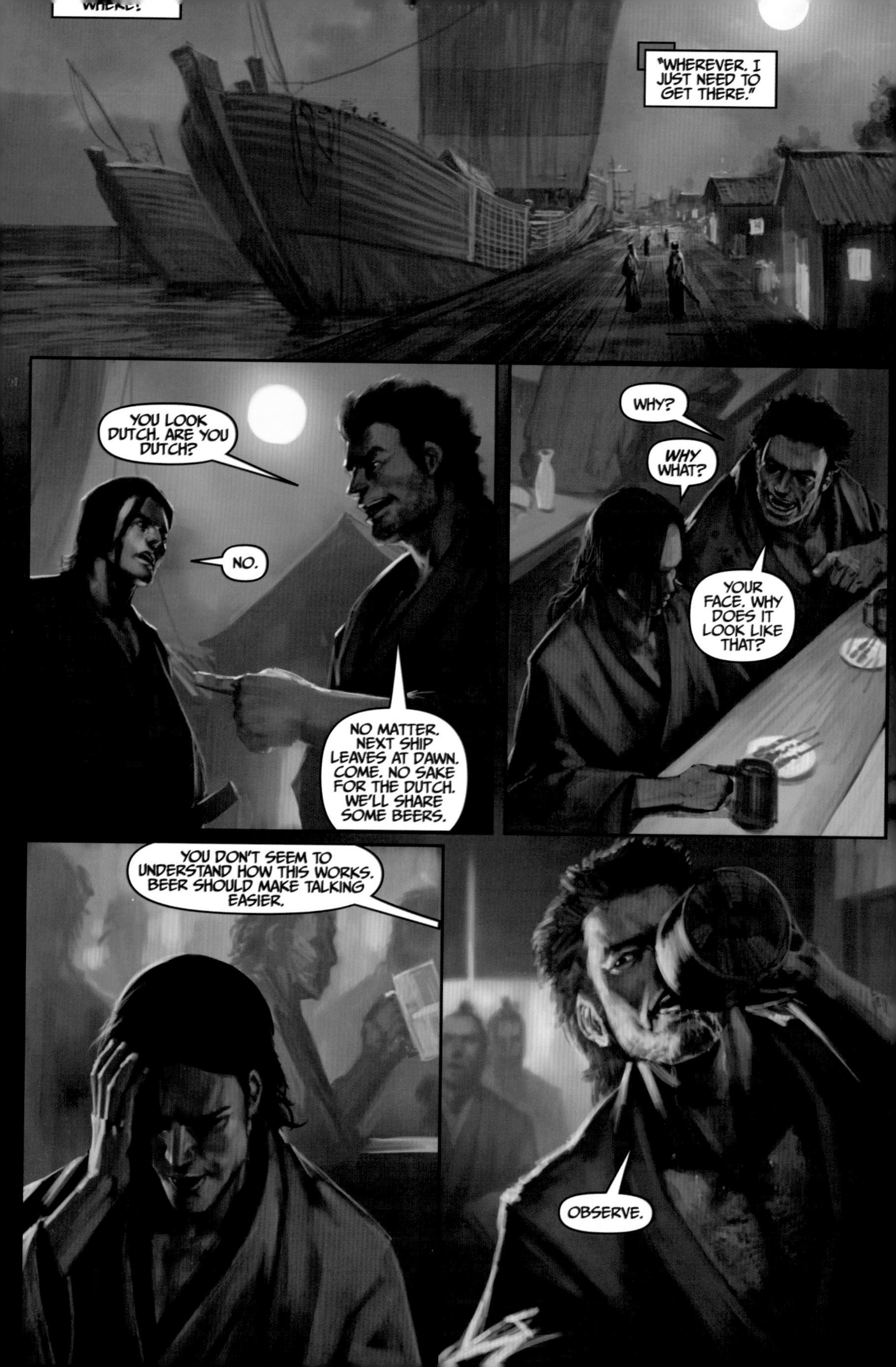
"WHEREVER. I JUST NEED TO GET THERE."
YOU LOOK DUTCH. ARE YOU DUTCH?
NO.
NO MATTER. NEXT SHIP LEAVES AT DAWN. COME. NO SAKE FOR THE DUTCH. WE'LL SHARE SOME BEERS.
WHY?
WHY WHAT?
YOUR FACE. WHY DOES IT LOOK LIKE THAT?
YOU DON'T SEEM TO UNDERSTAND HOW THIS WORKS. BEER SHOULD MAKE TALKING EASIER.
OBSERVE.

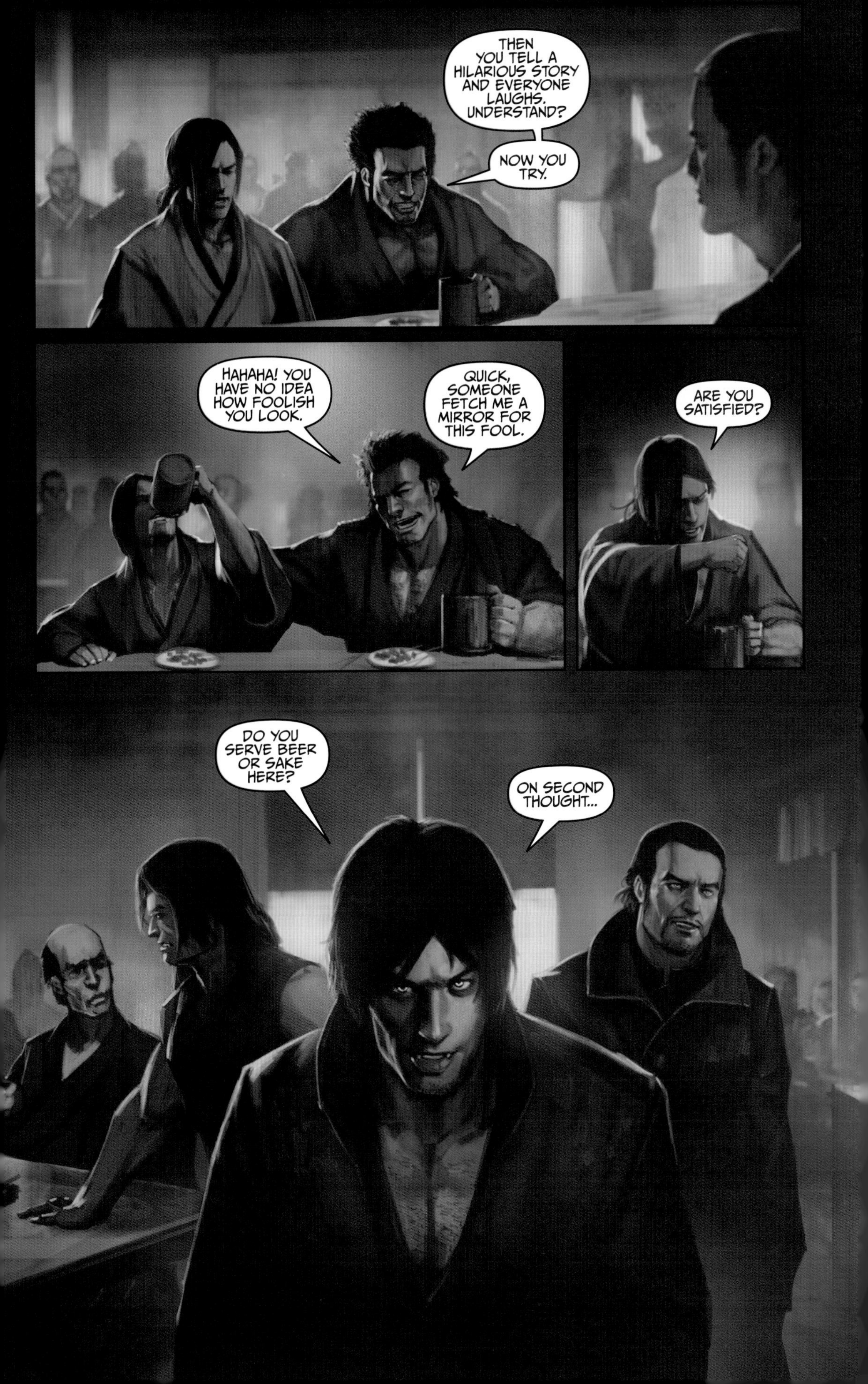
THEN YOU TELL A HILARIOUS STORY AND EVERYONE LAUGHS. UNDERSTAND?
NOW YOU TRY.
HAHAHA! YOU HAVE NO IDEA HOW FOOLISH YOU LOOK.
QUICK, SOMEONE FETCH ME A MIRROR FOR THIS FOOL.
ARE YOU SATISFIED?
DO YOU SERVE BEER OR SAKE HERE?
ON SECOND THOUGHT...

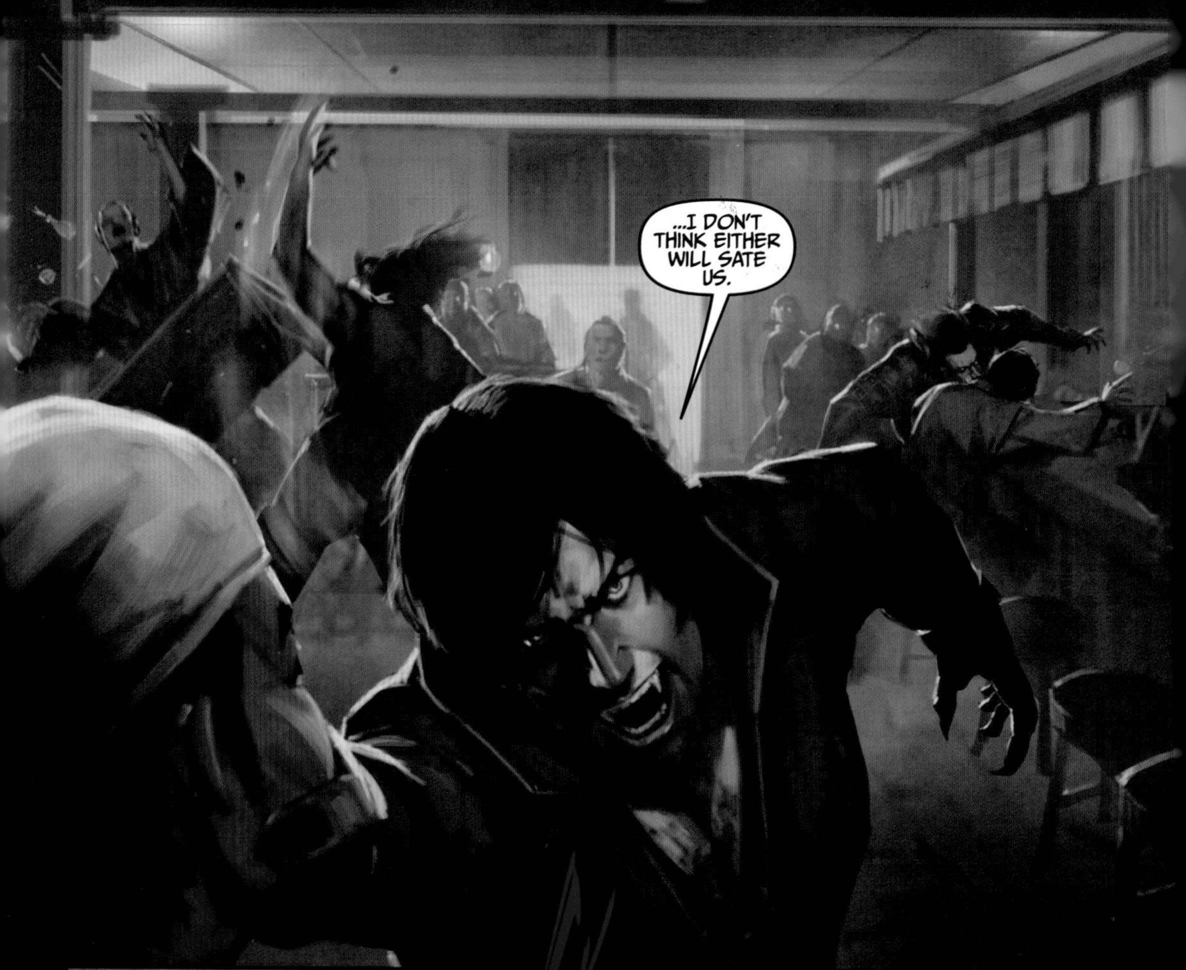
...I DON'T THINK EITHER WILL SATE US.

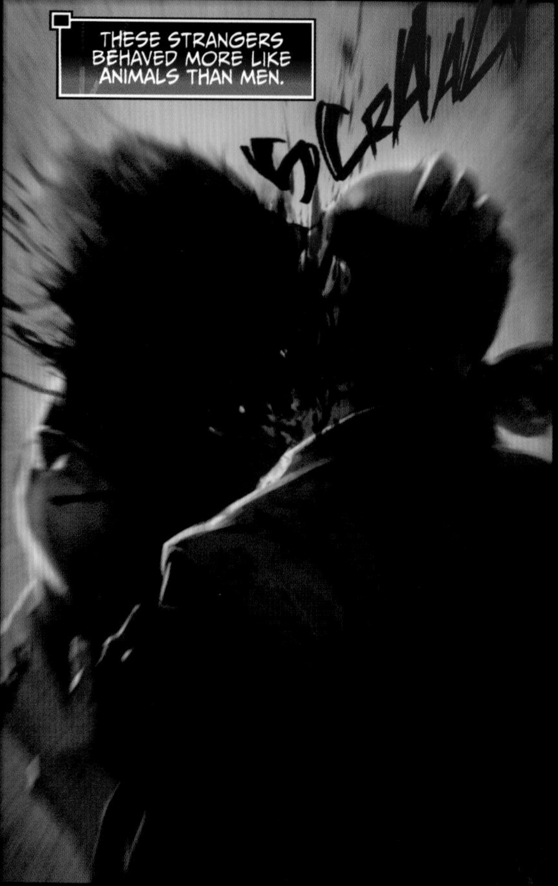
THESE STRANGERS BEHAVED MORE LIKE ANIMALS THAN MEN.

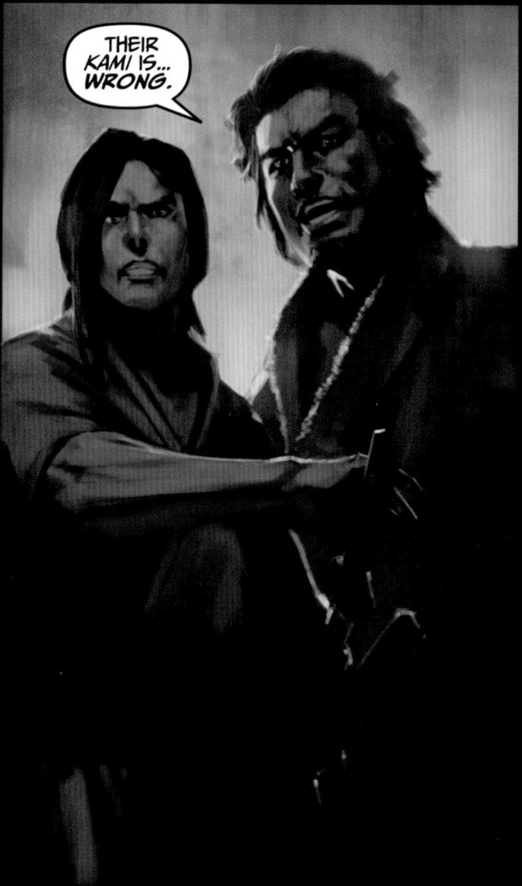
THEIR *KAMI* IS... **WRONG.**

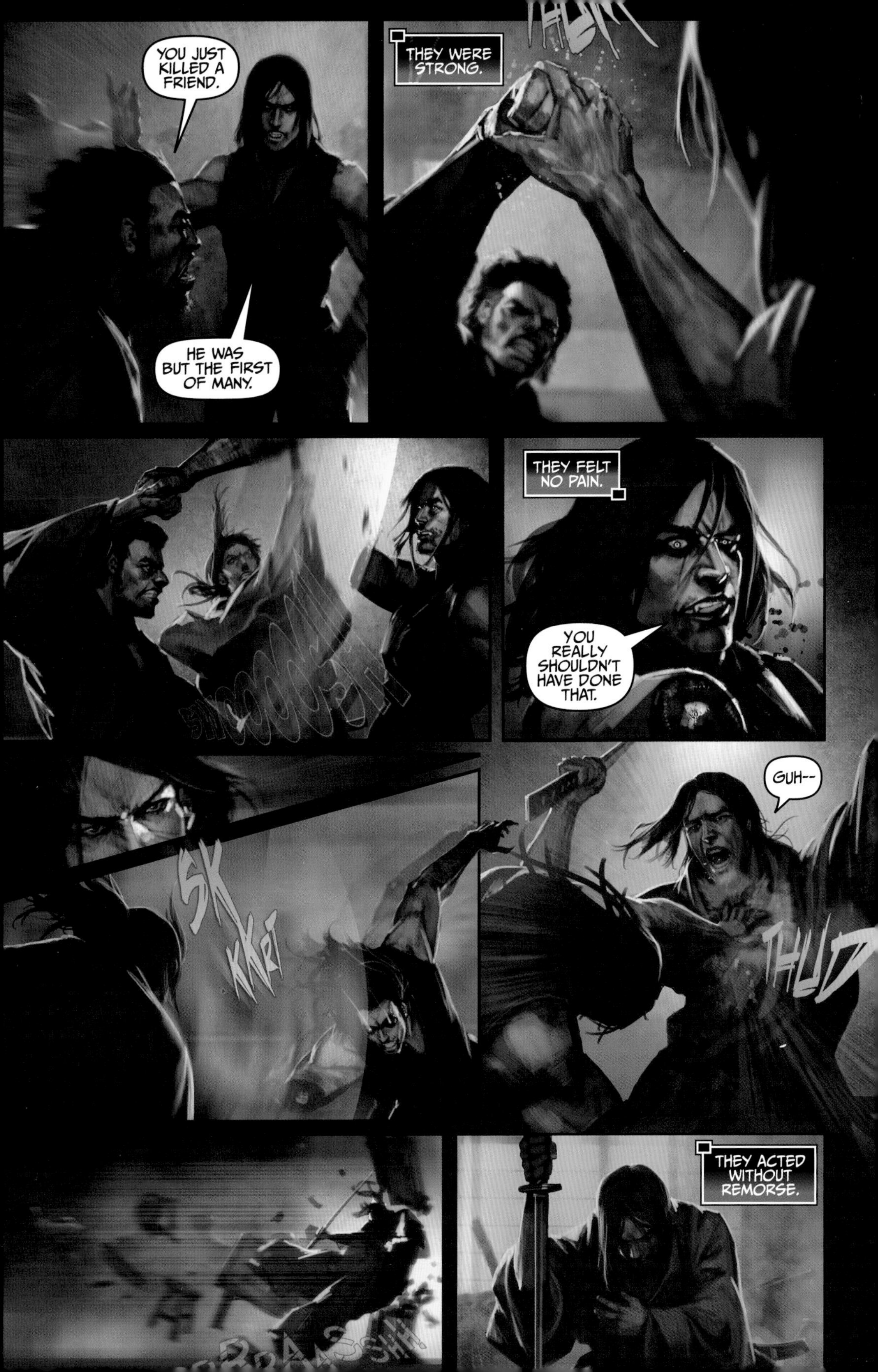
YOU JUST KILLED A FRIEND.
HE WAS BUT THE FIRST OF MANY.
THEY WERE STRONG.
THUNK
SHOOOOSH
THEY FELT NO PAIN.
YOU REALLY SHOULDN'T HAVE DONE THAT.
SK KKRT
GUH--
THUD
THEY ACTED WITHOUT REMORSE.

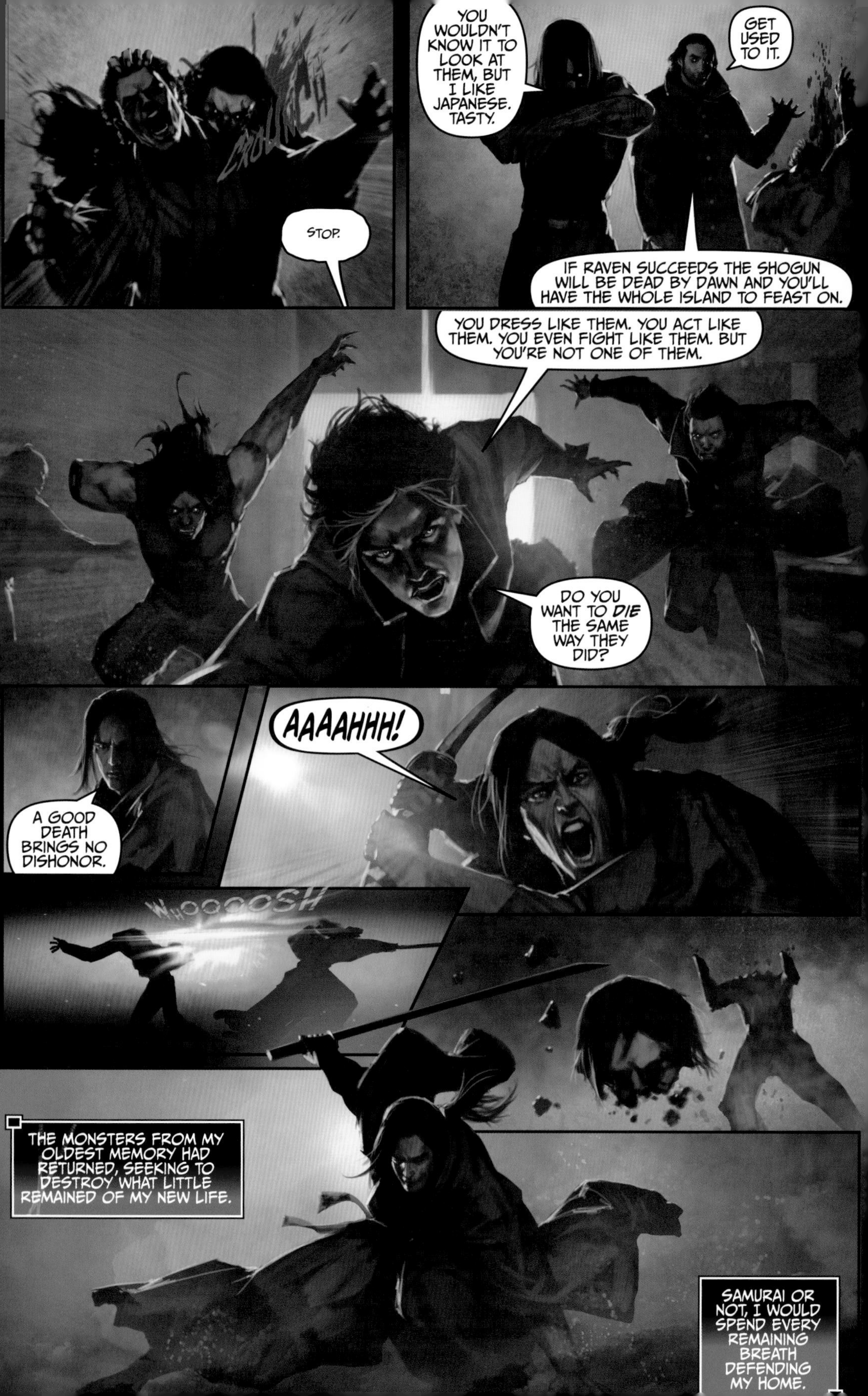
CROUNCH
STOP.
YOU WOULDN'T KNOW IT TO LOOK AT THEM, BUT I LIKE JAPANESE. TASTY.
GET USED TO IT.
IF RAVEN SUCCEEDS THE SHOGUN WILL BE DEAD BY DAWN AND YOU'LL HAVE THE WHOLE ISLAND TO FEAST ON.
YOU DRESS LIKE THEM. YOU ACT LIKE THEM. YOU EVEN FIGHT LIKE THEM. BUT YOU'RE NOT ONE OF THEM.
DO YOU WANT TO *DIE* THE SAME WAY THEY DID?
A GOOD DEATH BRINGS NO DISHONOR.
AAAAHHH!
WHOOOOOSH
THE MONSTERS FROM MY OLDEST MEMORY HAD RETURNED, SEEKING TO DESTROY WHAT LITTLE REMAINED OF MY NEW LIFE.
SAMURAI OR NOT, I WOULD SPEND EVERY REMAINING BREATH DEFENDING MY HOME.

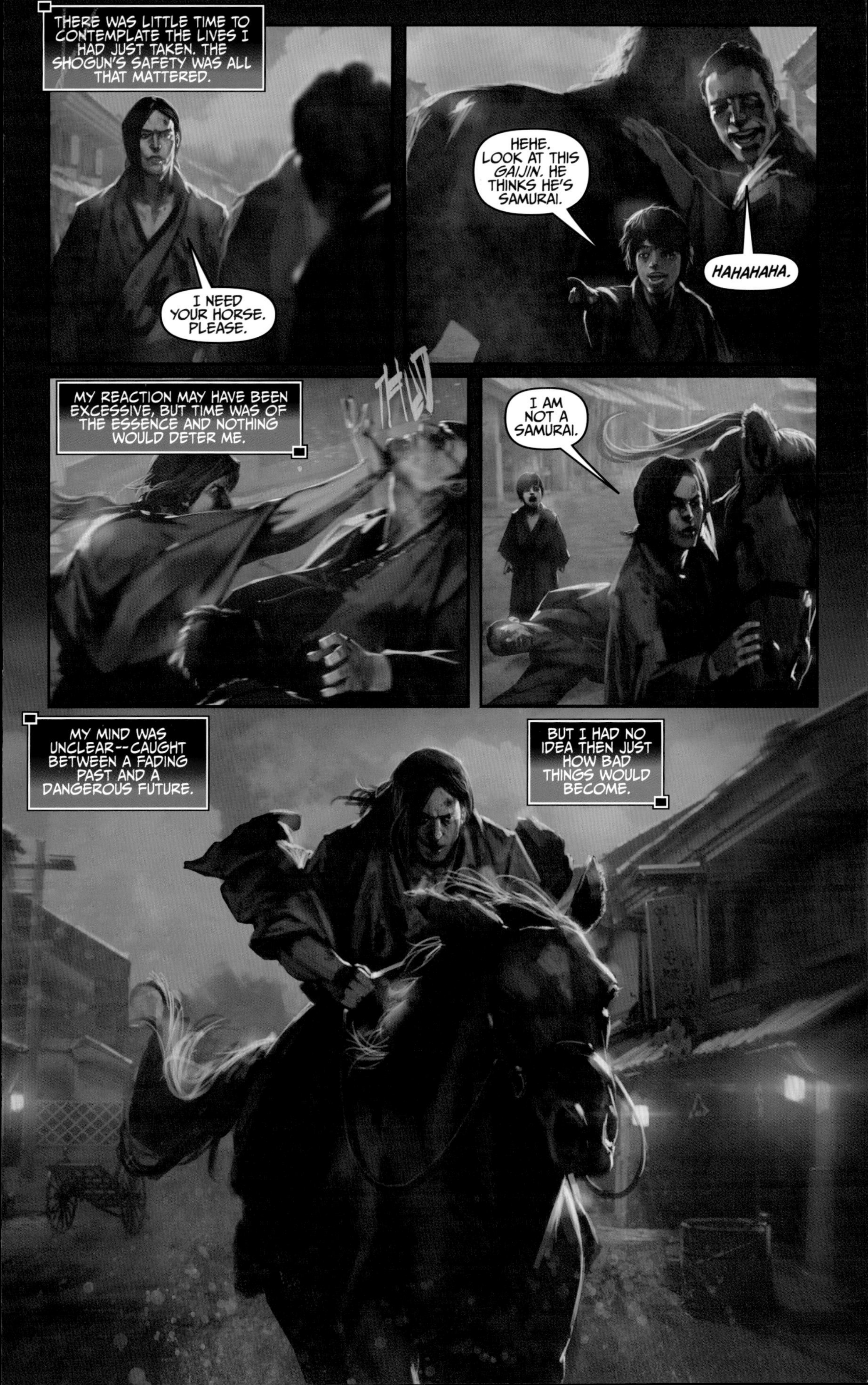

THERE WAS LITTLE TIME TO CONTEMPLATE THE LIVES I HAD JUST TAKEN. THE SHOGUN'S SAFETY WAS ALL THAT MATTERED.
I NEED YOUR HORSE. PLEASE.
HEHE. LOOK AT THIS *GAIJIN*. HE THINKS HE'S SAMURAI.
HAHAHAHA.
MY REACTION MAY HAVE BEEN EXCESSIVE, BUT TIME WAS OF THE ESSENCE AND NOTHING WOULD DETER ME.
THUD
I AM NOT A SAMURAI.
MY MIND WAS UNCLEAR--CAUGHT BETWEEN A FADING PAST AND A DANGEROUS FUTURE.
BUT I HAD NO IDEA THEN JUST HOW BAD THINGS WOULD BECOME.

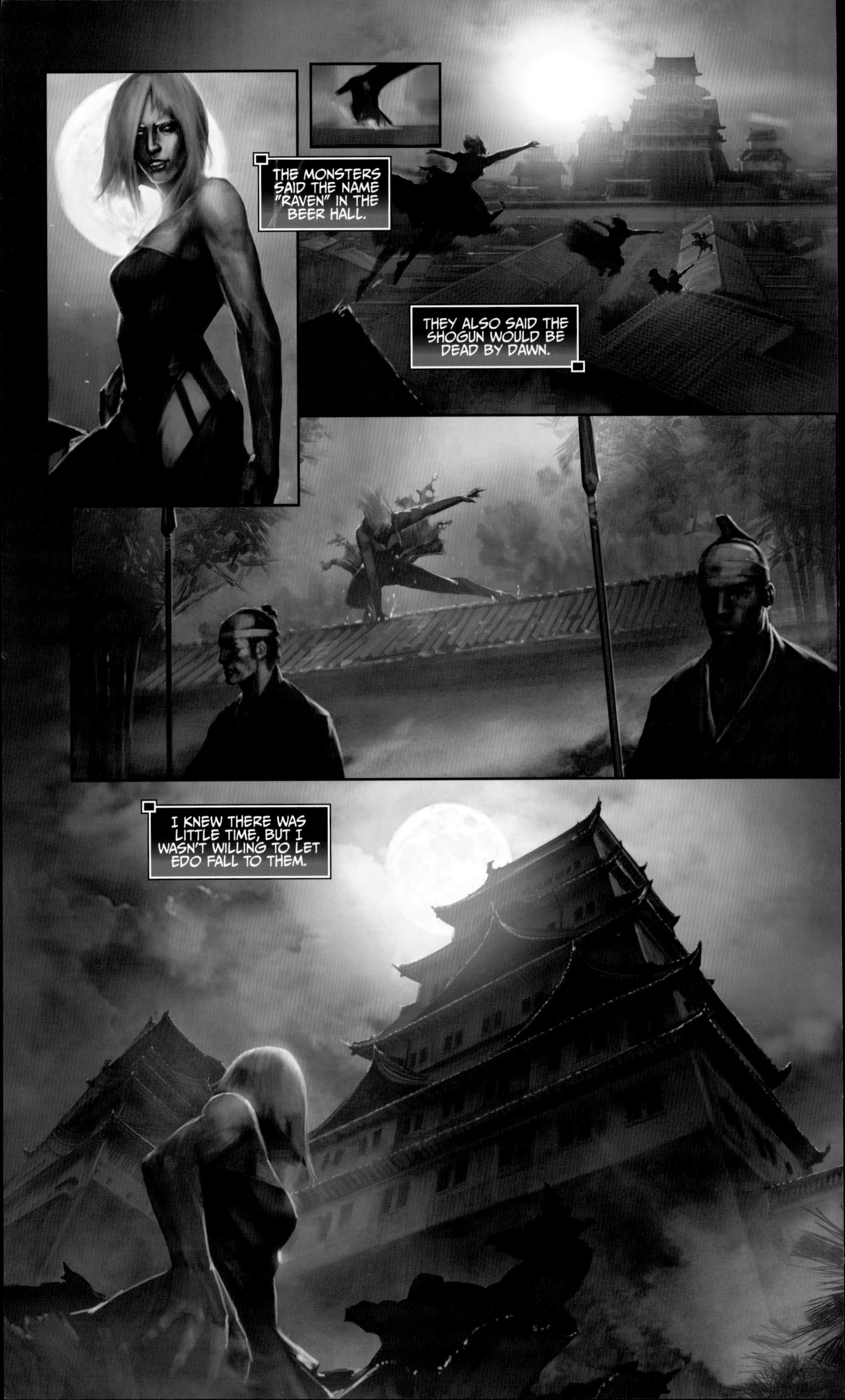
THE MONSTERS SAID THE NAME "RAVEN" IN THE BEER HALL.
THEY ALSO SAID THE SHOGUN WOULD BE DEAD BY DAWN.
I KNEW THERE WAS LITTLE TIME, BUT I WASN'T WILLING TO LET EDO FALL TO THEM.

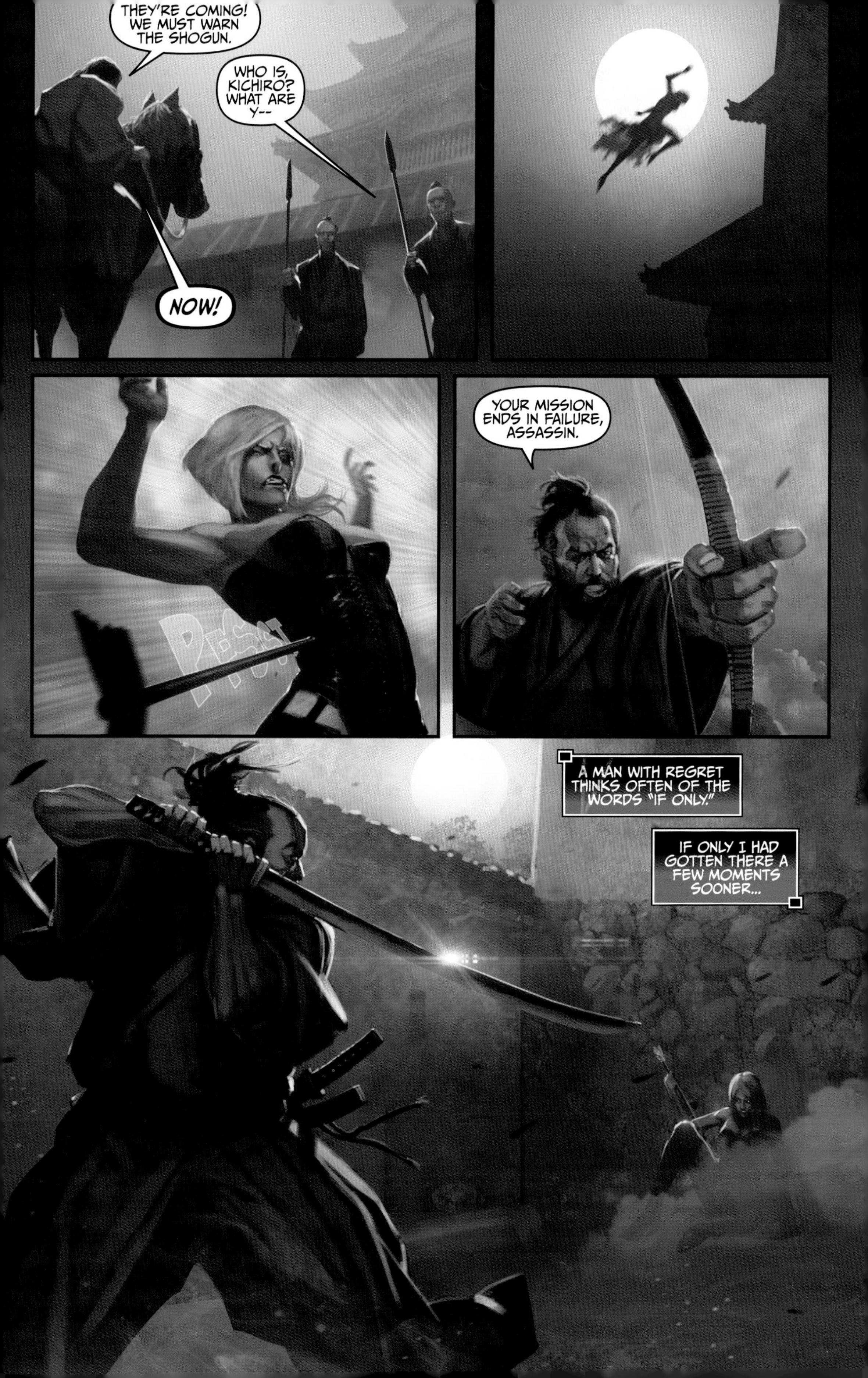

THEY'RE COMING! WE MUST WARN THE SHOGUN.
WHO IS, KICHIRO? WHAT ARE Y--
NOW!
PFSST
YOUR MISSION ENDS IN FAILURE, ASSASSIN.
A MAN WITH REGRET THINKS OFTEN OF THE WORDS "IF ONLY."
IF ONLY I HAD GOTTEN THERE A FEW MOMENTS SOONER...

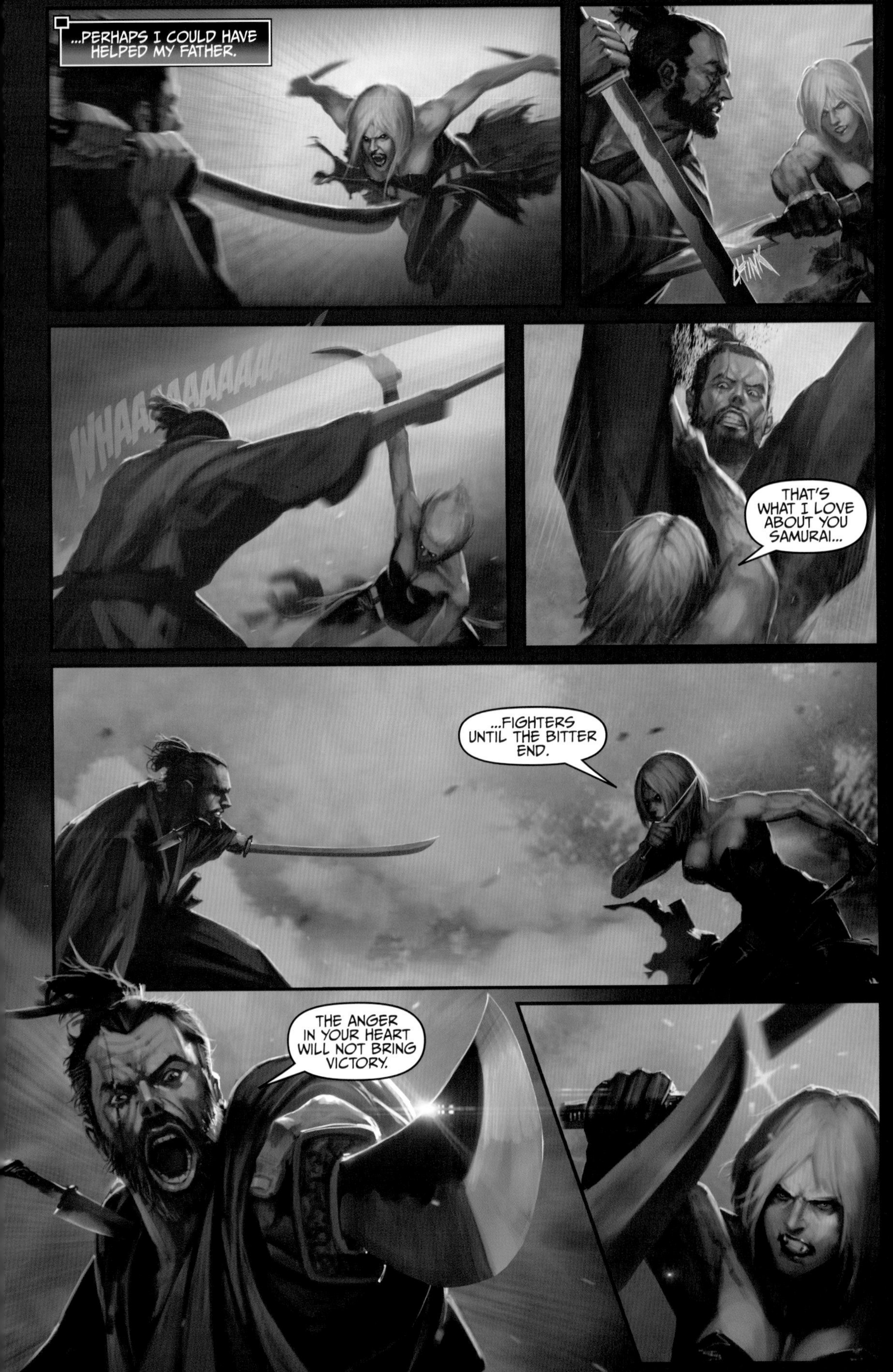
...PERHAPS I COULD HAVE HELPED MY FATHER.
CHINK
WHAAAAAAAAA
THAT'S WHAT I LOVE ABOUT YOU SAMURAI...
...FIGHTERS UNTIL THE BITTER END.
THE ANGER IN YOUR HEART WILL NOT BRING VICTORY.

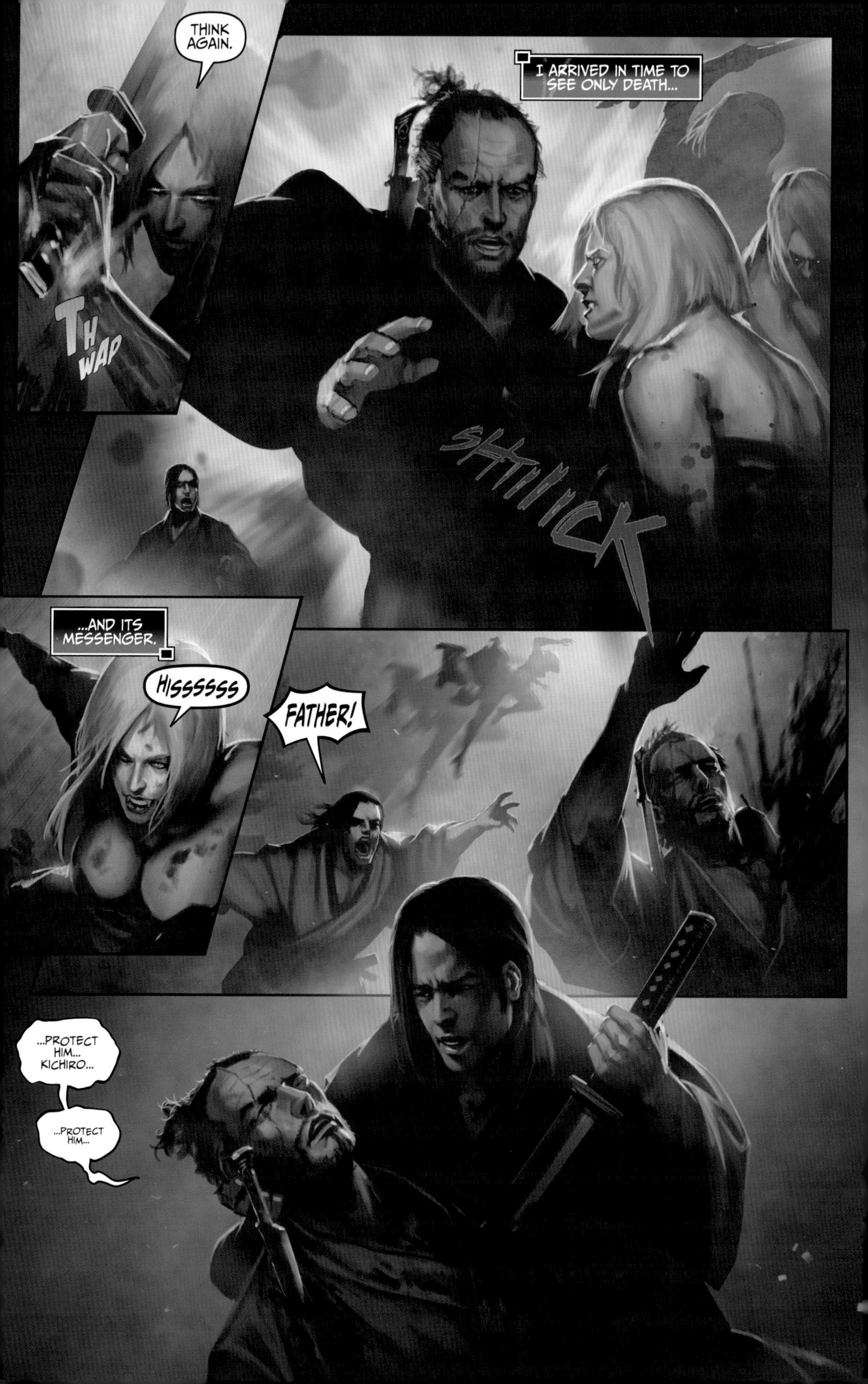
THINK AGAIN.
THWAP
I ARRIVED IN TIME TO SEE ONLY DEATH...
SHTHICK
...AND ITS MESSENGER.
HISSSSSS
FATHER!
...PROTECT HIM... KICHIRO...
...PROTECT HIM...

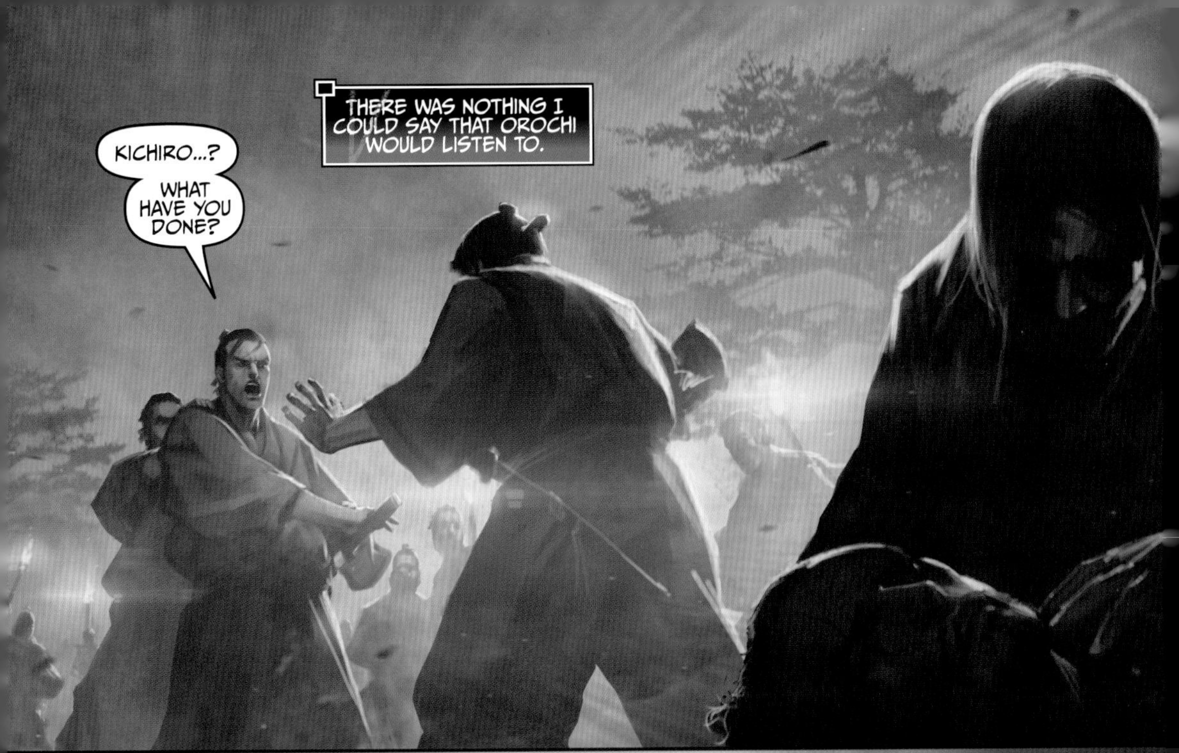
THERE WAS NOTHING I COULD SAY THAT OROCHI WOULD LISTEN TO.
KICHIRO...?
WHAT HAVE YOU DONE?
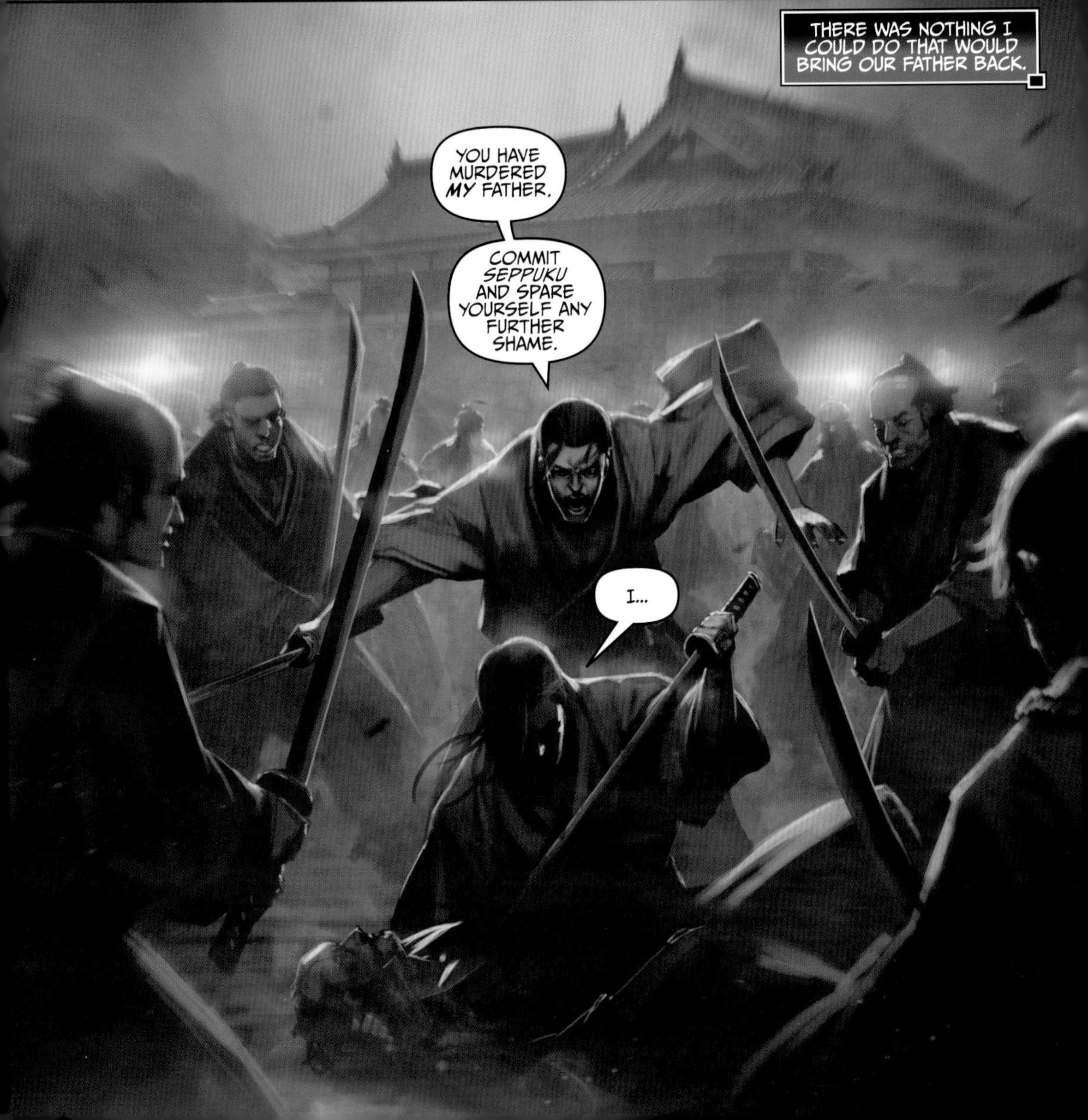
THERE WAS NOTHING I COULD DO THAT WOULD BRING OUR FATHER BACK.
YOU HAVE MURDERED *MY* FATHER.
COMMIT *SEPPUKU* AND SPARE YOURSELF ANY FURTHER SHAME.
I...

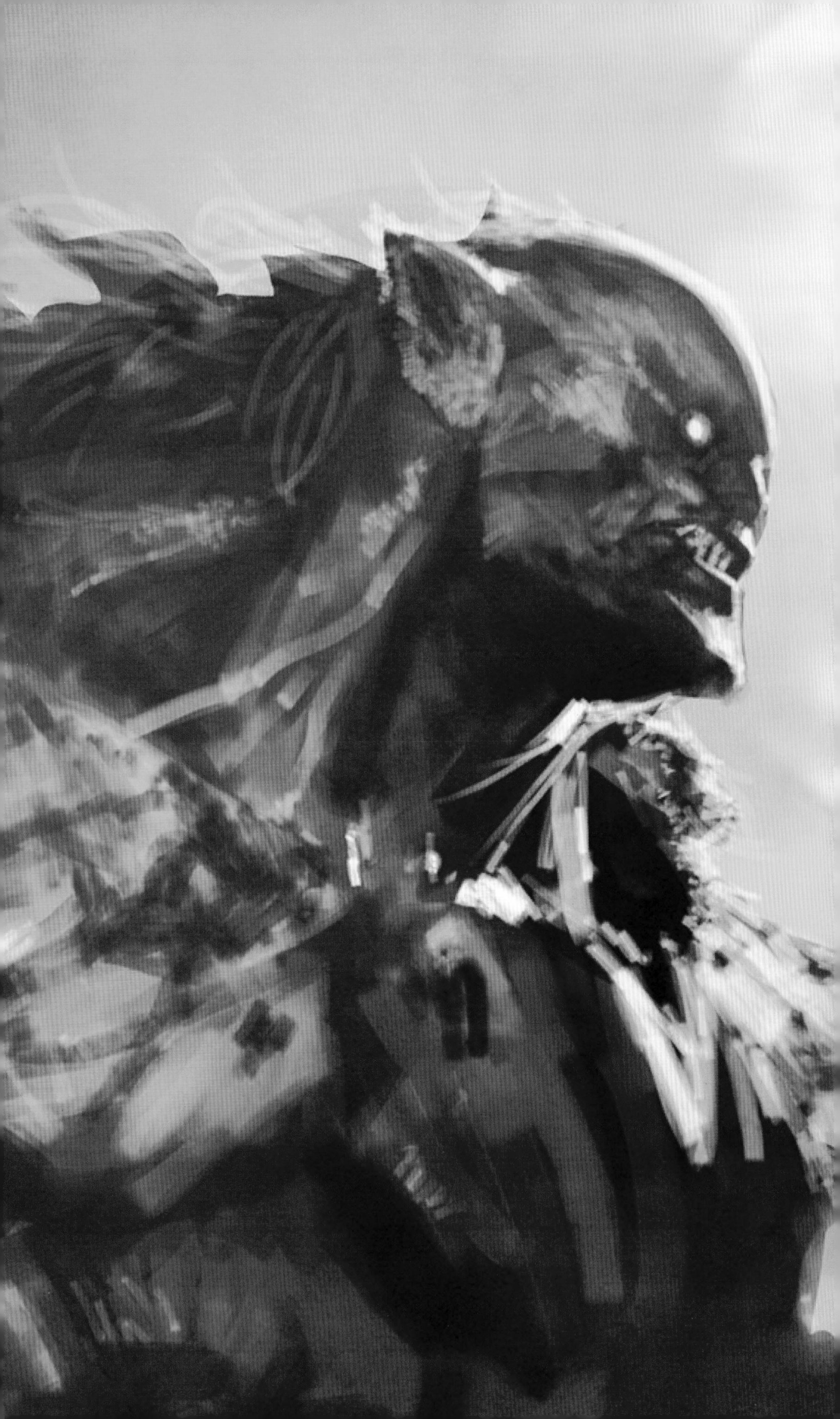

Chapter Two

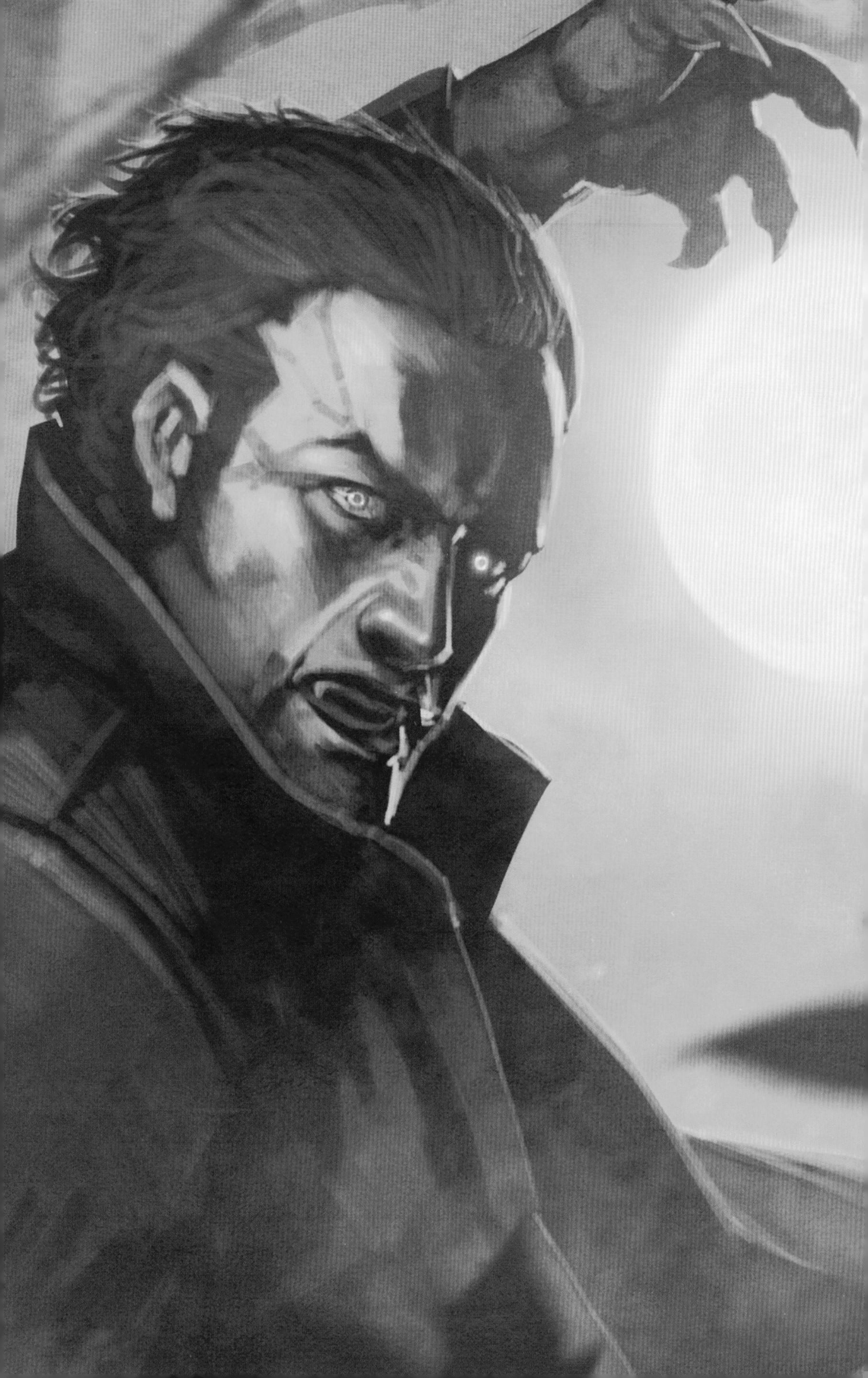

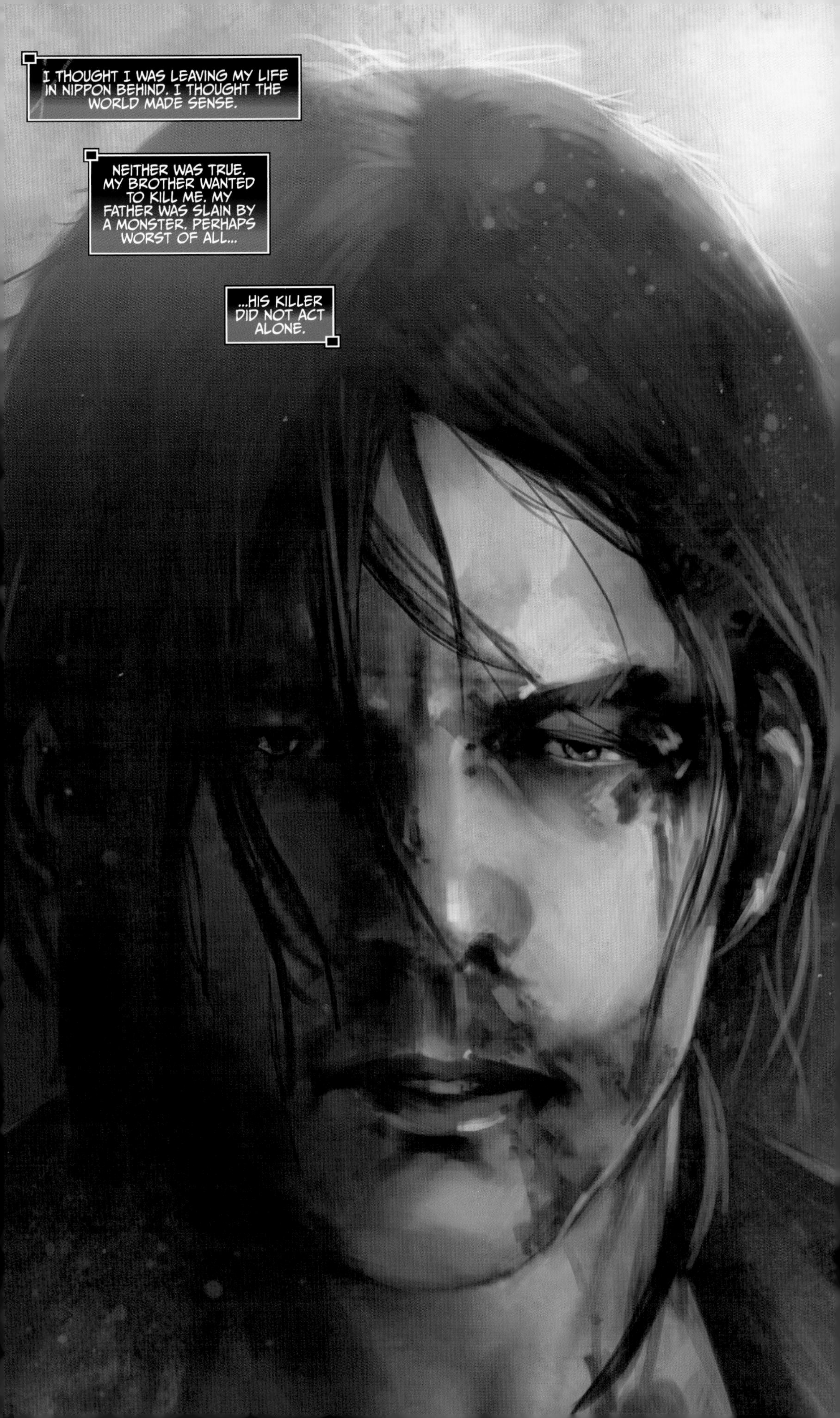
I THOUGHT I WAS LEAVING MY LIFE IN NIPPON BEHIND. I THOUGHT THE WORLD MADE SENSE.
NEITHER WAS TRUE. MY BROTHER WANTED TO KILL ME. MY FATHER WAS SLAIN BY A MONSTER. PERHAPS WORST OF ALL...
...HIS KILLER DID NOT ACT ALONE.

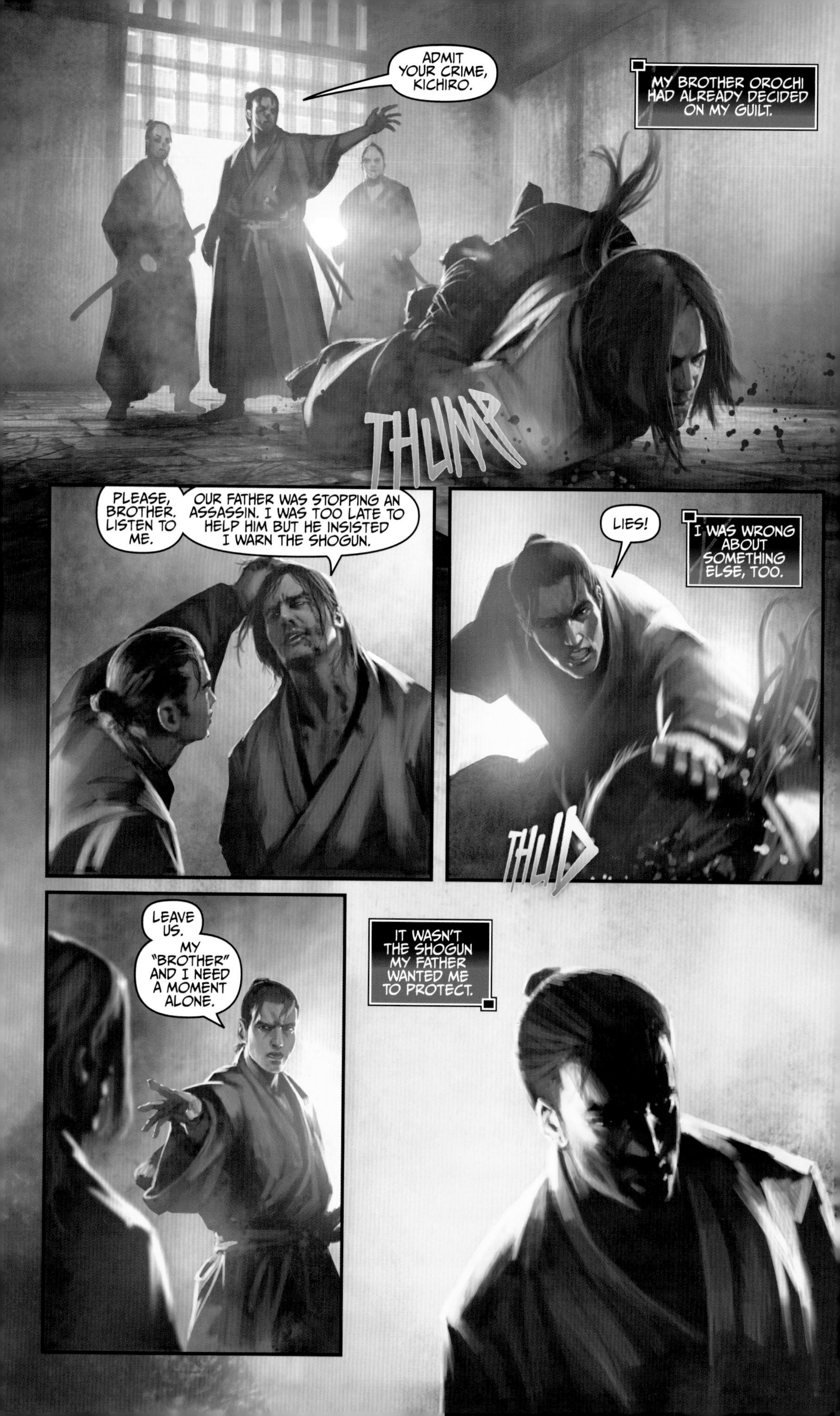
ADMIT YOUR CRIME, KICHIRO.
MY BROTHER OROCHI HAD ALREADY DECIDED ON MY GUILT.
THUMP
PLEASE, BROTHER. LISTEN TO ME.
OUR FATHER WAS STOPPING AN ASSASSIN. I WAS TOO LATE TO HELP HIM BUT HE INSISTED I WARN THE SHOGUN.
LIES!
I WAS WRONG ABOUT SOMETHING ELSE, TOO.
THUD
LEAVE US.
MY "BROTHER" AND I NEED A MOMENT ALONE.
IT WASN'T THE SHOGUN MY FATHER WANTED ME TO PROTECT.

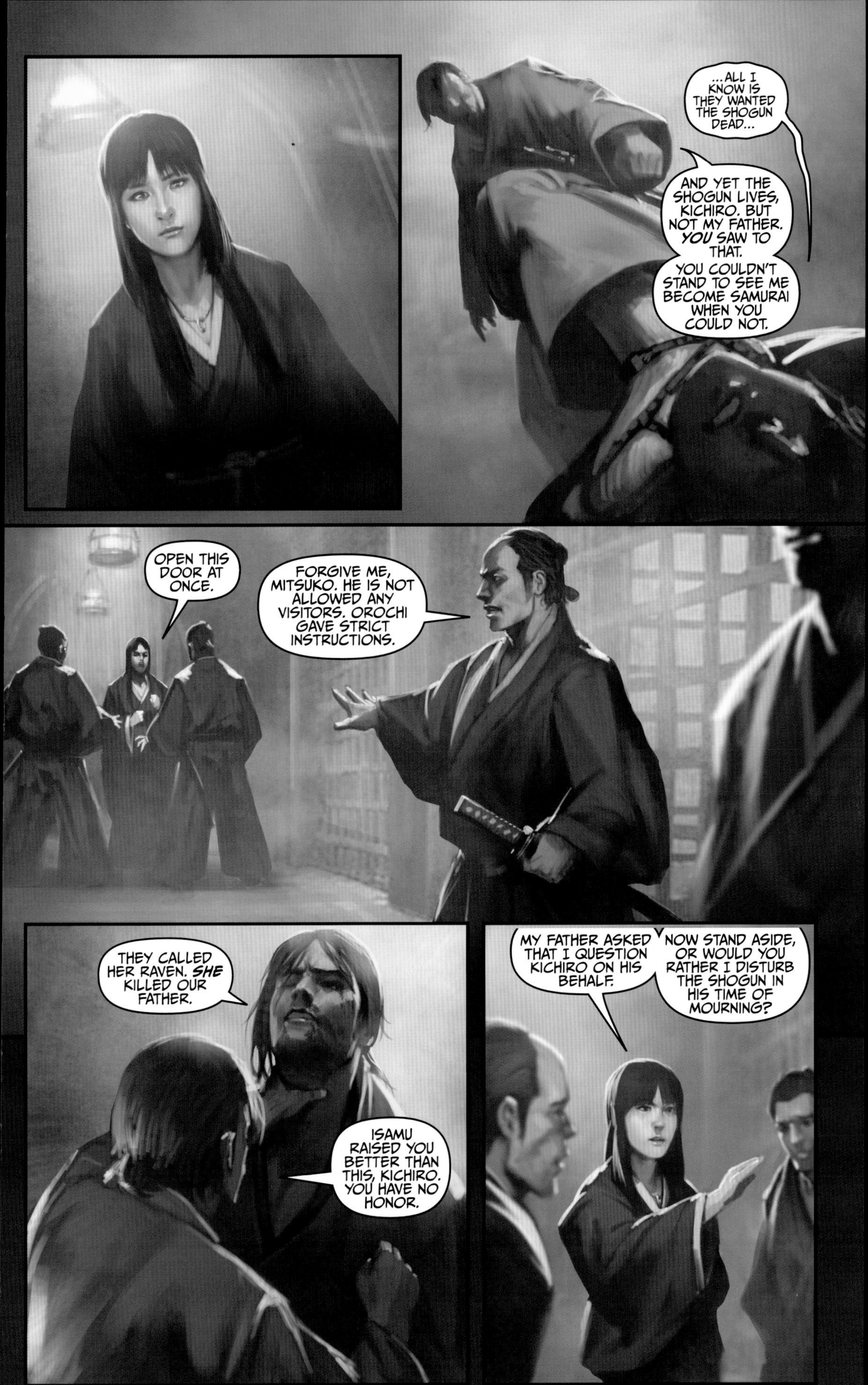
...ALL I KNOW IS THEY WANTED THE SHOGUN DEAD...
AND YET THE SHOGUN LIVES, KICHIRO. BUT NOT MY FATHER. *YOU* SAW TO THAT.
YOU COULDN'T STAND TO SEE ME BECOME SAMURAI WHEN YOU COULD NOT.
OPEN THIS DOOR AT ONCE.
FORGIVE ME, MITSUKO. HE IS NOT ALLOWED ANY VISITORS. OROCHI GAVE STRICT INSTRUCTIONS.
THEY CALLED HER RAVEN. ***SHE*** KILLED OUR FATHER.
ISAMU RAISED YOU BETTER THAN THIS, KICHIRO. YOU HAVE NO HONOR.
MY FATHER ASKED THAT I QUESTION KICHIRO ON HIS BEHALF.
NOW STAND ASIDE, OR WOULD YOU RATHER I DISTURB THE SHOGUN IN HIS TIME OF MOURNING?

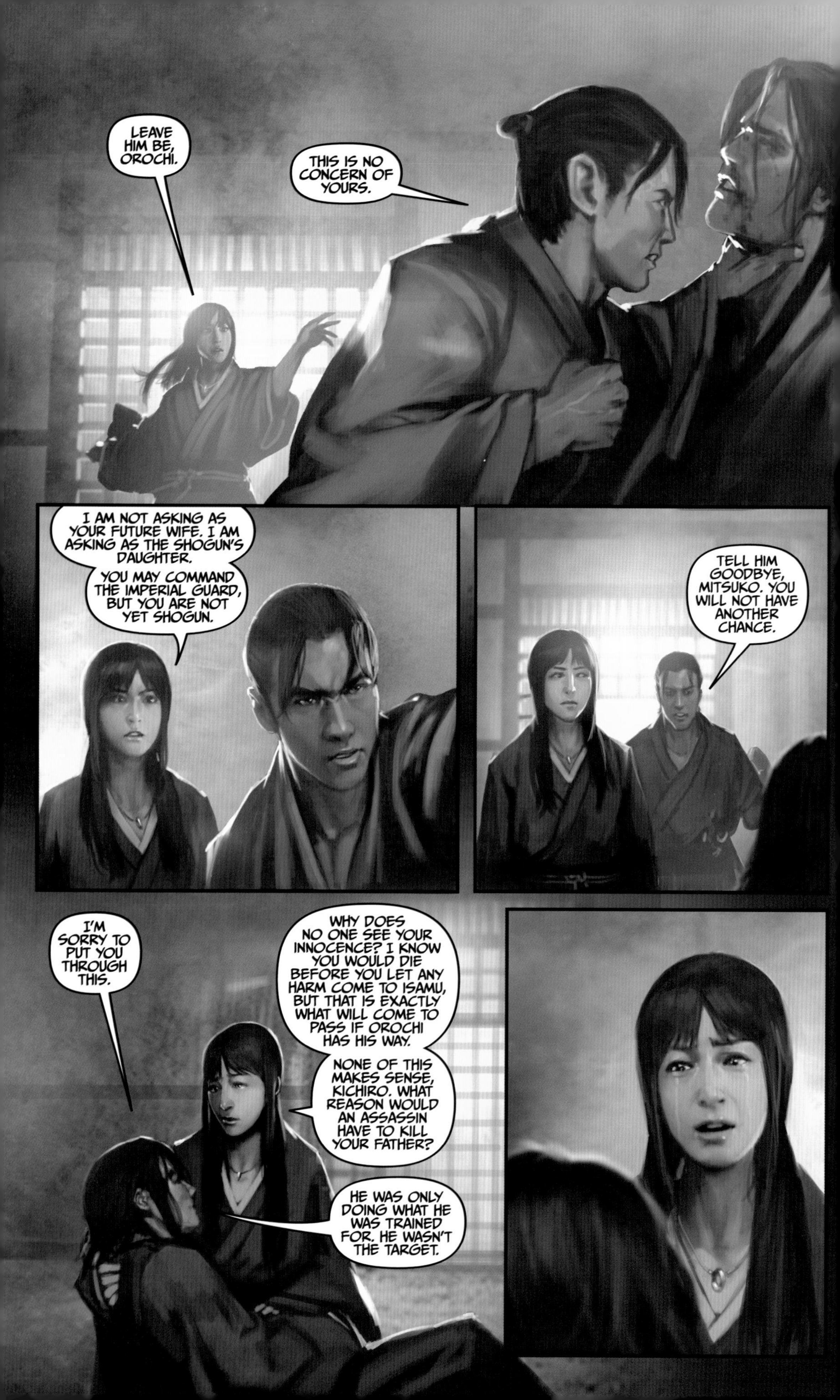
LEAVE HIM BE, OROCHI.
THIS IS NO CONCERN OF YOURS.
I AM NOT ASKING AS YOUR FUTURE WIFE. I AM ASKING AS THE SHOGUN'S DAUGHTER.
YOU MAY COMMAND THE IMPERIAL GUARD, BUT YOU ARE NOT YET SHOGUN.
TELL HIM GOODBYE, MITSUKO. YOU WILL NOT HAVE ANOTHER CHANCE.
I'M SORRY TO PUT YOU THROUGH THIS.
WHY DOES NO ONE SEE YOUR INNOCENCE? I KNOW YOU WOULD DIE BEFORE YOU LET ANY HARM COME TO ISAMU, BUT THAT IS EXACTLY WHAT WILL COME TO PASS IF OROCHI HAS HIS WAY.
NONE OF THIS MAKES SENSE, KICHIRO. WHAT REASON WOULD AN ASSASSIN HAVE TO KILL YOUR FATHER?
HE WAS ONLY DOING WHAT HE WAS TRAINED FOR. HE WASN'T THE TARGET.

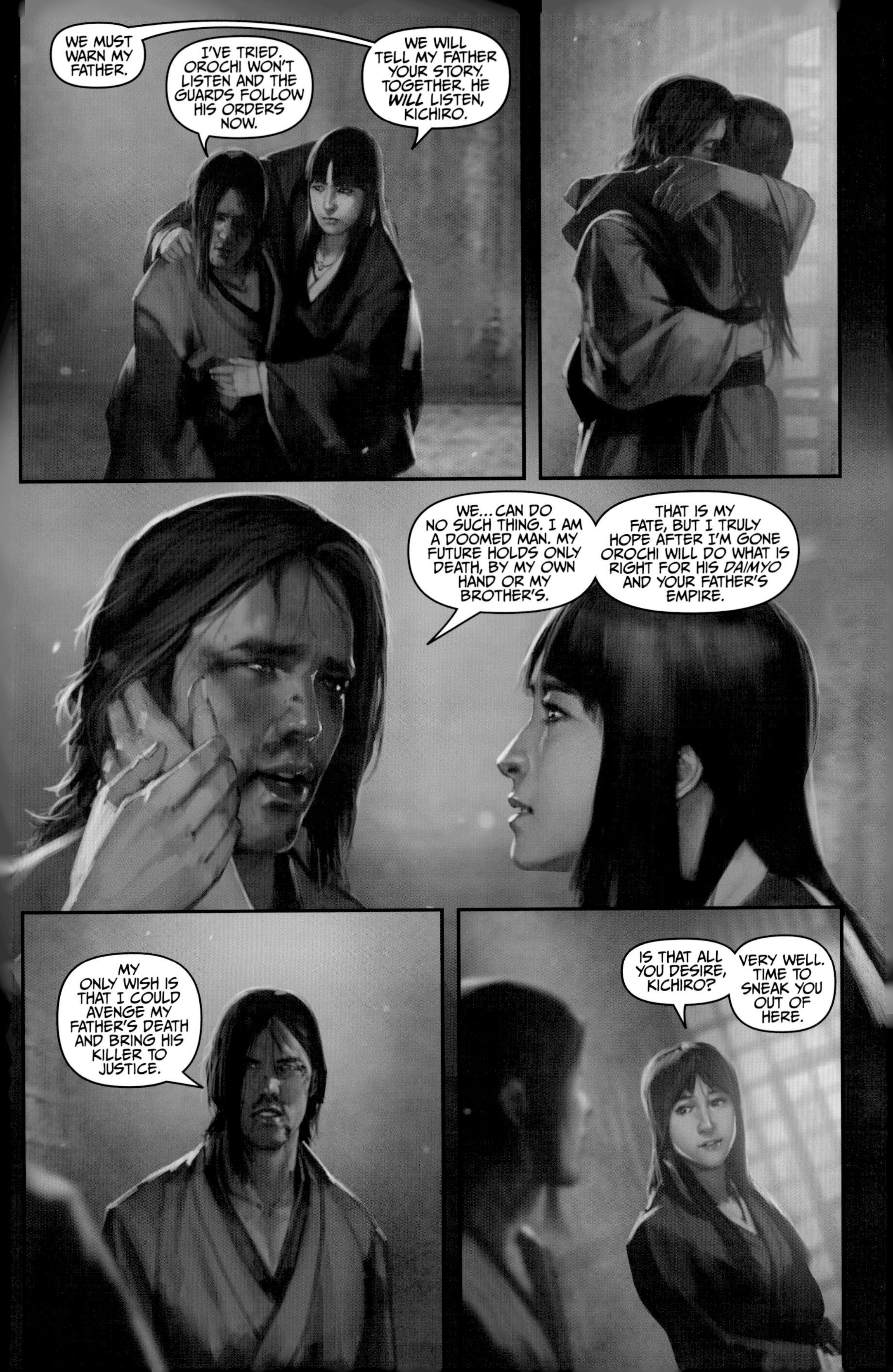
WE MUST WARN MY FATHER.
I'VE TRIED. OROCHI WON'T LISTEN AND THE GUARDS FOLLOW HIS ORDERS NOW.
WE WILL TELL MY FATHER YOUR STORY. TOGETHER. HE *WILL* LISTEN, KICHIRO.
WE... CAN DO NO SUCH THING. I AM A DOOMED MAN. MY FUTURE HOLDS ONLY DEATH, BY MY OWN HAND OR MY BROTHER'S.
THAT IS MY FATE, BUT I TRULY HOPE AFTER I'M GONE OROCHI WILL DO WHAT IS RIGHT FOR HIS *DAIMYO* AND YOUR FATHER'S EMPIRE.
MY ONLY WISH IS THAT I COULD AVENGE MY FATHER'S DEATH AND BRING HIS KILLER TO JUSTICE.
IS THAT ALL YOU DESIRE, KICHIRO?
VERY WELL. TIME TO SNEAK YOU OUT OF HERE.

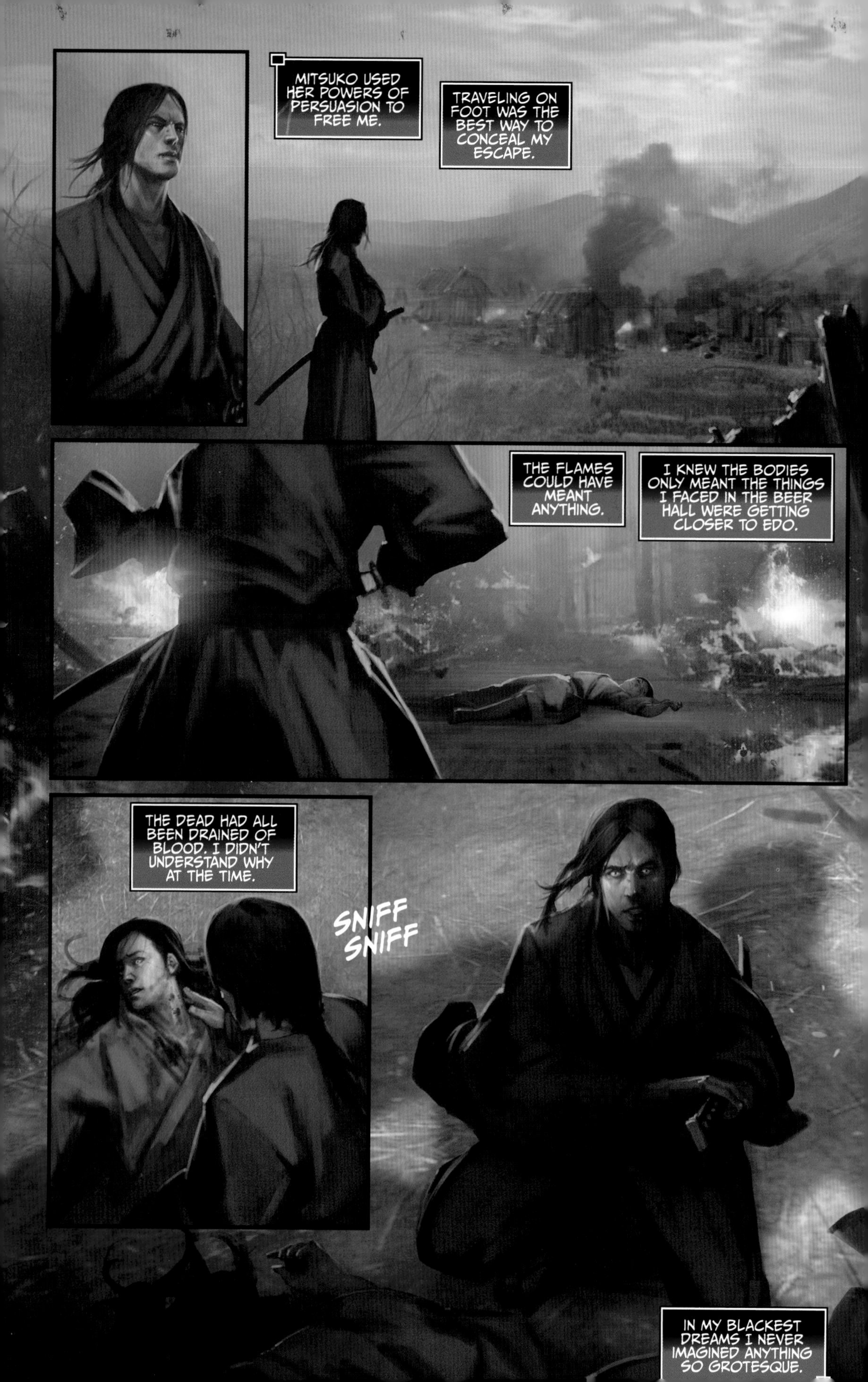
MITSUKO USED HER POWERS OF PERSUASION TO FREE ME.
TRAVELING ON FOOT WAS THE BEST WAY TO CONCEAL MY ESCAPE.
THE FLAMES COULD HAVE MEANT ANYTHING.
I KNEW THE BODIES ONLY MEANT THE THINGS I FACED IN THE BEER HALL WERE GETTING CLOSER TO EDO.
THE DEAD HAD ALL BEEN DRAINED OF BLOOD. I DIDN'T UNDERSTAND WHY AT THE TIME.
SNIFF SNIFF
IN MY BLACKEST DREAMS I NEVER IMAGINED ANYTHING SO GROTESQUE.

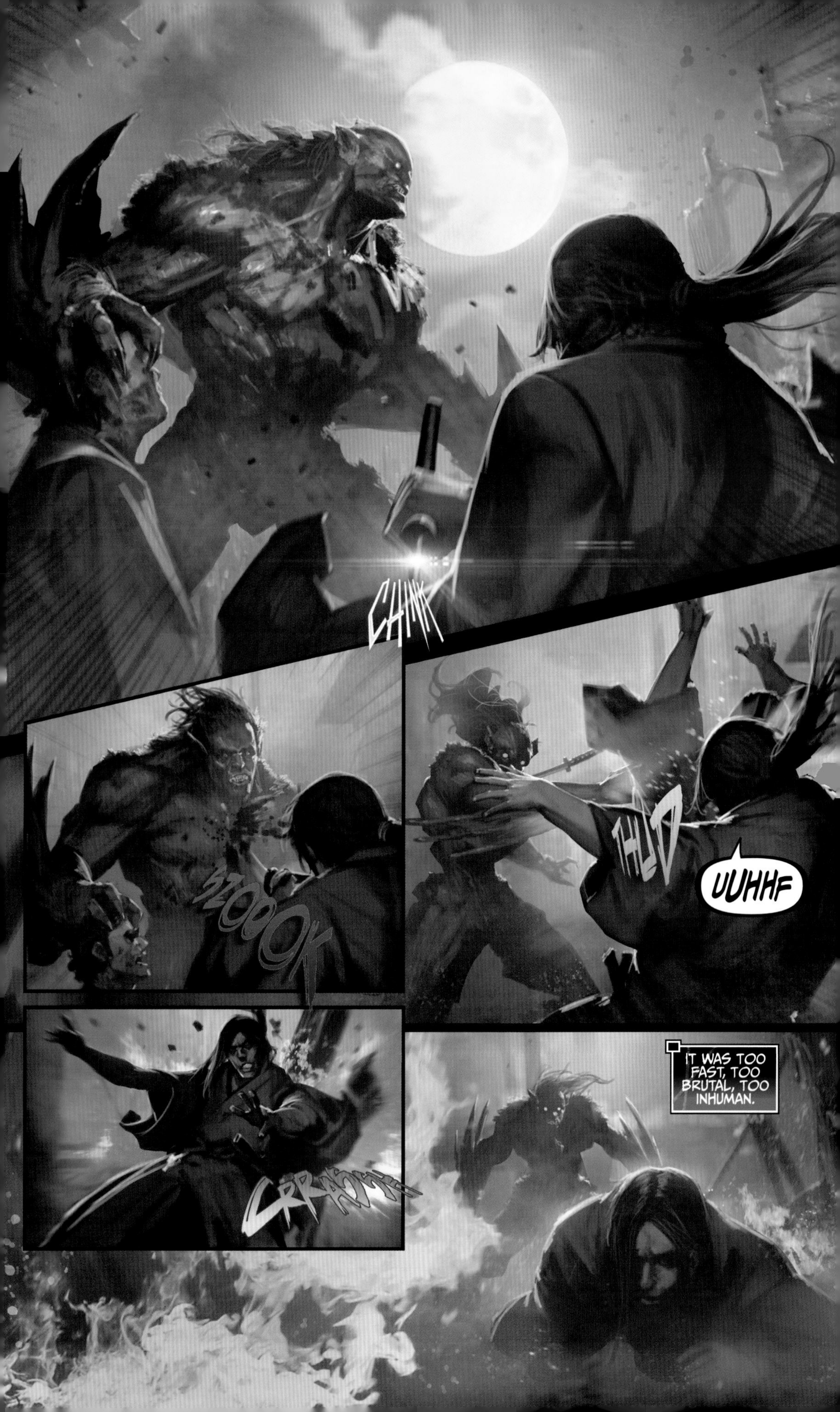
CHINK
BZOOOK
THUD
UUHHF
CRASH
IT WAS TOO FAST, TOO BRUTAL, TOO INHUMAN.

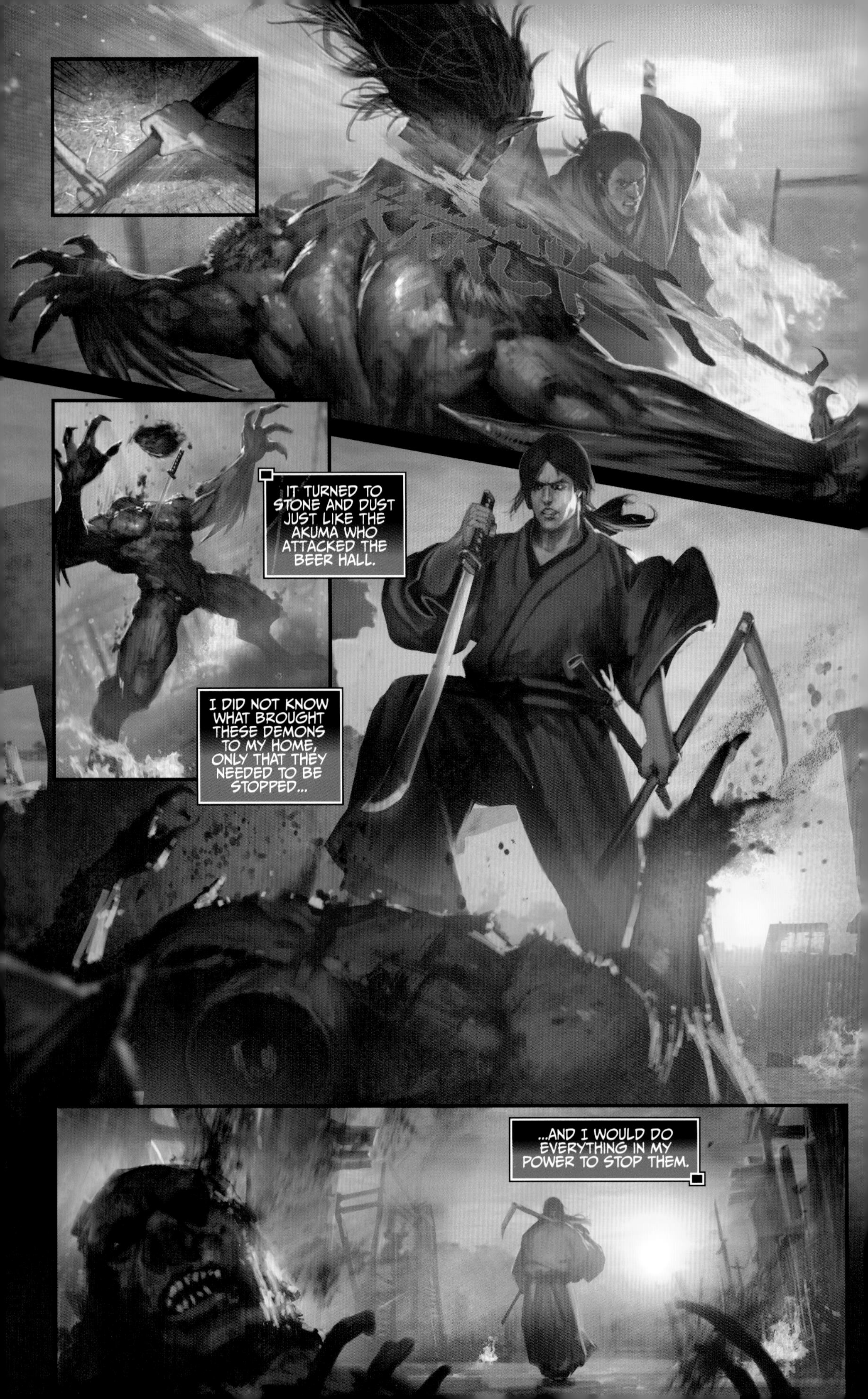
IT TURNED TO STONE AND DUST JUST LIKE THE AKUMA WHO ATTACKED THE BEER HALL.
I DID NOT KNOW WHAT BROUGHT THESE DEMONS TO MY HOME, ONLY THAT THEY NEEDED TO BE STOPPED...
...AND I WOULD DO EVERYTHING IN MY POWER TO STOP THEM.

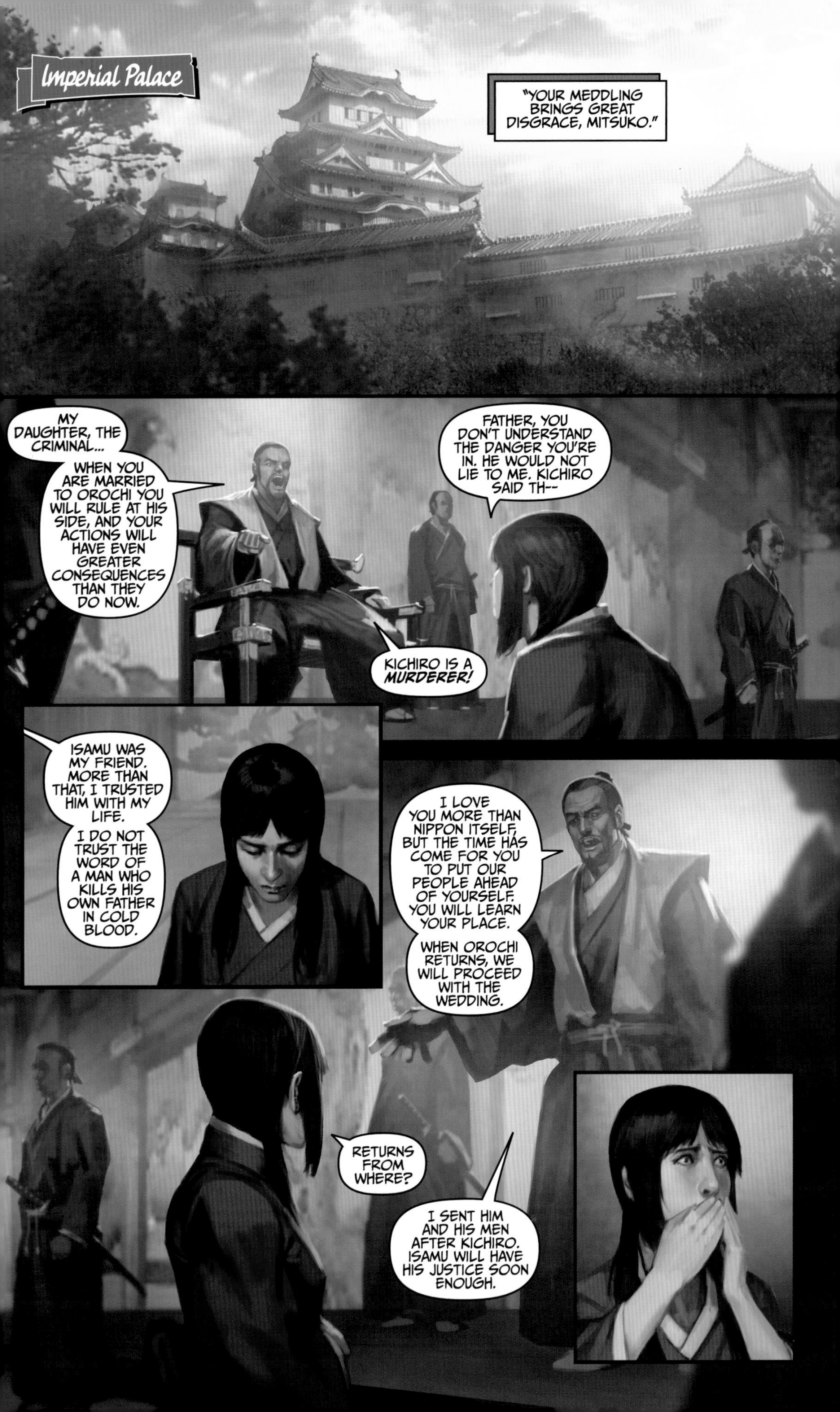
Imperial Palace
"YOUR MEDDLING BRINGS GREAT DISGRACE, MITSUKO."
MY DAUGHTER, THE CRIMINAL...
WHEN YOU ARE MARRIED TO OROCHI YOU WILL RULE AT HIS SIDE, AND YOUR ACTIONS WILL HAVE EVEN GREATER CONSEQUENCES THAN THEY DO NOW.
FATHER, YOU DON'T UNDERSTAND THE DANGER YOU'RE IN. HE WOULD NOT LIE TO ME. KICHIRO SAID TH--
KICHIRO IS A MURDERER!
ISAMU WAS MY FRIEND. MORE THAN THAT, I TRUSTED HIM WITH MY LIFE.
I DO NOT TRUST THE WORD OF A MAN WHO KILLS HIS OWN FATHER IN COLD BLOOD.
I LOVE YOU MORE THAN NIPPON ITSELF, BUT THE TIME HAS COME FOR YOU TO PUT OUR PEOPLE AHEAD OF YOURSELF. YOU WILL LEARN YOUR PLACE.
WHEN OROCHI RETURNS, WE WILL PROCEED WITH THE WEDDING.
RETURNS FROM WHERE?
I SENT HIM AND HIS MEN AFTER KICHIRO. ISAMU WILL HAVE HIS JUSTICE SOON ENOUGH.

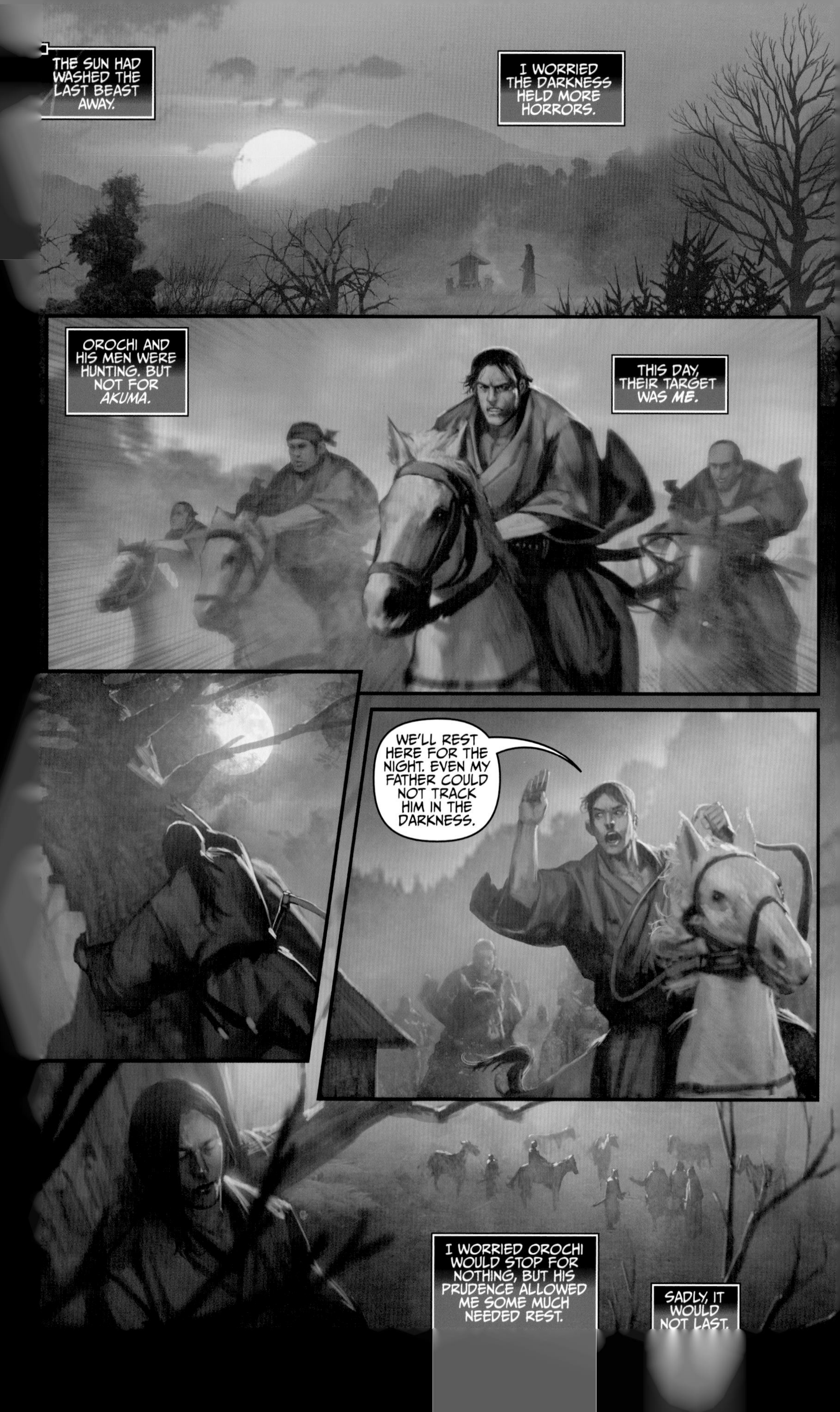
THE SUN HAD WASHED THE LAST BEAST AWAY.
I WORRIED THE DARKNESS HELD MORE HORRORS.
OROCHI AND HIS MEN WERE HUNTING. BUT NOT FOR *AKUMA.*
THIS DAY, THEIR TARGET WAS *ME.*
WE'LL REST HERE FOR THE NIGHT. EVEN MY FATHER COULD NOT TRACK HIM IN THE DARKNESS.
I WORRIED OROCHI WOULD STOP FOR NOTHING, BUT HIS PRUDENCE ALLOWED ME SOME MUCH NEEDED REST.
SADLY, IT WOULD NOT LAST.

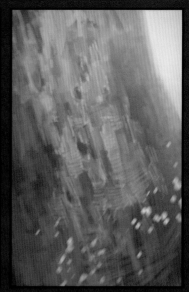

YOU *REALLY* SHOULD HAVE KILLED ME WHEN YOU HAD THE CHANCE.

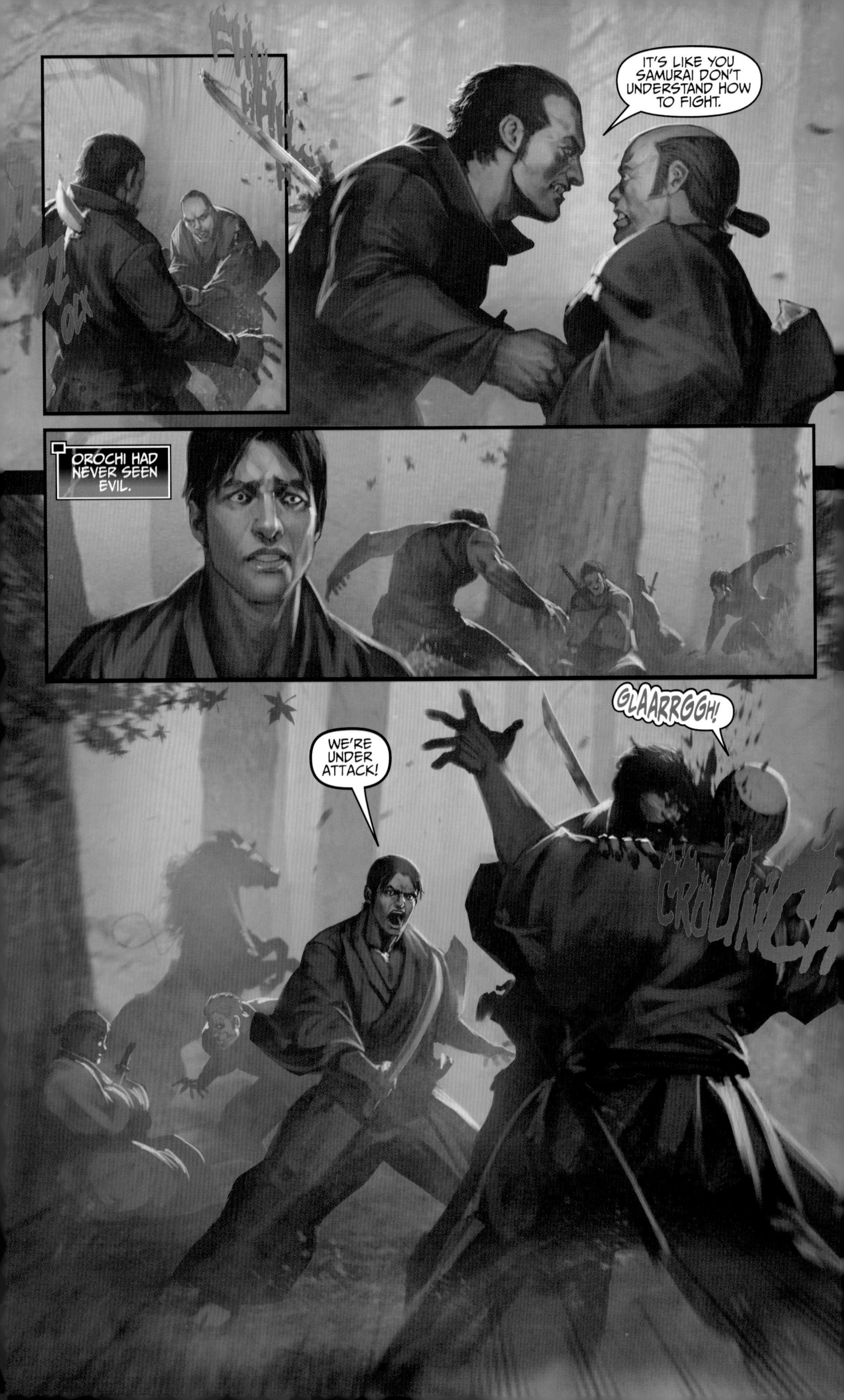

IT'S LIKE YOU SAMURAI DON'T UNDERSTAND HOW TO FIGHT.
OROCHI HAD NEVER SEEN EVIL.
GLAARRGGH!
WE'RE UNDER ATTACK!

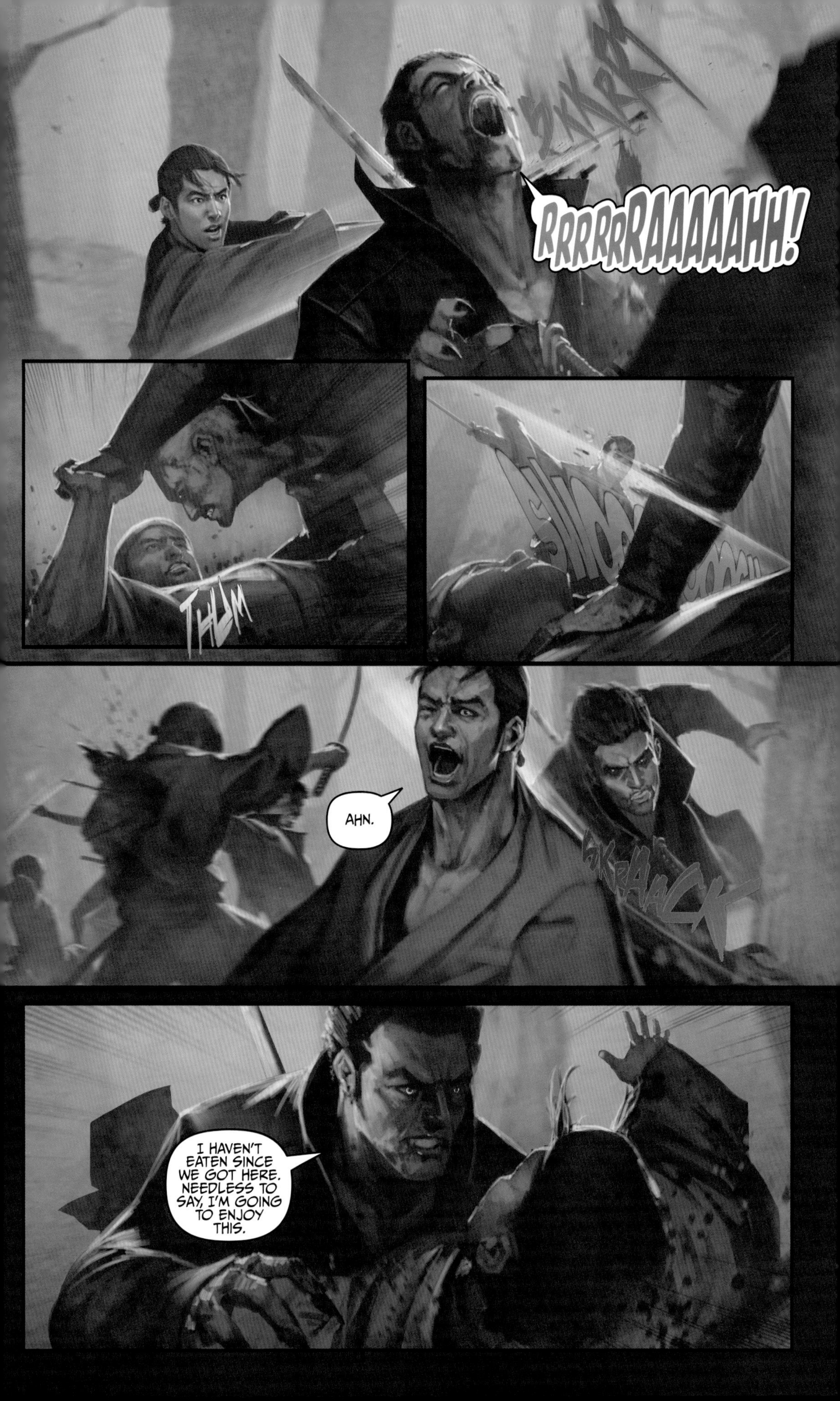
RRRRRAAAAAHH!
THUM
AHN.
I HAVEN'T EATEN SINCE WE GOT HERE. NEEDLESS TO SAY, I'M GOING TO ENJOY THIS.

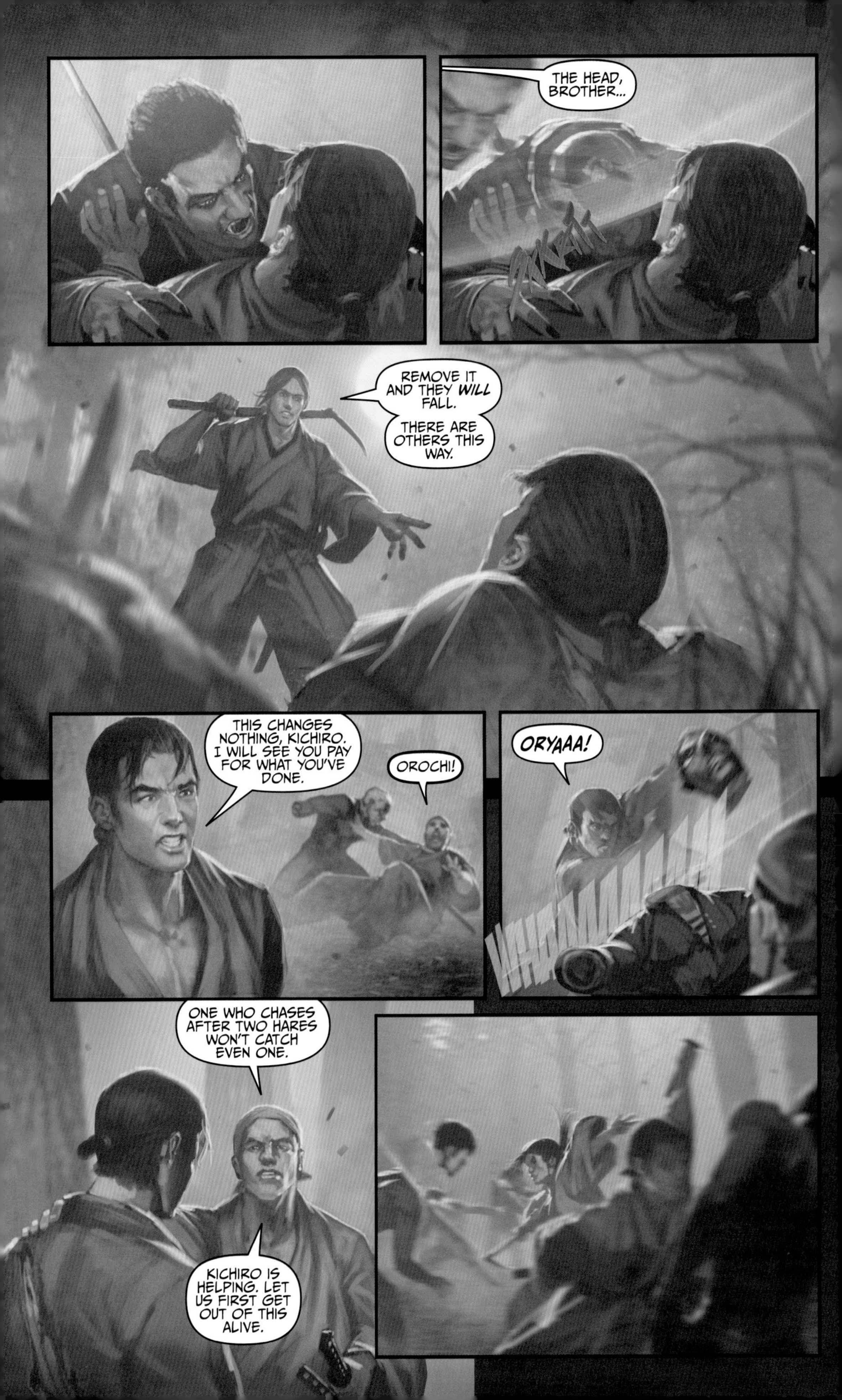
THE HEAD, BROTHER...
ZZKAT
REMOVE IT AND THEY WILL FALL.
THERE ARE OTHERS THIS WAY.
THIS CHANGES NOTHING, KICHIRO. I WILL SEE YOU PAY FOR WHAT YOU'VE DONE.
OROCHI!
ORYAAA!
ONE WHO CHASES AFTER TWO HARES WON'T CATCH EVEN ONE.
KICHIRO IS HELPING. LET US FIRST GET OUT OF THIS ALIVE.

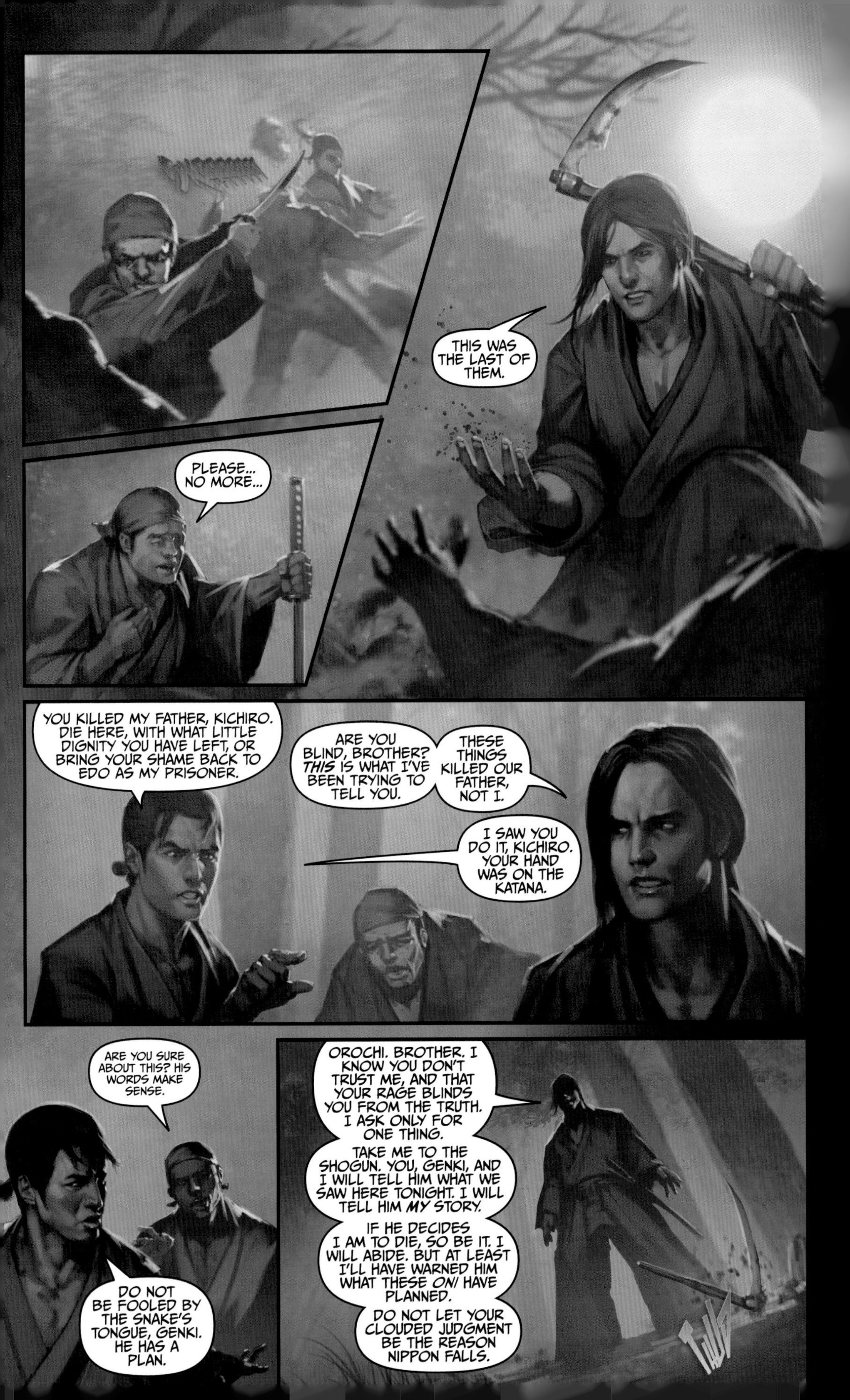
THIS WAS THE LAST OF THEM.
PLEASE... NO MORE...
YOU KILLED MY FATHER, KICHIRO. DIE HERE, WITH WHAT LITTLE DIGNITY YOU HAVE LEFT, OR BRING YOUR SHAME BACK TO EDO AS MY PRISONER.
ARE YOU BLIND, BROTHER? *THIS* IS WHAT I'VE BEEN TRYING TO TELL YOU.
THESE THINGS KILLED OUR FATHER, NOT I.
I SAW YOU DO IT, KICHIRO. YOUR HAND WAS ON THE KATANA.
ARE YOU SURE ABOUT THIS? HIS WORDS MAKE SENSE.
DO NOT BE FOOLED BY THE SNAKE'S TONGUE, GENKI. HE HAS A PLAN.
OROCHI. BROTHER. I KNOW YOU DON'T TRUST ME, AND THAT YOUR RAGE BLINDS YOU FROM THE TRUTH. I ASK ONLY FOR ONE THING.
TAKE ME TO THE SHOGUN. YOU, GENKI, AND I WILL TELL HIM WHAT WE SAW HERE TONIGHT. I WILL TELL HIM *MY* STORY.
IF HE DECIDES I AM TO DIE, SO BE IT. I WILL ABIDE. BUT AT LEAST I'LL HAVE WARNED HIM WHAT THESE *ONI* HAVE PLANNED.
DO NOT LET YOUR CLOUDED JUDGMENT BE THE REASON NIPPON FALLS.

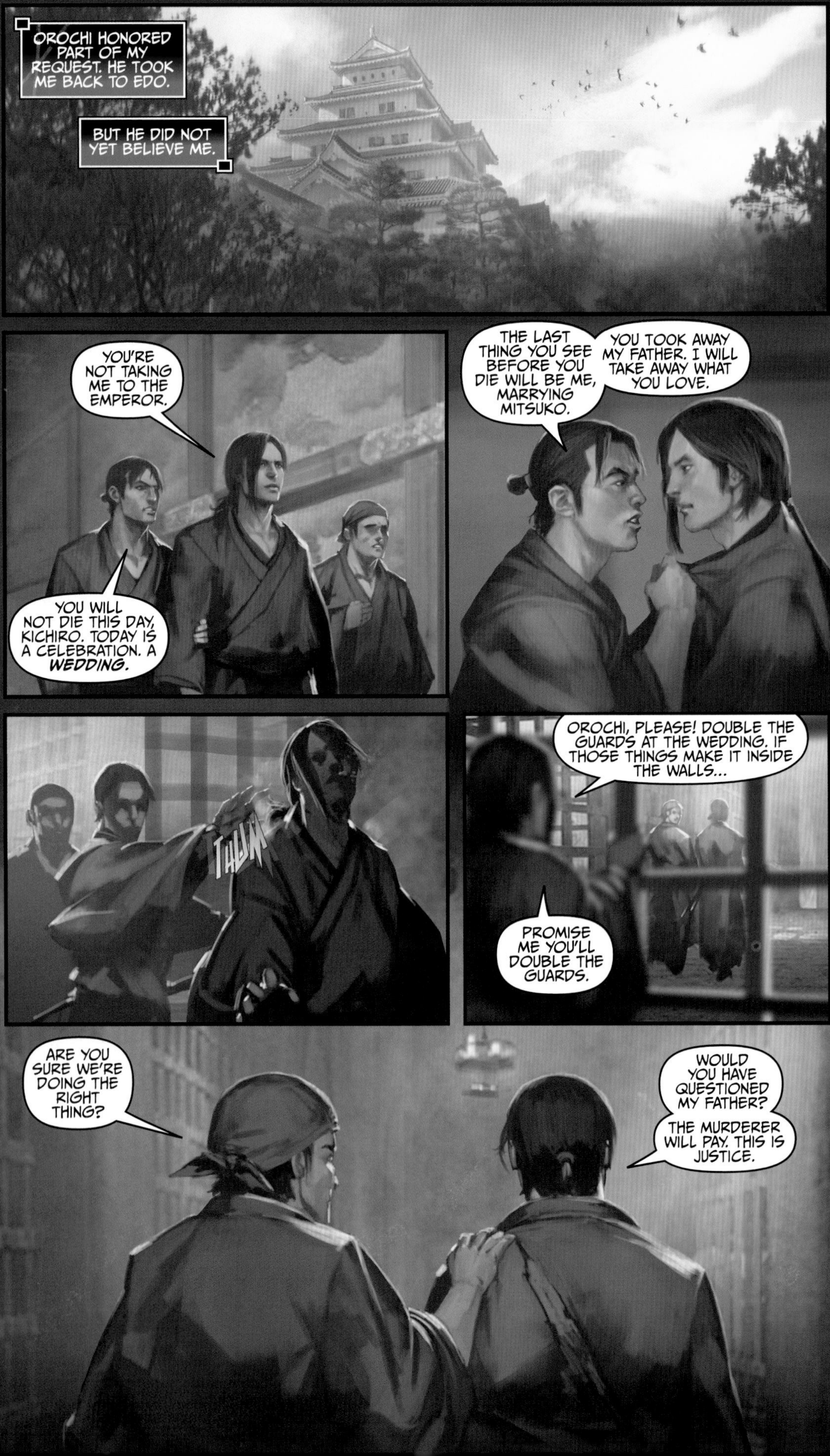
OROCHI HONORED PART OF MY REQUEST. HE TOOK ME BACK TO EDO.
BUT HE DID NOT YET BELIEVE ME.
YOU'RE NOT TAKING ME TO THE EMPEROR.
YOU WILL NOT DIE THIS DAY, KICHIRO. TODAY IS A CELEBRATION. A WEDDING.
THE LAST THING YOU SEE BEFORE YOU DIE WILL BE ME, MARRYING MITSUKO.
YOU TOOK AWAY MY FATHER. I WILL TAKE AWAY WHAT YOU LOVE.
THUM
OROCHI, PLEASE! DOUBLE THE GUARDS AT THE WEDDING. IF THOSE THINGS MAKE IT INSIDE THE WALLS...
PROMISE ME YOU'LL DOUBLE THE GUARDS.
ARE YOU SURE WE'RE DOING THE RIGHT THING?
WOULD YOU HAVE QUESTIONED MY FATHER?
THE MURDERER WILL PAY. THIS IS JUSTICE.

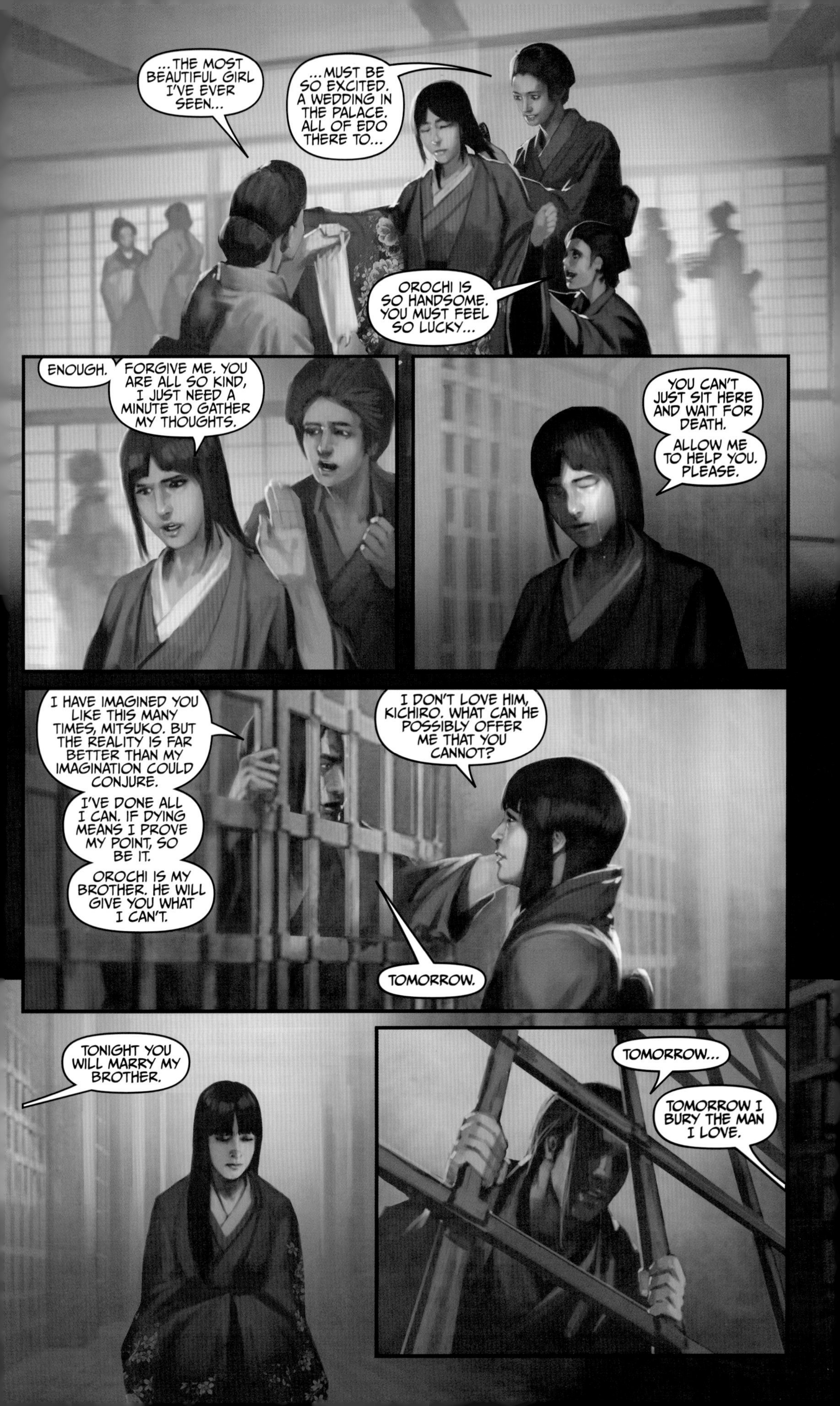
...THE MOST BEAUTIFUL GIRL I'VE EVER SEEN...
...MUST BE SO EXCITED. A WEDDING IN THE PALACE. ALL OF EDO THERE TO...
OROCHI IS SO HANDSOME. YOU MUST FEEL SO LUCKY...
ENOUGH.
FORGIVE ME. YOU ARE ALL SO KIND, I JUST NEED A MINUTE TO GATHER MY THOUGHTS.
YOU CAN'T JUST SIT HERE AND WAIT FOR DEATH.
ALLOW ME TO HELP YOU. PLEASE.
I HAVE IMAGINED YOU LIKE THIS MANY TIMES, MITSUKO. BUT THE REALITY IS FAR BETTER THAN MY IMAGINATION COULD CONJURE.
I DON'T LOVE HIM, KICHIRO. WHAT CAN HE POSSIBLY OFFER ME THAT YOU CANNOT?
I'VE DONE ALL I CAN. IF DYING MEANS I PROVE MY POINT, SO BE IT.
OROCHI IS MY BROTHER. HE WILL GIVE YOU WHAT I CAN'T.
TOMORROW.
TONIGHT YOU WILL MARRY MY BROTHER.
TOMORROW...
TOMORROW I BURY THE MAN I LOVE.

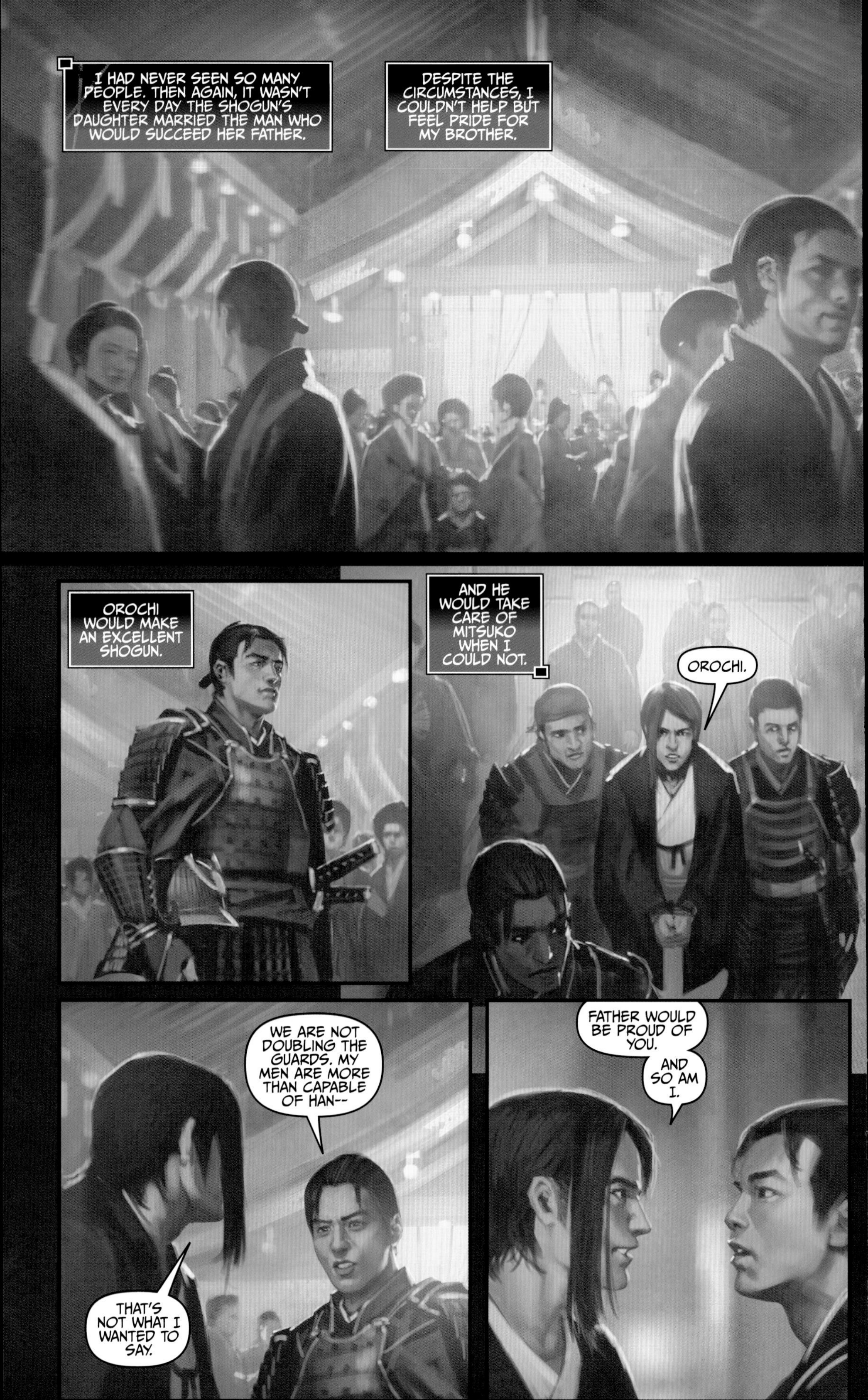
I HAD NEVER SEEN SO MANY PEOPLE. THEN AGAIN, IT WASN'T EVERY DAY THE SHOGUN'S DAUGHTER MARRIED THE MAN WHO WOULD SUCCEED HER FATHER.
DESPITE THE CIRCUMSTANCES, I COULDN'T HELP BUT FEEL PRIDE FOR MY BROTHER.
OROCHI WOULD MAKE AN EXCELLENT SHOGUN.
AND HE WOULD TAKE CARE OF MITSUKO WHEN I COULD NOT.
OROCHI.
WE ARE NOT DOUBLING THE GUARDS. MY MEN ARE MORE THAN CAPABLE OF HAN--
THAT'S NOT WHAT I WANTED TO SAY.
FATHER WOULD BE PROUD OF YOU.
AND SO AM I.

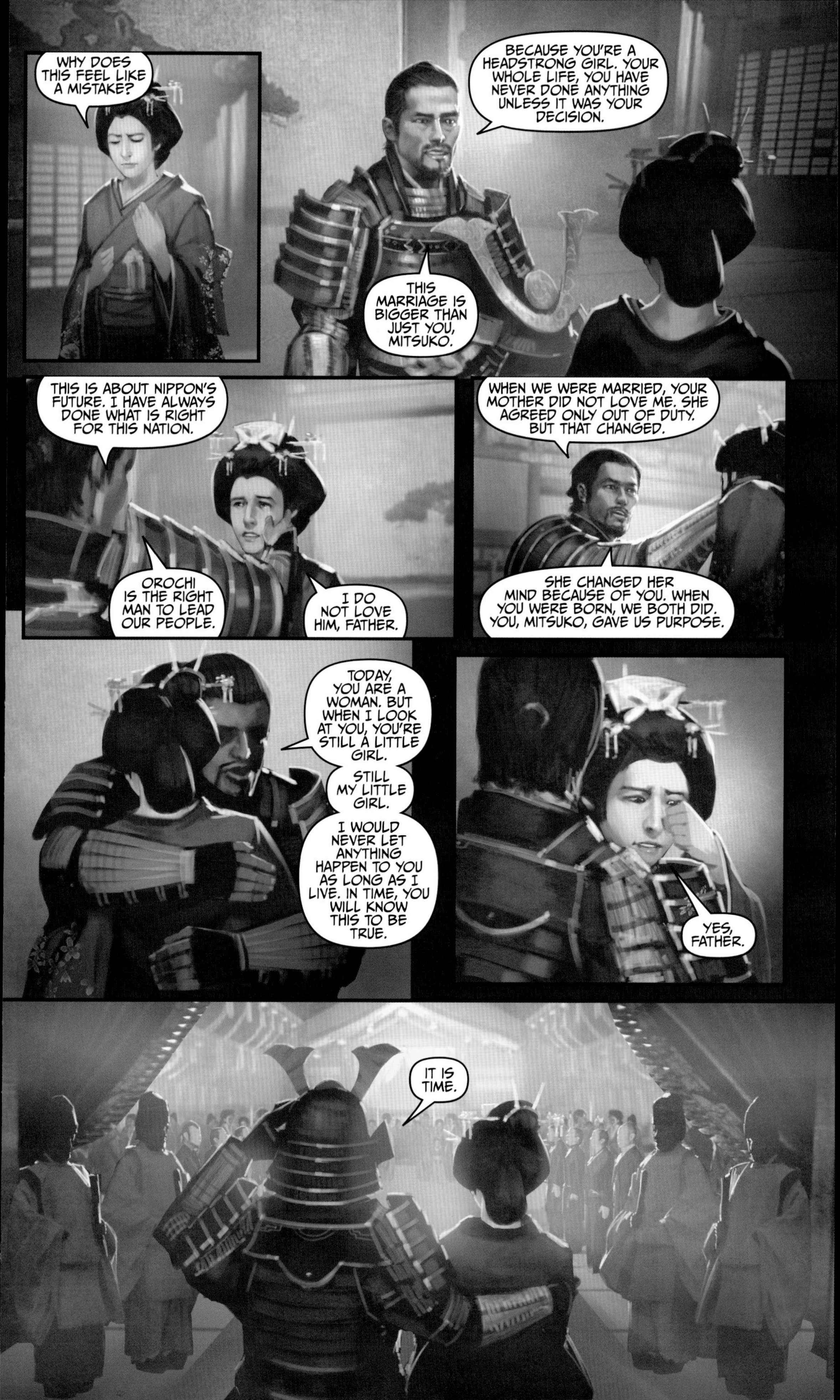
WHY DOES THIS FEEL LIKE A MISTAKE?
BECAUSE YOU'RE A HEADSTRONG GIRL. YOUR WHOLE LIFE, YOU HAVE NEVER DONE ANYTHING UNLESS IT WAS YOUR DECISION.
THIS MARRIAGE IS BIGGER THAN JUST YOU, MITSUKO.
THIS IS ABOUT NIPPON'S FUTURE. I HAVE ALWAYS DONE WHAT IS RIGHT FOR THIS NATION.
OROCHI IS THE RIGHT MAN TO LEAD OUR PEOPLE.
I DO NOT LOVE HIM, FATHER.
WHEN WE WERE MARRIED, YOUR MOTHER DID NOT LOVE ME. SHE AGREED ONLY OUT OF DUTY. BUT THAT CHANGED.
SHE CHANGED HER MIND BECAUSE OF YOU. WHEN YOU WERE BORN, WE BOTH DID. YOU, MITSUKO, GAVE US PURPOSE.
TODAY, YOU ARE A WOMAN. BUT WHEN I LOOK AT YOU, YOU'RE STILL A LITTLE GIRL.
STILL MY LITTLE GIRL.
I WOULD NEVER LET ANYTHING HAPPEN TO YOU AS LONG AS I LIVE. IN TIME, YOU WILL KNOW THIS TO BE TRUE.
YES, FATHER.
IT IS TIME.

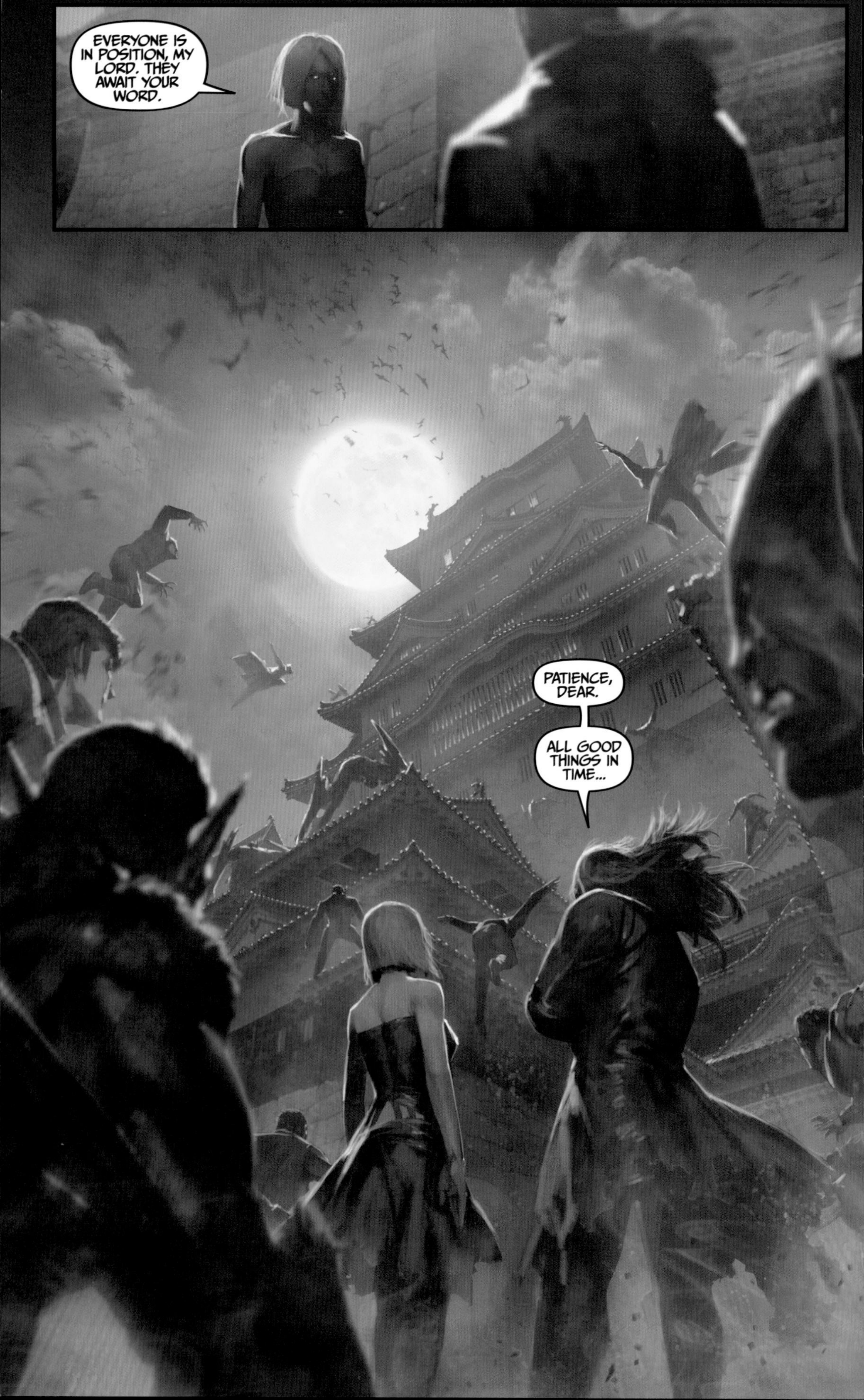
EVERYONE IS IN POSITION, MY LORD. THEY AWAIT YOUR WORD.
PATIENCE, DEAR.
ALL GOOD THINGS IN TIME...

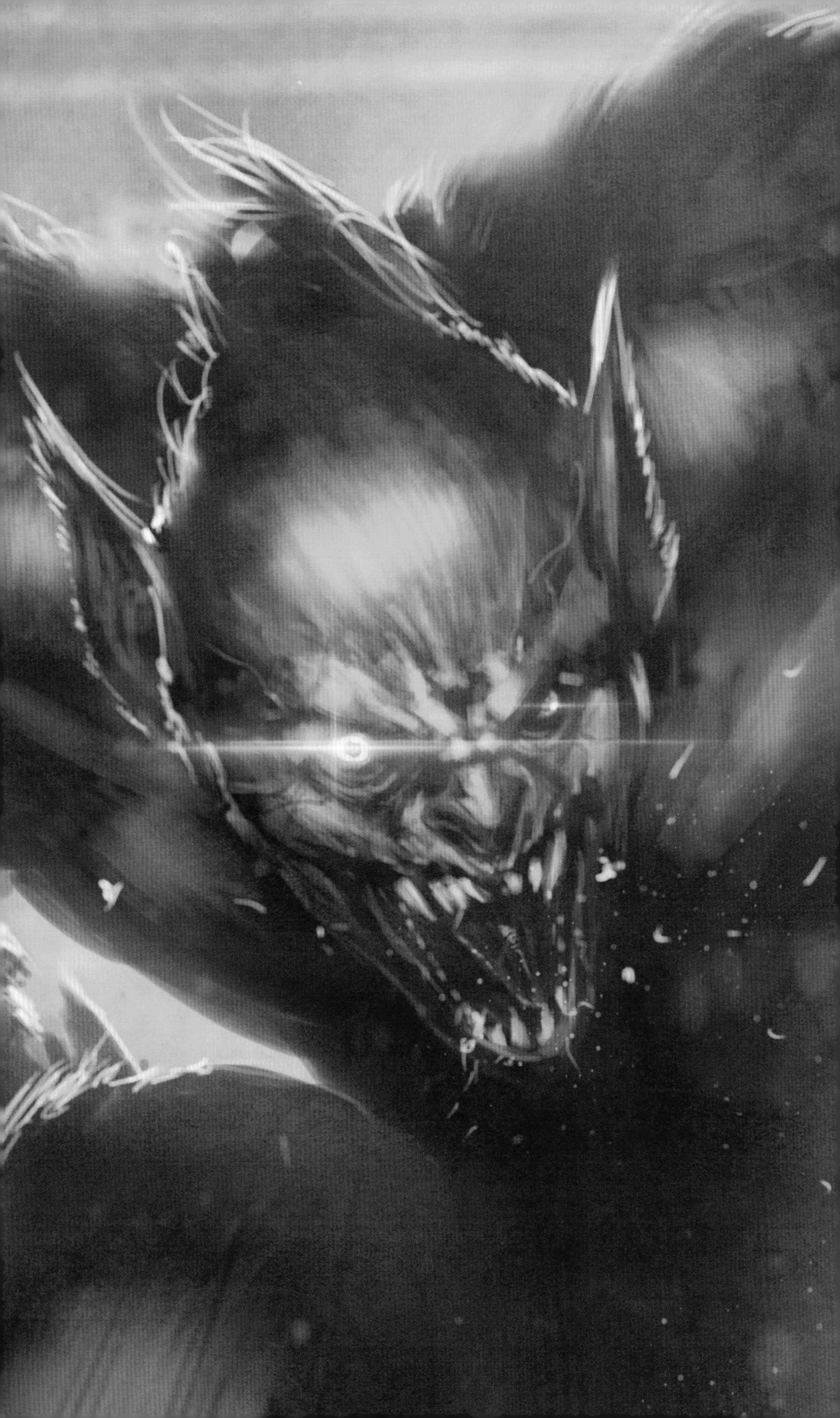

Chapter Three

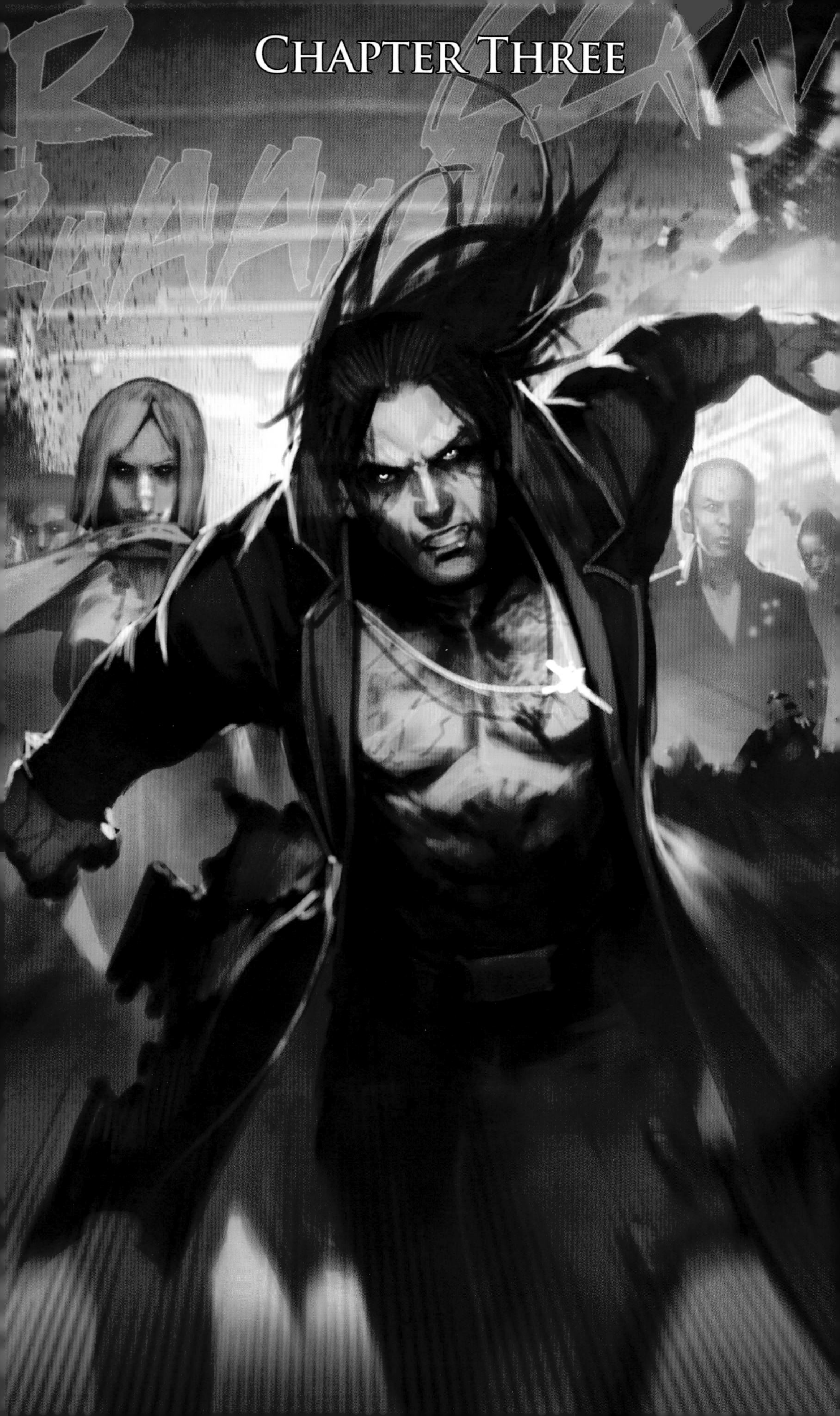

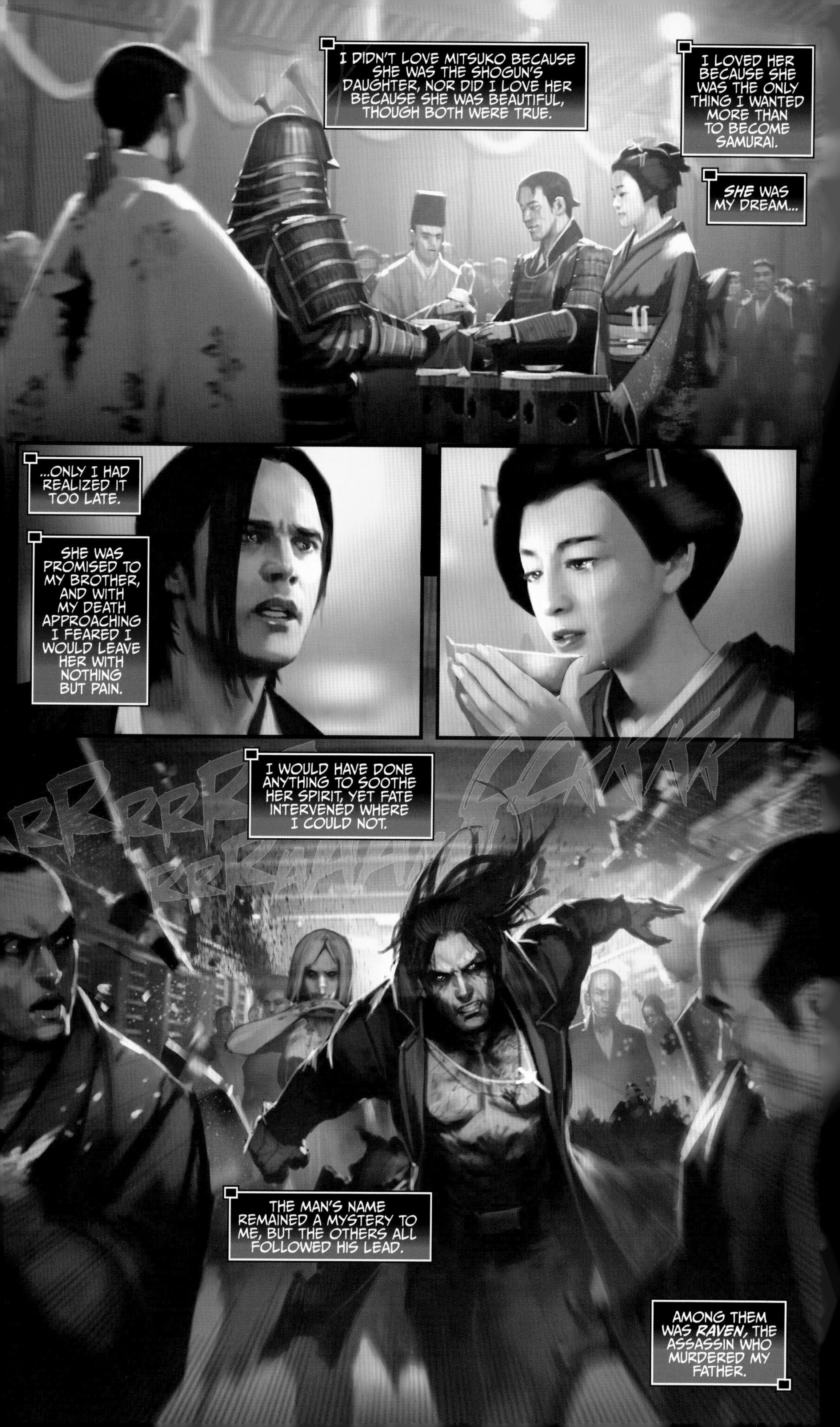
I DIDN'T LOVE MITSUKO BECAUSE SHE WAS THE SHOGUN'S DAUGHTER, NOR DID I LOVE HER BECAUSE SHE WAS BEAUTIFUL, THOUGH BOTH WERE TRUE.
I LOVED HER BECAUSE SHE WAS THE ONLY THING I WANTED MORE THAN TO BECOME SAMURAI.
SHE WAS MY DREAM...
...ONLY I HAD REALIZED IT TOO LATE.
SHE WAS PROMISED TO MY BROTHER, AND WITH MY DEATH APPROACHING I FEARED I WOULD LEAVE HER WITH NOTHING BUT PAIN.
I WOULD HAVE DONE ANYTHING TO SOOTHE HER SPIRIT, YET FATE INTERVENED WHERE I COULD NOT.
THE MAN'S NAME REMAINED A MYSTERY TO ME, BUT THE OTHERS ALL FOLLOWED HIS LEAD.
AMONG THEM WAS *RAVEN*, THE ASSASSIN WHO MURDERED MY FATHER.

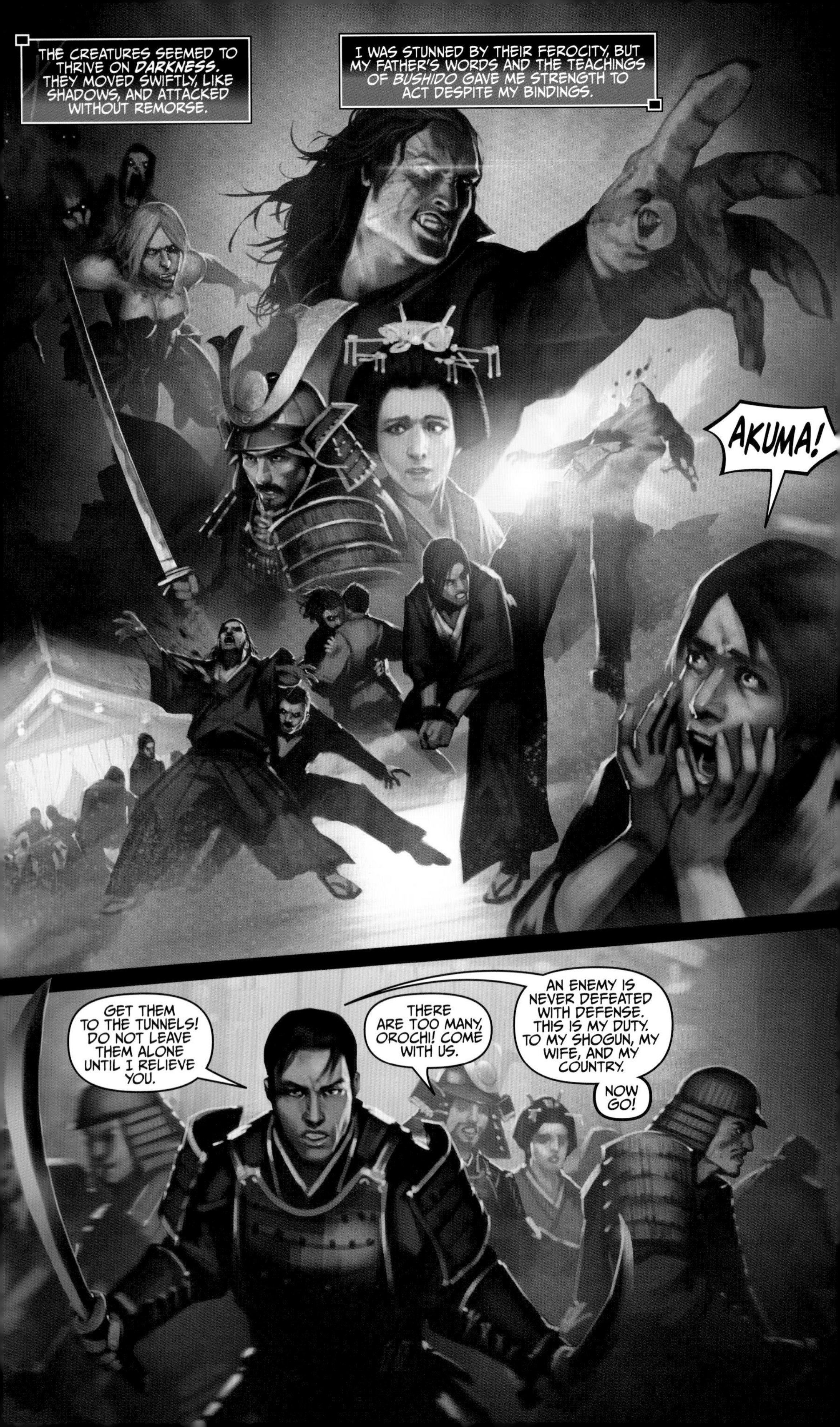
THE CREATURES SEEMED TO THRIVE ON *DARKNESS.* THEY MOVED SWIFTLY, LIKE SHADOWS, AND ATTACKED WITHOUT REMORSE.
I WAS STUNNED BY THEIR FEROCITY, BUT MY FATHER'S WORDS AND THE TEACHINGS OF *BUSHIDO* GAVE ME STRENGTH TO ACT DESPITE MY BINDINGS.
AKUMA!
GET THEM TO THE TUNNELS! DO NOT LEAVE THEM ALONE UNTIL I RELIEVE YOU.
THERE ARE TOO MANY, OROCHI! COME WITH US.
AN ENEMY IS NEVER DEFEATED WITH DEFENSE. THIS IS MY DUTY. TO MY SHOGUN, MY WIFE, AND MY COUNTRY.
NOW GO!

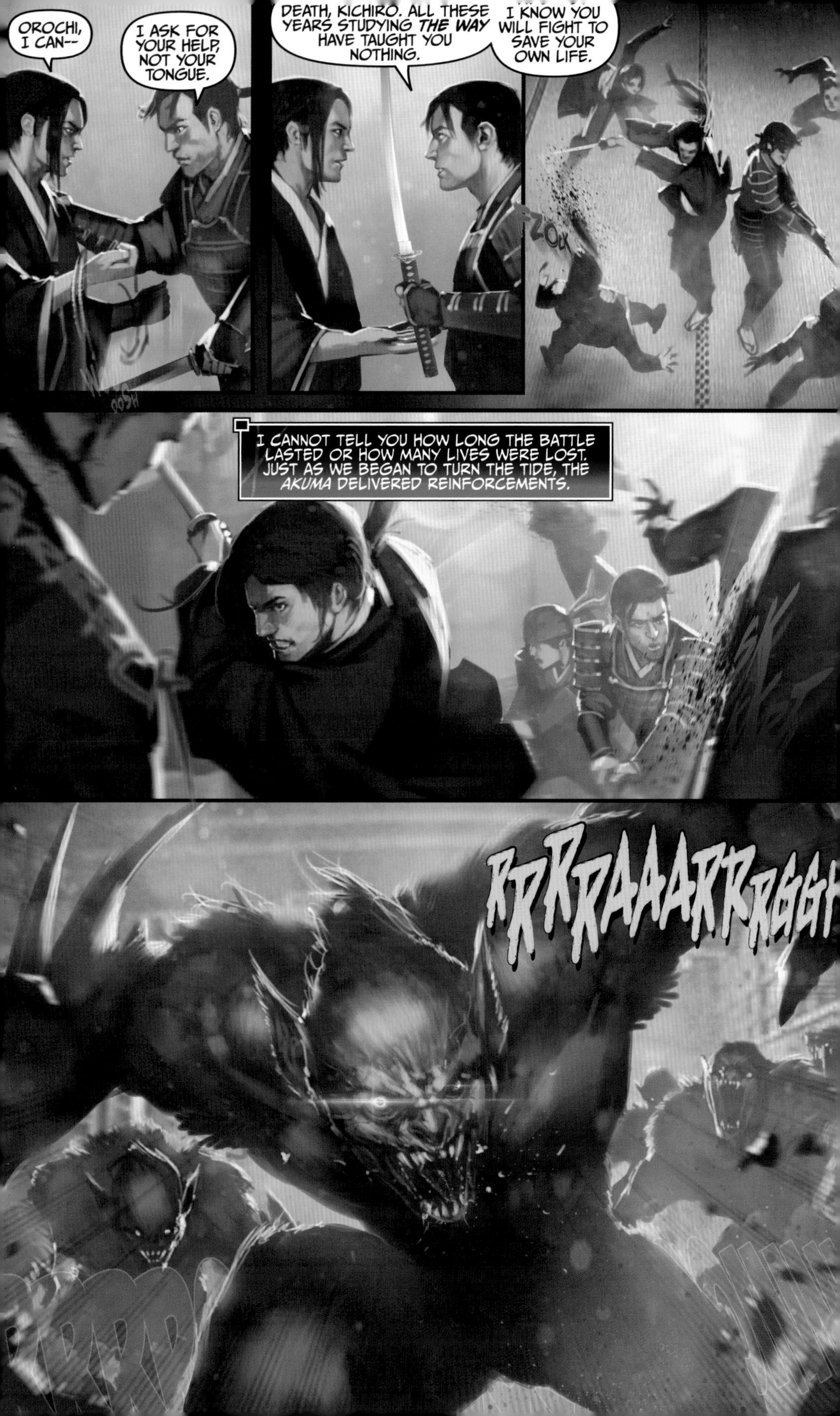
OROCHI, I CAN--
I ASK FOR YOUR HELP, NOT YOUR TONGUE.
DEATH, KICHIRO. ALL THESE YEARS STUDYING THE WAY HAVE TAUGHT YOU NOTHING.
I KNOW YOU WILL FIGHT TO SAVE YOUR OWN LIFE.
I CANNOT TELL YOU HOW LONG THE BATTLE LASTED OR HOW MANY LIVES WERE LOST. JUST AS WE BEGAN TO TURN THE TIDE, THE AKUMA DELIVERED REINFORCEMENTS.
RRRRAAARRRGGH

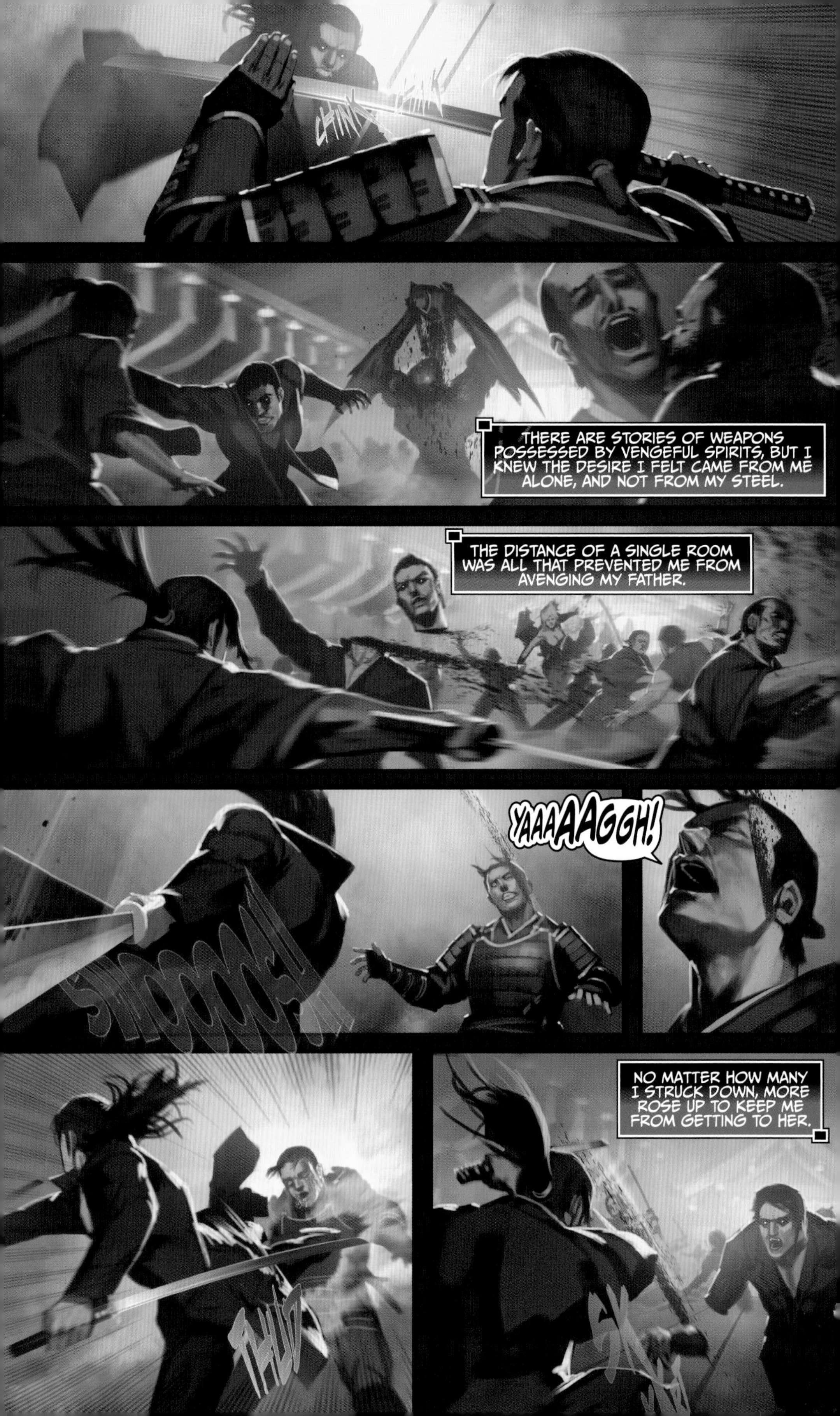

CHINK CHINK
THERE ARE STORIES OF WEAPONS POSSESSED BY VENGEFUL SPIRITS, BUT I KNEW THE DESIRE I FELT CAME FROM ME ALONE, AND NOT FROM MY STEEL.
THE DISTANCE OF A SINGLE ROOM WAS ALL THAT PREVENTED ME FROM AVENGING MY FATHER.
YAAAAAGGH!
NO MATTER HOW MANY I STRUCK DOWN, MORE ROSE UP TO KEEP ME FROM GETTING TO HER.
THUD

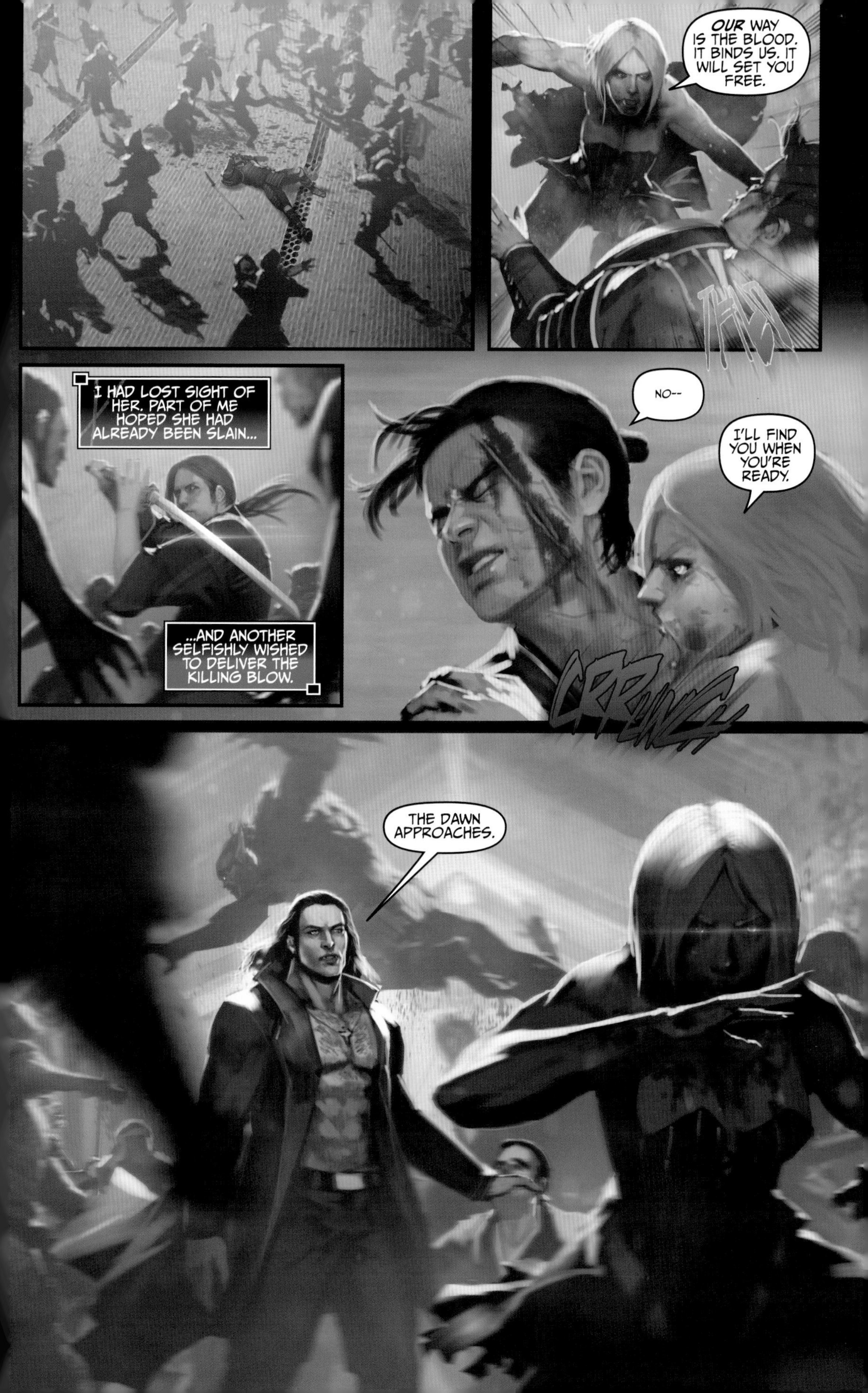
OUR WAY IS THE BLOOD. IT BINDS US. IT WILL SET YOU FREE.
I HAD LOST SIGHT OF HER. PART OF ME HOPED SHE HAD ALREADY BEEN SLAIN...
...AND ANOTHER SELFISHLY WISHED TO DELIVER THE KILLING BLOW.
NO--
I'LL FIND YOU WHEN YOU'RE READY.
THE DAWN APPROACHES.

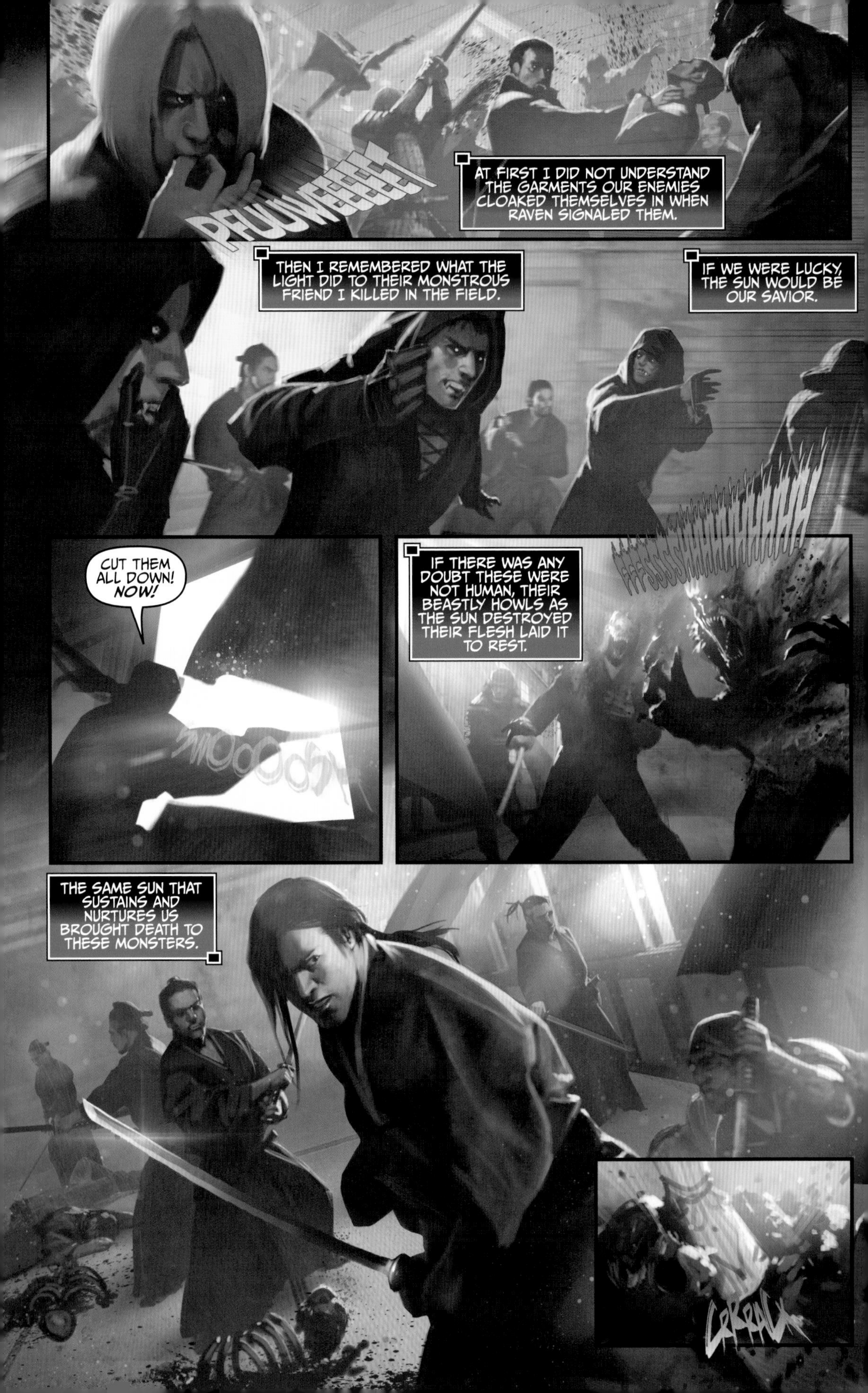
PFUUWEEEET
AT FIRST I DID NOT UNDERSTAND THE GARMENTS OUR ENEMIES CLOAKED THEMSELVES IN WHEN RAVEN SIGNALED THEM.
THEN I REMEMBERED WHAT THE LIGHT DID TO THEIR MONSTROUS FRIEND I KILLED IN THE FIELD.
IF WE WERE LUCKY, THE SUN WOULD BE OUR SAVIOR.
CUT THEM ALL DOWN! NOW!
SWOOOOSH
IF THERE WAS ANY DOUBT THESE WERE NOT HUMAN, THEIR BEASTLY HOWLS AS THE SUN DESTROYED THEIR FLESH LAID IT TO REST.
FFFSSSSHHHHHHHHHHH
THE SAME SUN THAT SUSTAINS AND NURTURES US BROUGHT DEATH TO THESE MONSTERS.
CRKRACK

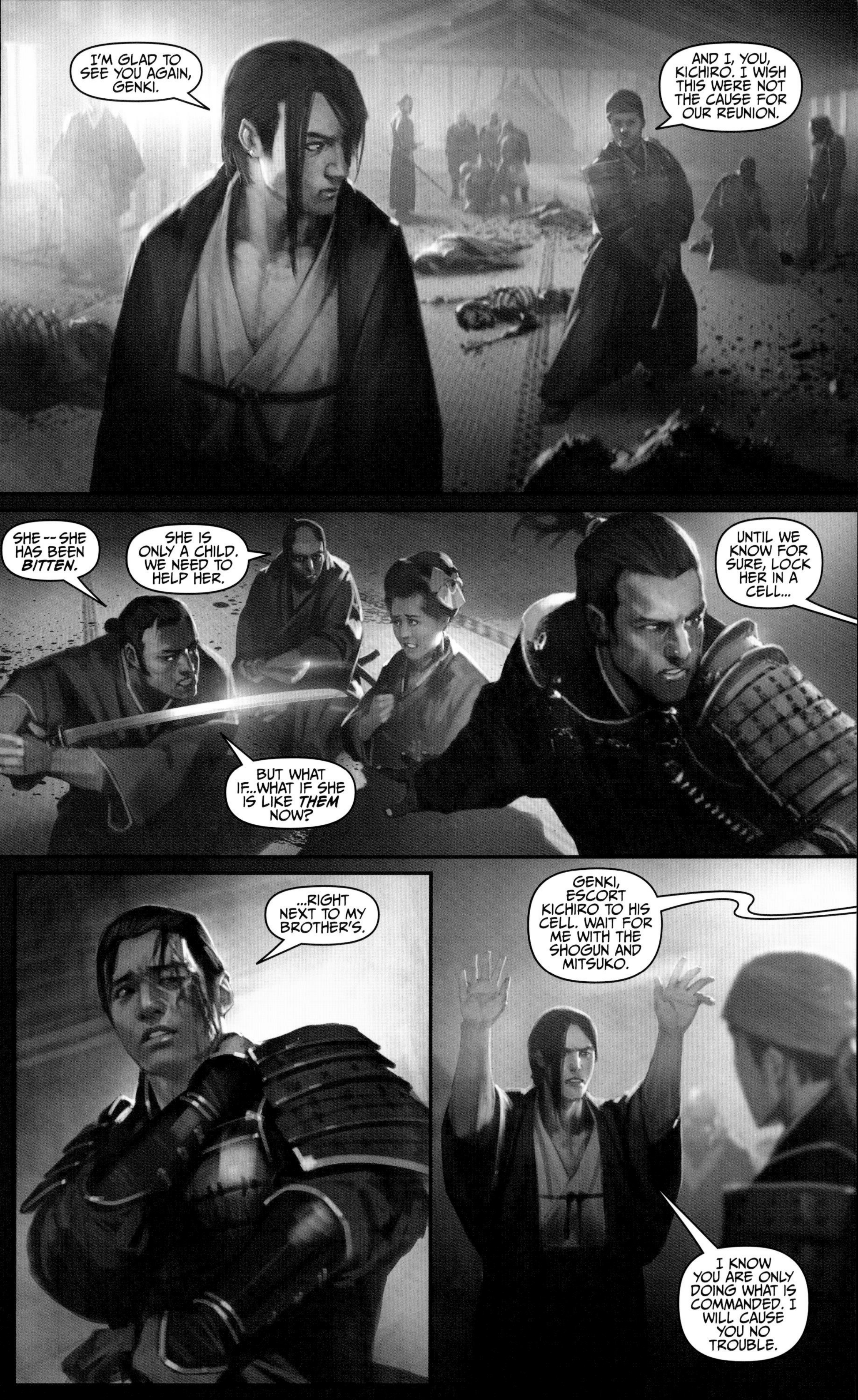
I'M GLAD TO SEE YOU AGAIN, GENKI.
AND I, YOU, KICHIRO. I WISH THIS WERE NOT THE CAUSE FOR OUR REUNION.
SHE -- SHE HAS BEEN *BITTEN.*
SHE IS ONLY A CHILD. WE NEED TO HELP HER.
BUT WHAT IF...WHAT IF SHE IS LIKE *THEM* NOW?
UNTIL WE KNOW FOR SURE, LOCK HER IN A CELL...
...RIGHT NEXT TO MY BROTHER'S.
GENKI, ESCORT KICHIRO TO HIS CELL. WAIT FOR ME WITH THE SHOGUN AND MITSUKO.
I KNOW YOU ARE ONLY DOING WHAT IS COMMANDED. I WILL CAUSE YOU NO TROUBLE.

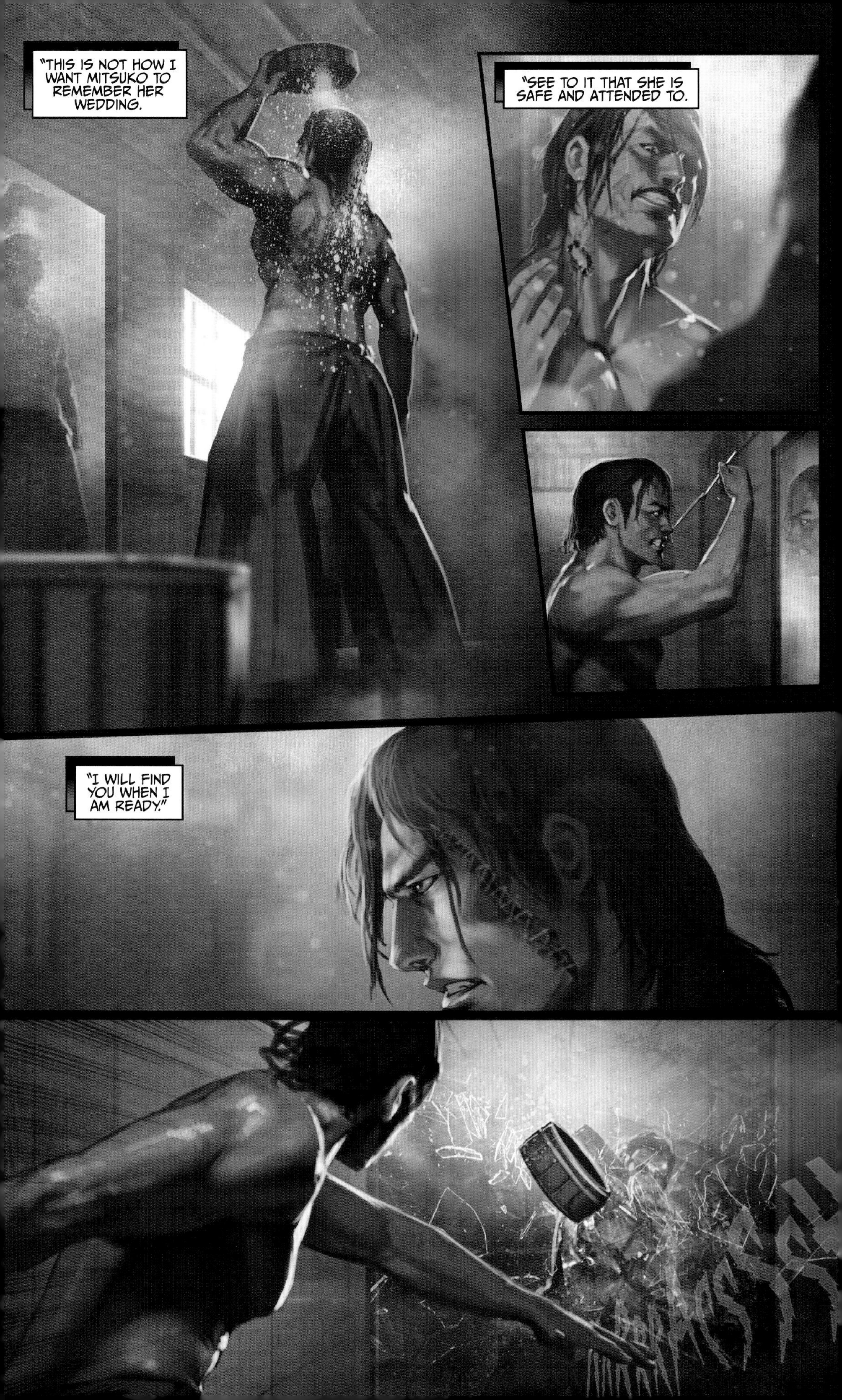
"THIS IS NOT HOW I WANT MITSUKO TO REMEMBER HER WEDDING.
"SEE TO IT THAT SHE IS SAFE AND ATTENDED TO.
"I WILL FIND YOU WHEN I AM READY."

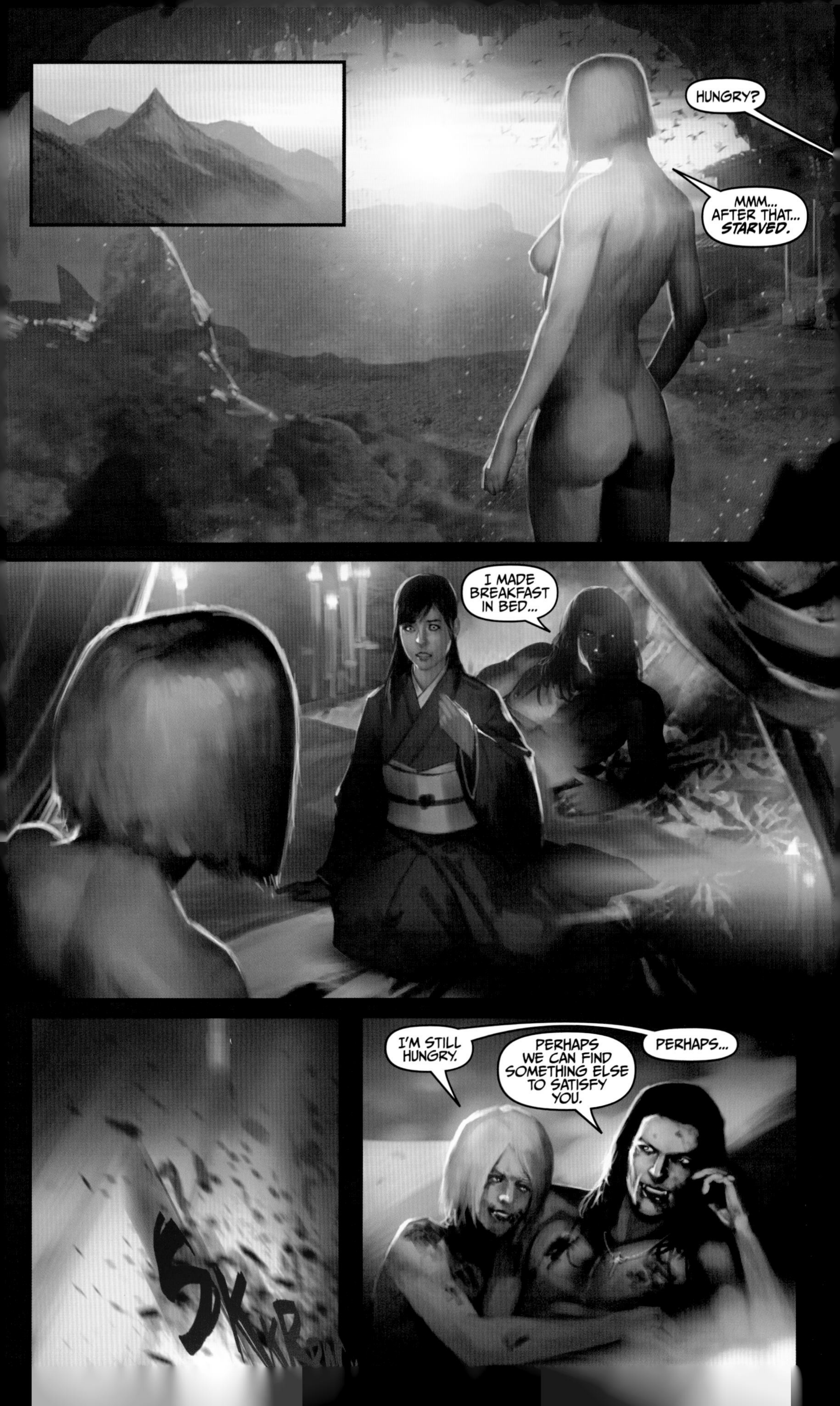
HUNGRY?
MMM... AFTER THAT... STARVED.
I MADE BREAKFAST IN BED...
I'M STILL HUNGRY.
PERHAPS...
PERHAPS WE CAN FIND SOMETHING ELSE TO SATISFY YOU.

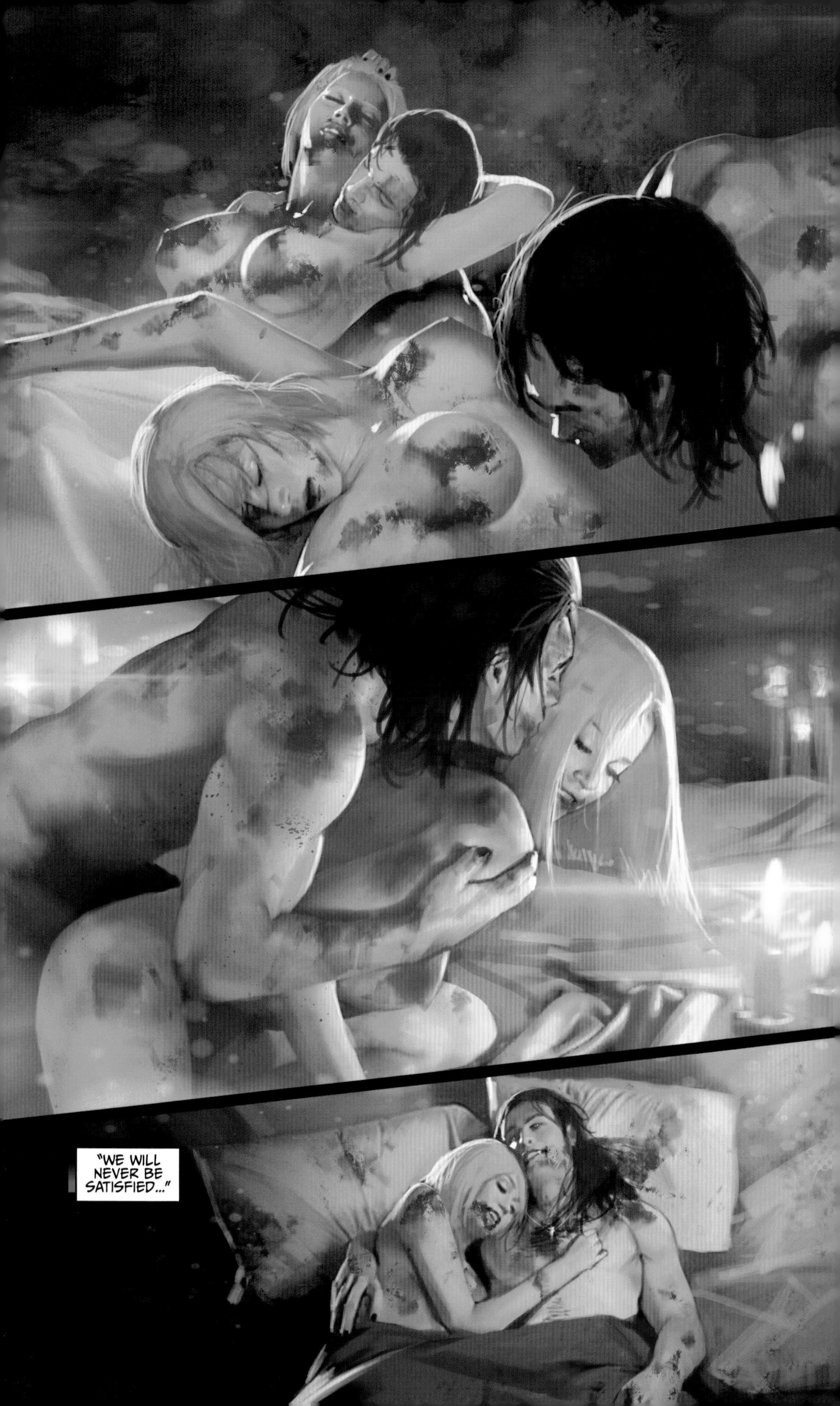
"WE WILL NEVER BE SATISFIED..."

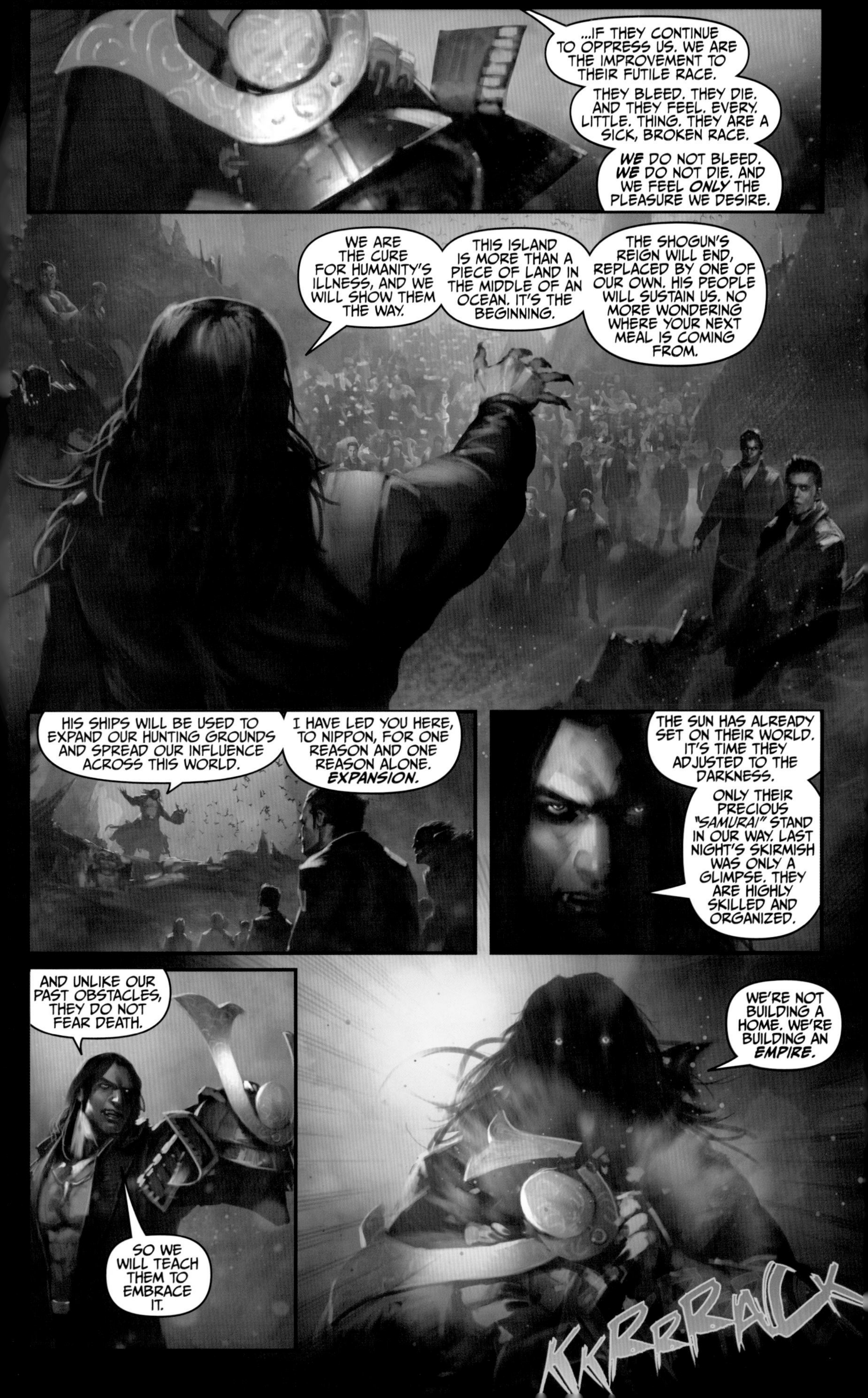
...IF THEY CONTINUE TO OPPRESS US. WE ARE THE IMPROVEMENT TO THEIR FUTILE RACE.
THEY BLEED. THEY DIE. AND THEY FEEL. EVERY. LITTLE. THING. THEY ARE A SICK, BROKEN RACE.
WE DO NOT BLEED. WE DO NOT DIE. AND WE FEEL ONLY THE PLEASURE WE DESIRE.
WE ARE THE CURE FOR HUMANITY'S ILLNESS, AND WE WILL SHOW THEM THE WAY.
THIS ISLAND IS MORE THAN A PIECE OF LAND IN THE MIDDLE OF AN OCEAN. IT'S THE BEGINNING.
THE SHOGUN'S REIGN WILL END, REPLACED BY ONE OF OUR OWN. HIS PEOPLE WILL SUSTAIN US. NO MORE WONDERING WHERE YOUR NEXT MEAL IS COMING FROM.
HIS SHIPS WILL BE USED TO EXPAND OUR HUNTING GROUNDS AND SPREAD OUR INFLUENCE ACROSS THIS WORLD.
I HAVE LED YOU HERE, TO NIPPON, FOR ONE REASON AND ONE REASON ALONE. EXPANSION.
THE SUN HAS ALREADY SET ON THEIR WORLD. IT'S TIME THEY ADJUSTED TO THE DARKNESS.
ONLY THEIR PRECIOUS "SAMURAI" STAND IN OUR WAY. LAST NIGHT'S SKIRMISH WAS ONLY A GLIMPSE. THEY ARE HIGHLY SKILLED AND ORGANIZED.
AND UNLIKE OUR PAST OBSTACLES, THEY DO NOT FEAR DEATH.
SO WE WILL TEACH THEM TO EMBRACE IT.
WE'RE NOT BUILDING A HOME. WE'RE BUILDING AN EMPIRE.
KKRRRACK

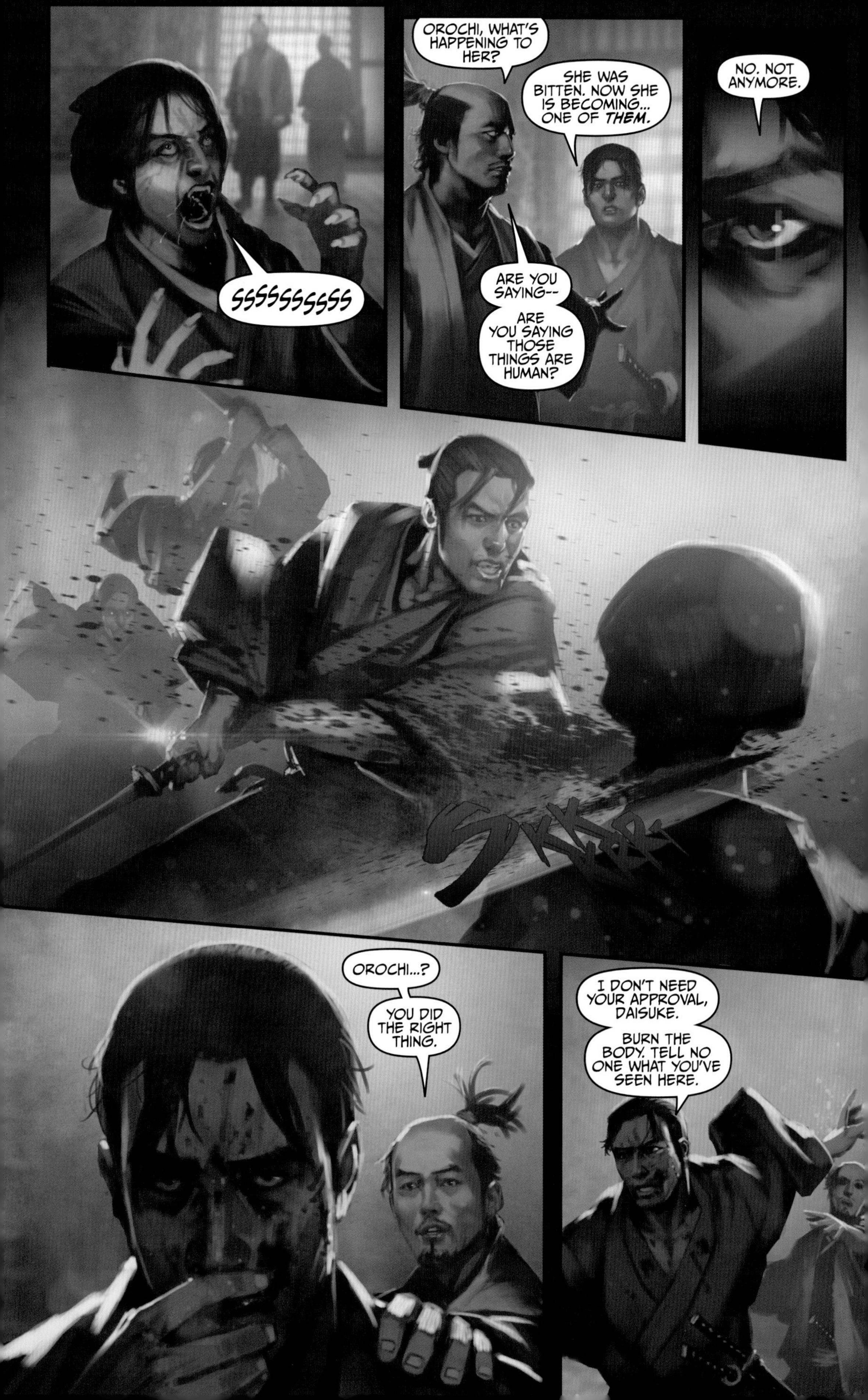
SSSSSSSSSS
OROCHI, WHAT'S HAPPENING TO HER?
SHE WAS BITTEN. NOW SHE IS BECOMING... ONE OF *THEM.*
ARE YOU SAYING--
ARE YOU SAYING THOSE THINGS ARE HUMAN?
NO. NOT ANYMORE.
SKKSH
OROCHI...?
YOU DID THE RIGHT THING.
I DON'T NEED YOUR APPROVAL, DAISUKE.
BURN THE BODY. TELL NO ONE WHAT YOU'VE SEEN HERE.

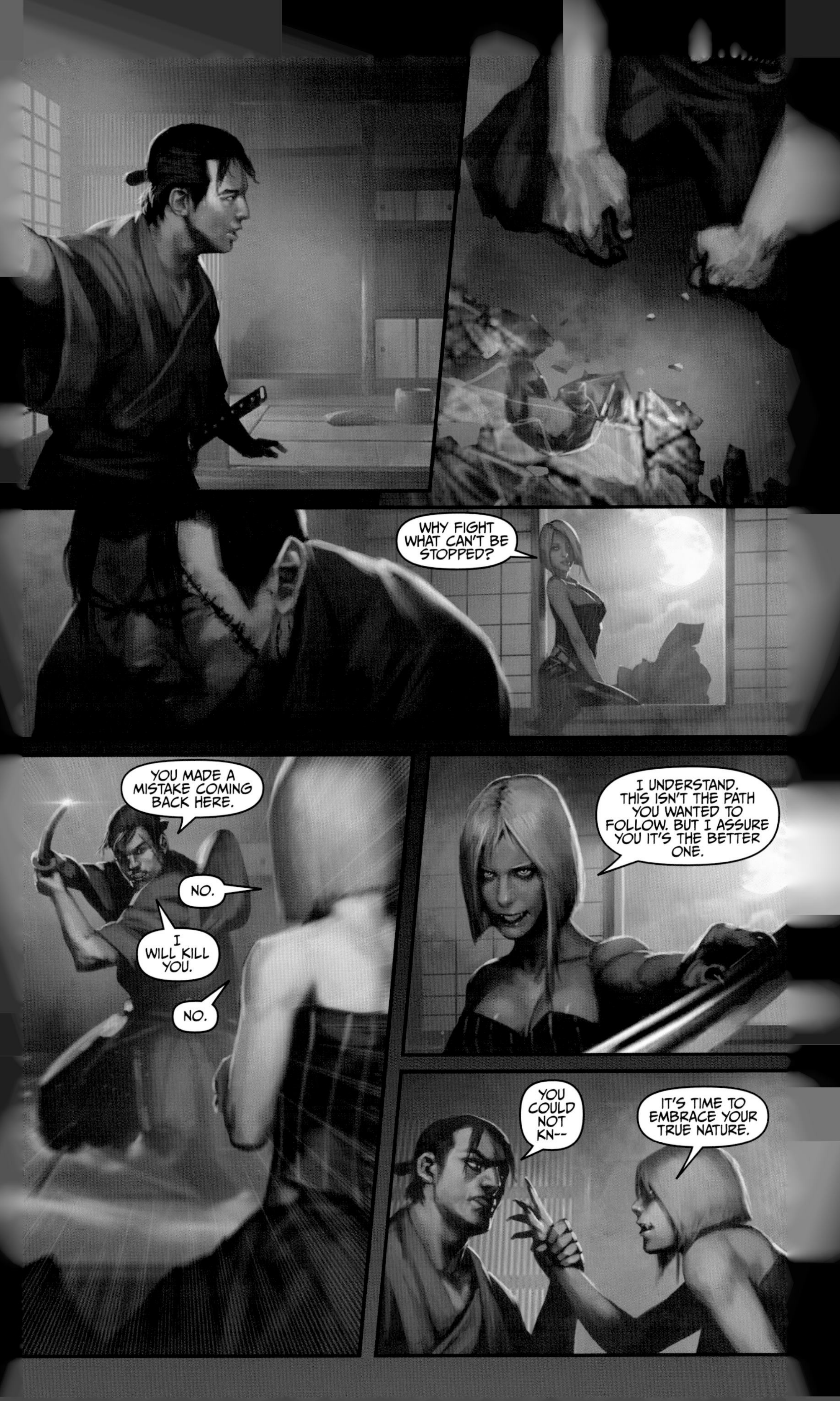
WHY FIGHT WHAT CAN'T BE STOPPED?
YOU MADE A MISTAKE COMING BACK HERE.
NO.
I WILL KILL YOU.
NO.
I UNDERSTAND. THIS ISN'T THE PATH YOU WANTED TO FOLLOW. BUT I ASSURE YOU IT'S THE BETTER ONE.
YOU COULD NOT KN--
IT'S TIME TO EMBRACE YOUR TRUE NATURE.

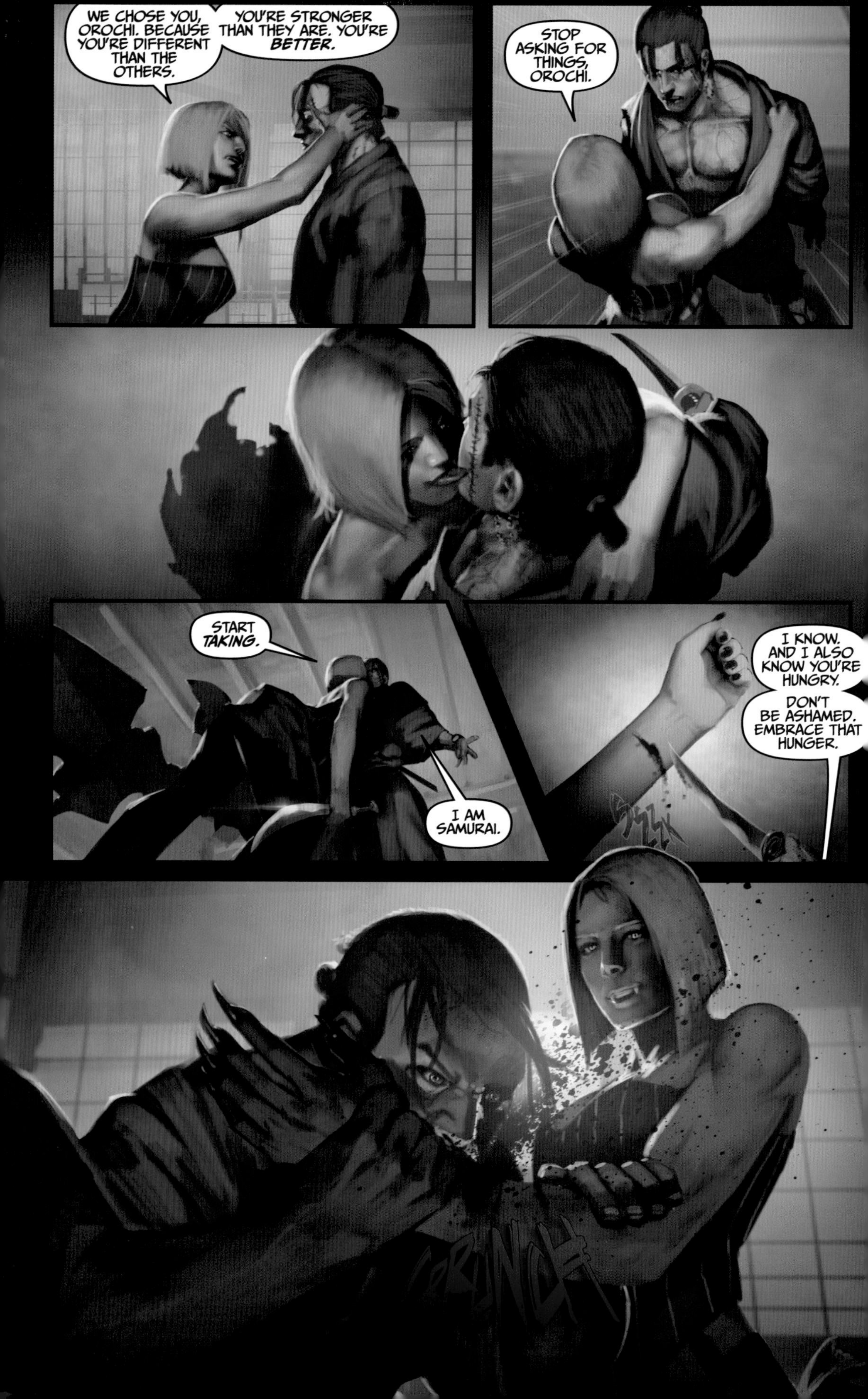
WE CHOSE YOU, OROCHI. BECAUSE YOU'RE DIFFERENT THAN THE OTHERS.
YOU'RE STRONGER THAN THEY ARE. YOU'RE *BETTER.*
STOP ASKING FOR THINGS, OROCHI.
START *TAKING.*
I AM SAMURAI.
I KNOW. AND I ALSO KNOW YOU'RE HUNGRY.
DON'T BE ASHAMED. EMBRACE THAT HUNGER.
SZZZK
CRUNCH

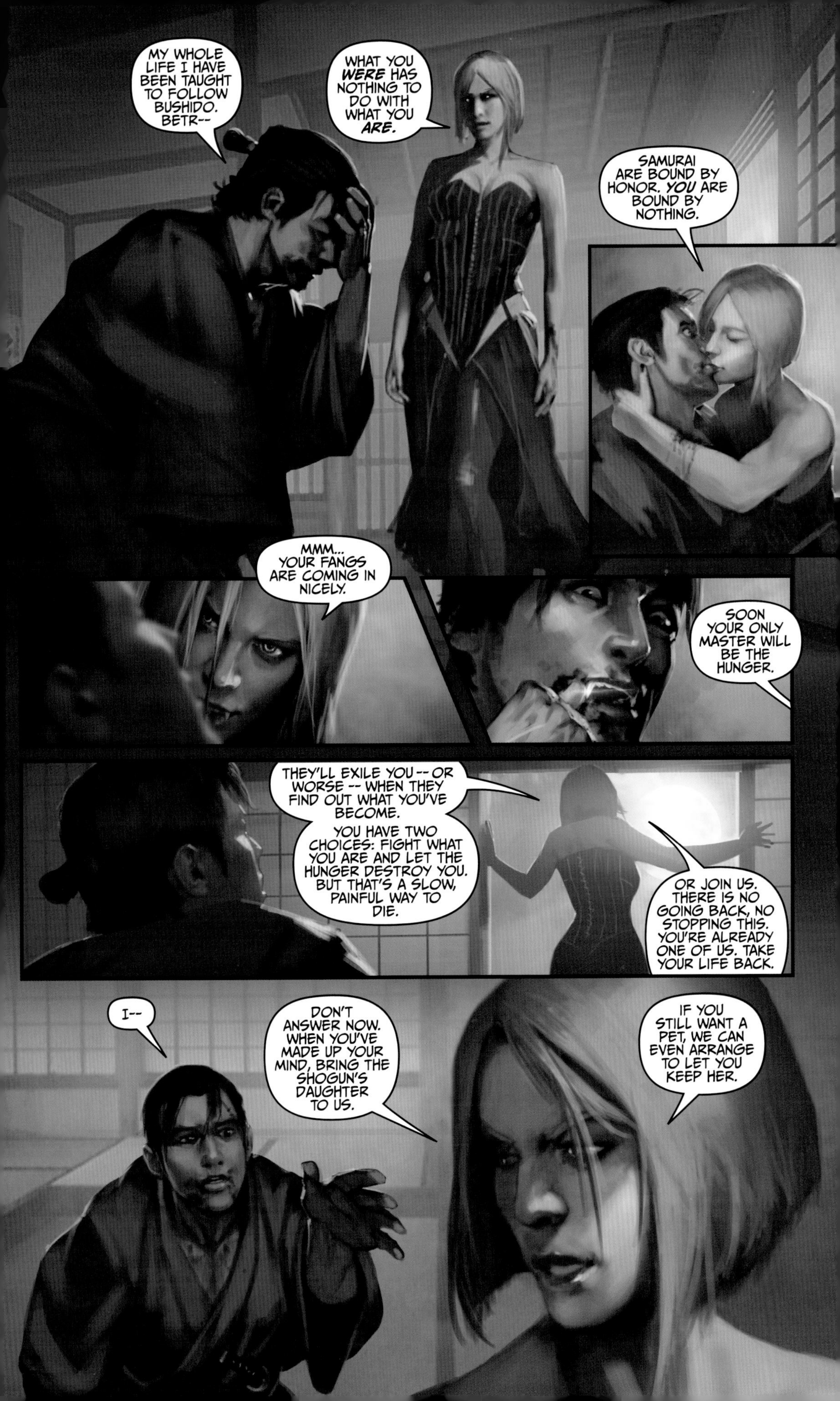
MY WHOLE LIFE I HAVE BEEN TAUGHT TO FOLLOW BUSHIDO. BETR--
WHAT YOU **WERE** HAS NOTHING TO DO WITH WHAT YOU **ARE.**
SAMURAI ARE BOUND BY HONOR. **YOU** ARE BOUND BY NOTHING.
MMM... YOUR FANGS ARE COMING IN NICELY.
SOON YOUR ONLY MASTER WILL BE THE HUNGER.
THEY'LL EXILE YOU -- OR WORSE -- WHEN THEY FIND OUT WHAT YOU'VE BECOME.
YOU HAVE TWO CHOICES: FIGHT WHAT YOU ARE AND LET THE HUNGER DESTROY YOU. BUT THAT'S A SLOW, PAINFUL WAY TO DIE.
OR JOIN US. THERE IS NO GOING BACK, NO STOPPING THIS. YOU'RE ALREADY ONE OF US. TAKE YOUR LIFE BACK.
I--
DON'T ANSWER NOW. WHEN YOU'VE MADE UP YOUR MIND, BRING THE SHOGUN'S DAUGHTER TO US.
IF YOU STILL WANT A PET, WE CAN EVEN ARRANGE TO LET YOU KEEP HER.

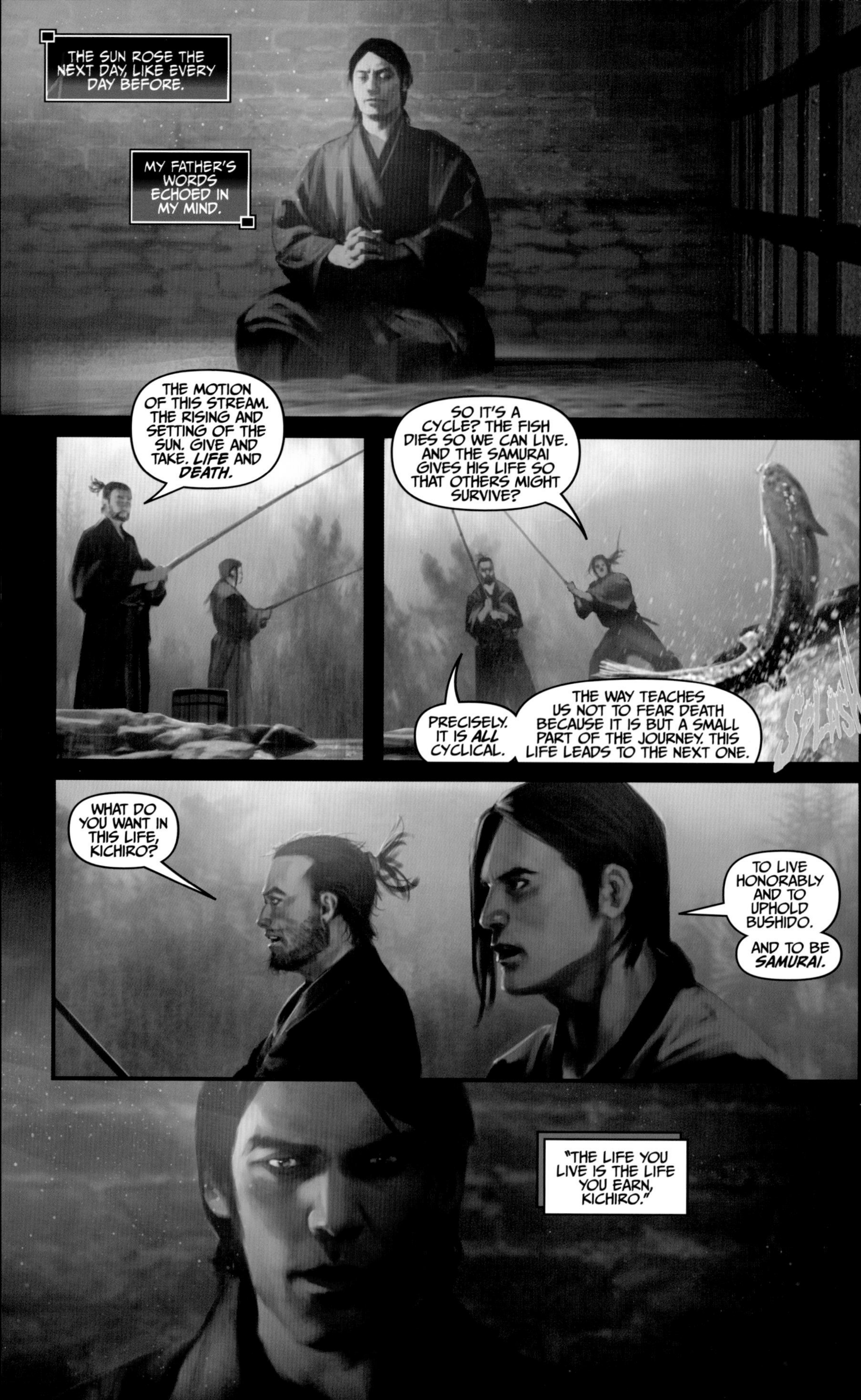
THE SUN ROSE THE NEXT DAY, LIKE EVERY DAY BEFORE.
MY FATHER'S WORDS ECHOED IN MY MIND.
THE MOTION OF THIS STREAM. THE RISING AND SETTING OF THE SUN. GIVE AND TAKE. LIFE AND DEATH.
SO IT'S A CYCLE? THE FISH DIES SO WE CAN LIVE. AND THE SAMURAI GIVES HIS LIFE SO THAT OTHERS MIGHT SURVIVE?
PRECISELY. IT IS ALL CYCLICAL.
THE WAY TEACHES US NOT TO FEAR DEATH BECAUSE IT IS BUT A SMALL PART OF THE JOURNEY. THIS LIFE LEADS TO THE NEXT ONE.
SPLASH
WHAT DO YOU WANT IN THIS LIFE, KICHIRO?
TO LIVE HONORABLY AND TO UPHOLD BUSHIDO.
AND TO BE SAMURAI.
"THE LIFE YOU LIVE IS THE LIFE YOU EARN, KICHIRO."

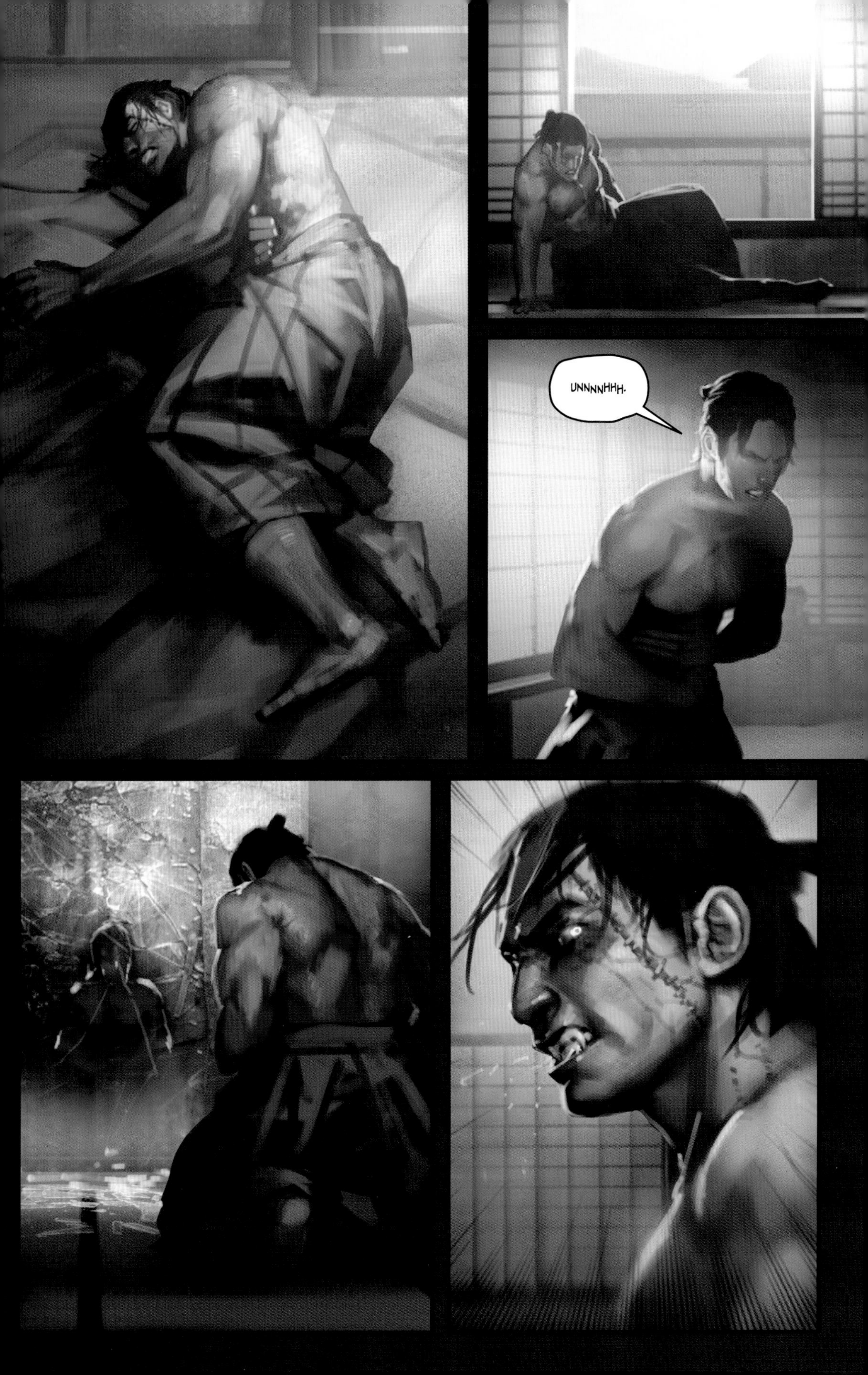
UNNNNHHH.

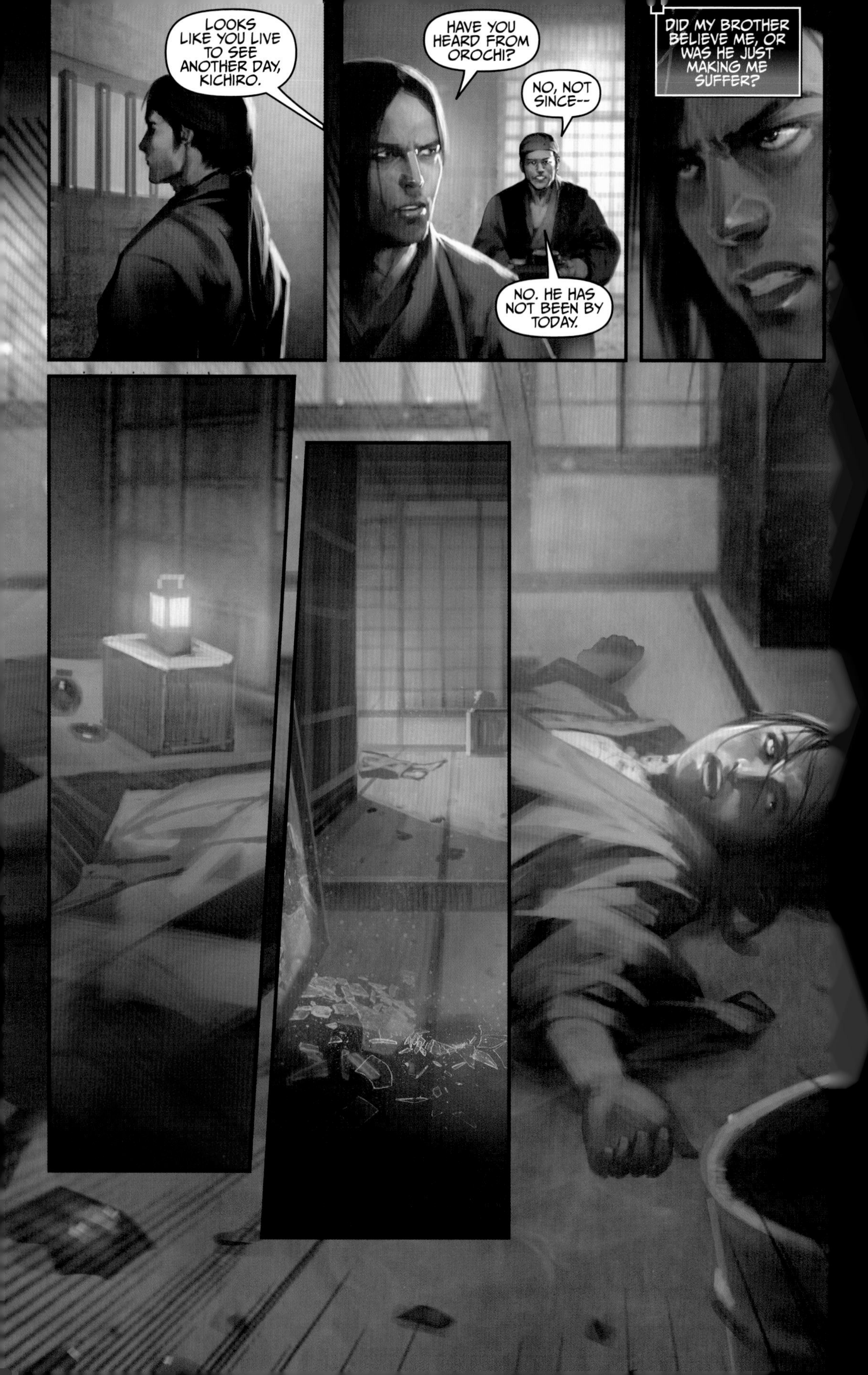
LOOKS LIKE YOU LIVE TO SEE ANOTHER DAY, KICHIRO.
HAVE YOU HEARD FROM OROCHI?
NO, NOT SINCE--
NO. HE HAS NOT BEEN BY TODAY.
DID MY BROTHER BELIEVE ME, OR WAS HE JUST MAKING ME SUFFER?

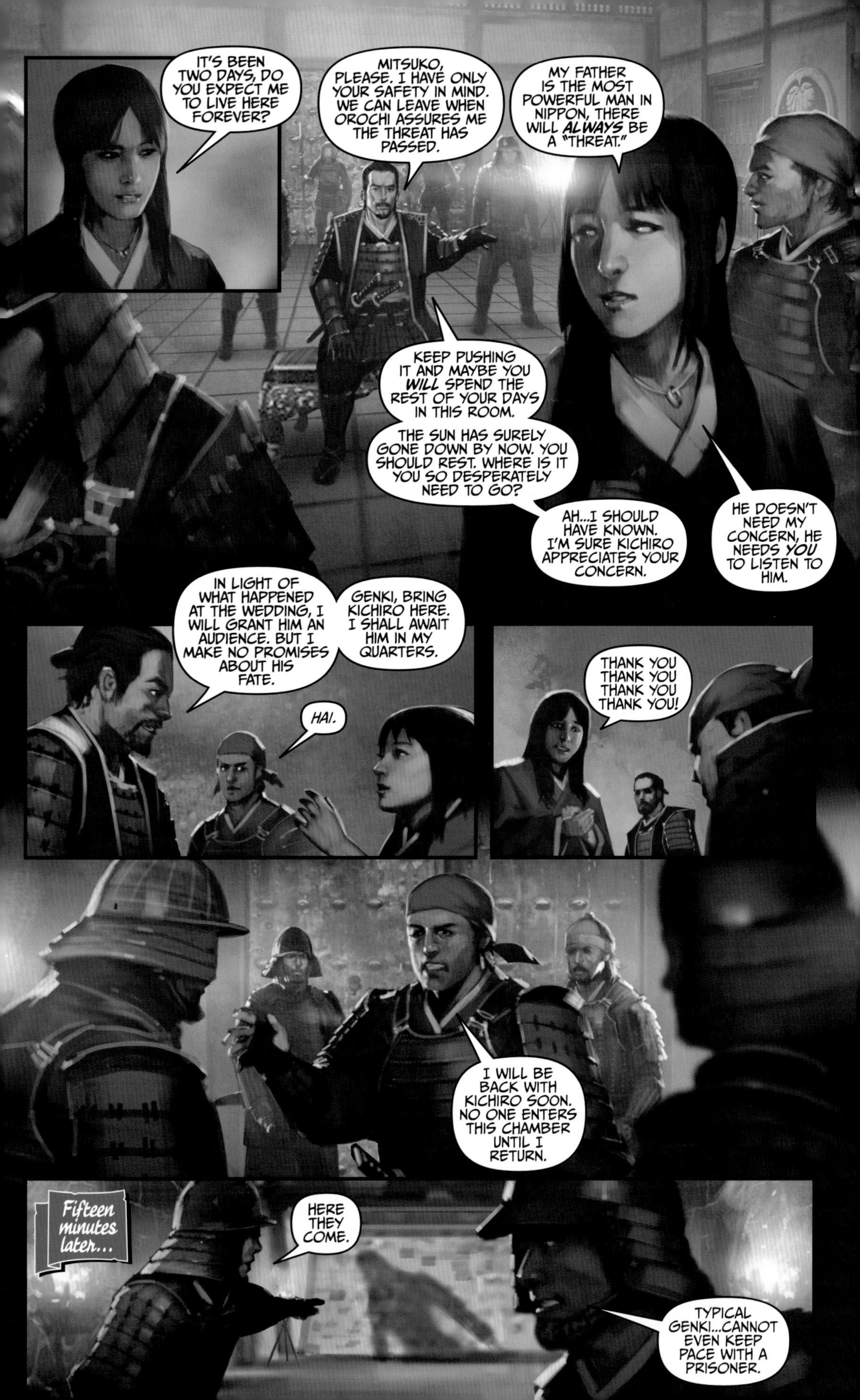
IT'S BEEN TWO DAYS, DO YOU EXPECT ME TO LIVE HERE FOREVER?
MITSUKO, PLEASE. I HAVE ONLY YOUR SAFETY IN MIND. WE CAN LEAVE WHEN OROCHI ASSURES ME THE THREAT HAS PASSED.
MY FATHER IS THE MOST POWERFUL MAN IN NIPPON, THERE WILL ALWAYS BE A "THREAT."
KEEP PUSHING IT AND MAYBE YOU WILL SPEND THE REST OF YOUR DAYS IN THIS ROOM.
THE SUN HAS SURELY GONE DOWN BY NOW. YOU SHOULD REST. WHERE IS IT YOU SO DESPERATELY NEED TO GO?
AH...I SHOULD HAVE KNOWN. I'M SURE KICHIRO APPRECIATES YOUR CONCERN.
HE DOESN'T NEED MY CONCERN, HE NEEDS YOU TO LISTEN TO HIM.
IN LIGHT OF WHAT HAPPENED AT THE WEDDING, I WILL GRANT HIM AN AUDIENCE. BUT I MAKE NO PROMISES ABOUT HIS FATE.
GENKI, BRING KICHIRO HERE. I SHALL AWAIT HIM IN MY QUARTERS.
HAI.
THANK YOU THANK YOU THANK YOU THANK YOU!
I WILL BE BACK WITH KICHIRO SOON. NO ONE ENTERS THIS CHAMBER UNTIL I RETURN.
Fifteen minutes later...
HERE THEY COME.
TYPICAL GENKI...CANNOT EVEN KEEP PACE WITH A PRISONER.

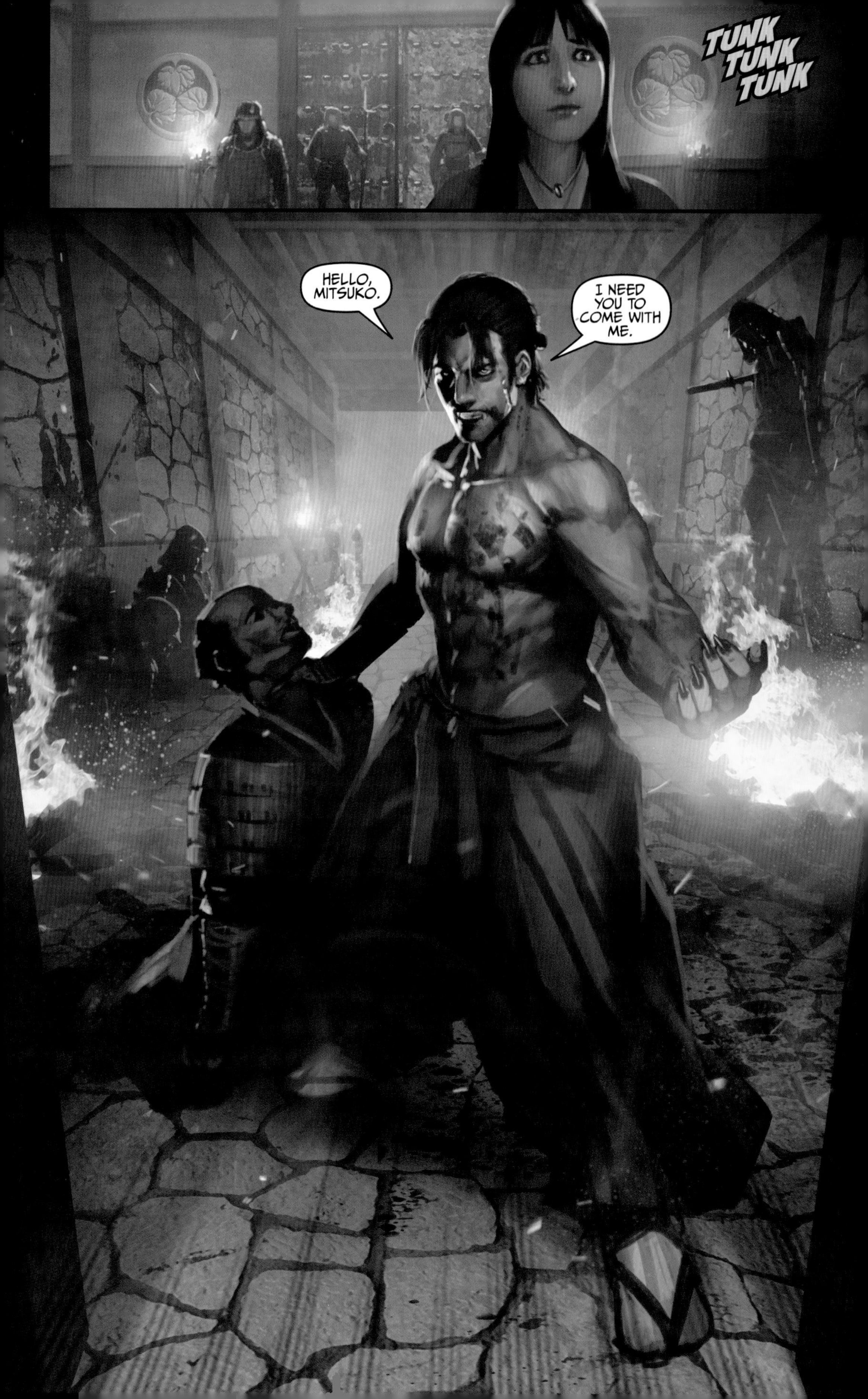
TUNK TUNK TUNK
HELLO, MITSUKO.
I NEED YOU TO COME WITH ME.

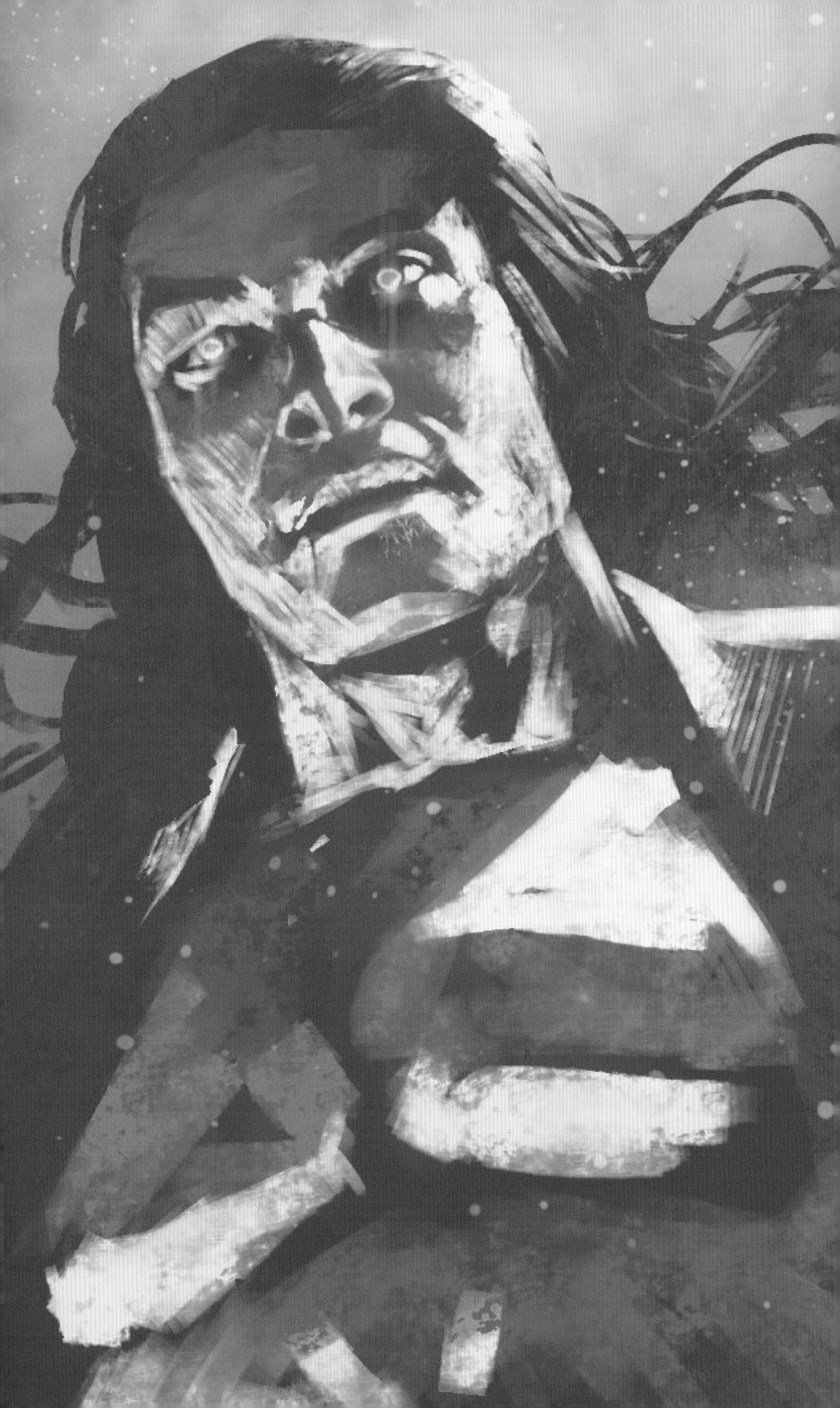

Chapter Four

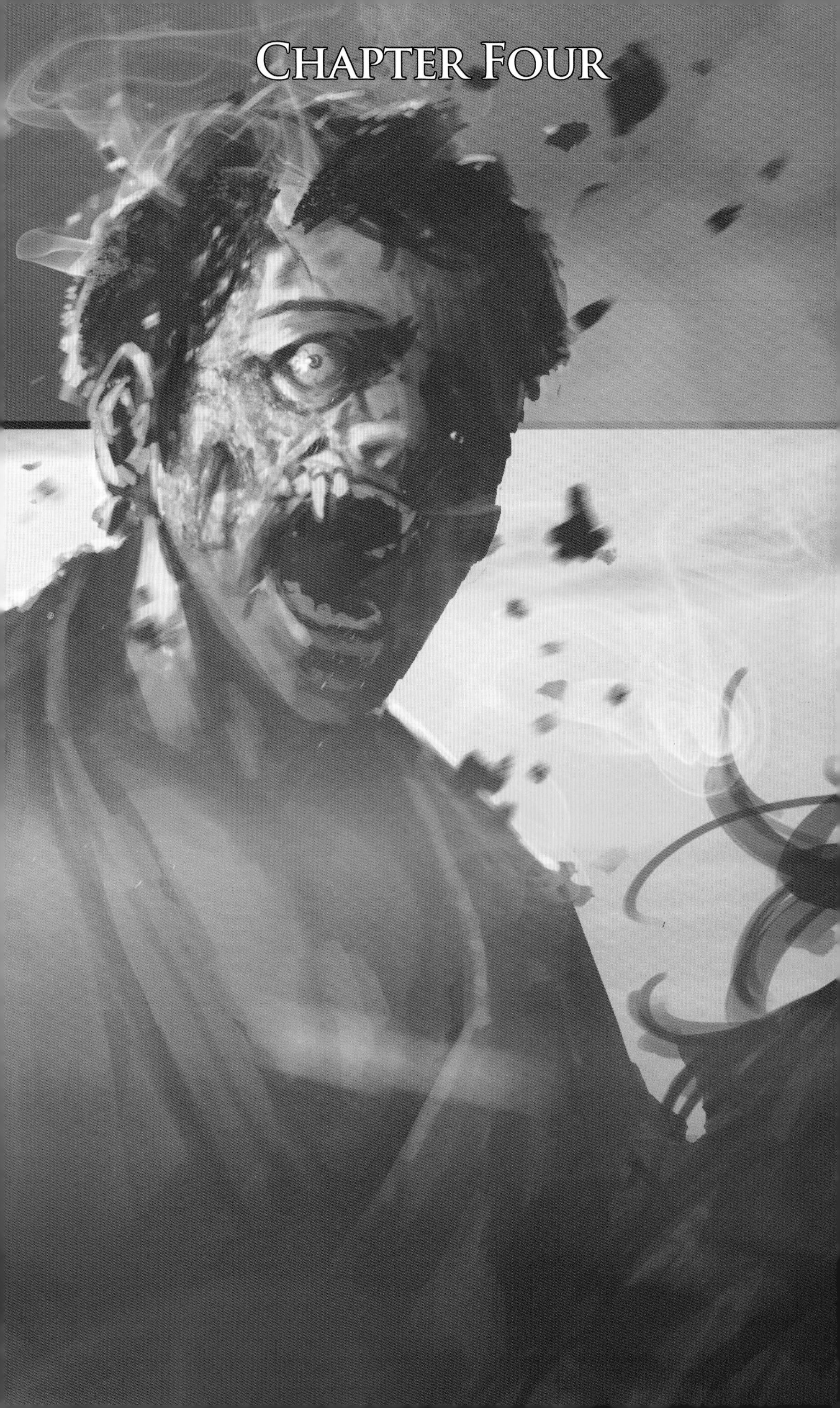

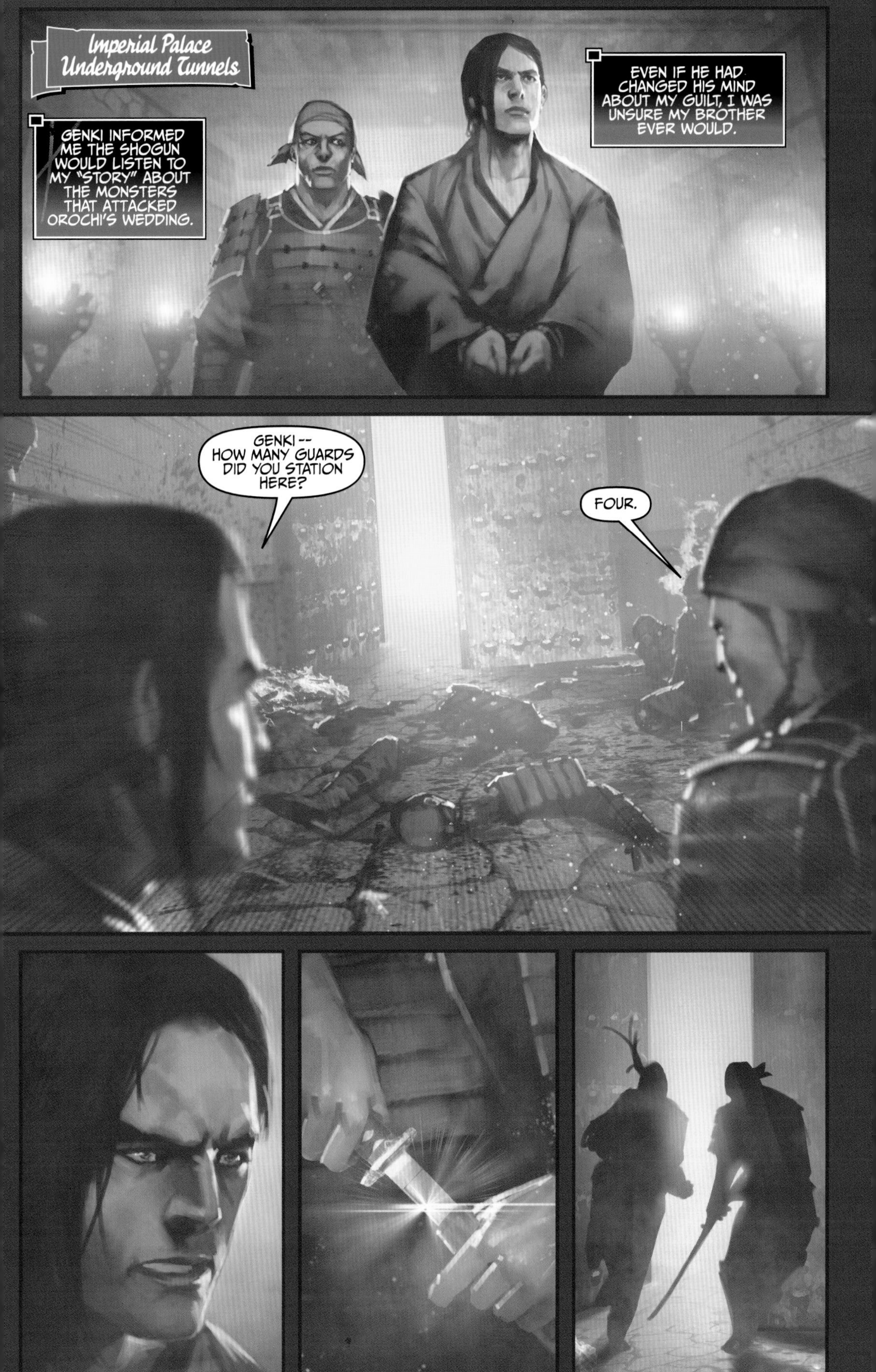
Imperial Palace Underground Tunnels
GENKI INFORMED ME THE SHOGUN WOULD LISTEN TO MY "STORY" ABOUT THE MONSTERS THAT ATTACKED OROCHI'S WEDDING.
EVEN IF HE HAD CHANGED HIS MIND ABOUT MY GUILT, I WAS UNSURE MY BROTHER EVER WOULD.
GENKI -- HOW MANY GUARDS DID YOU STATION HERE?
FOUR.

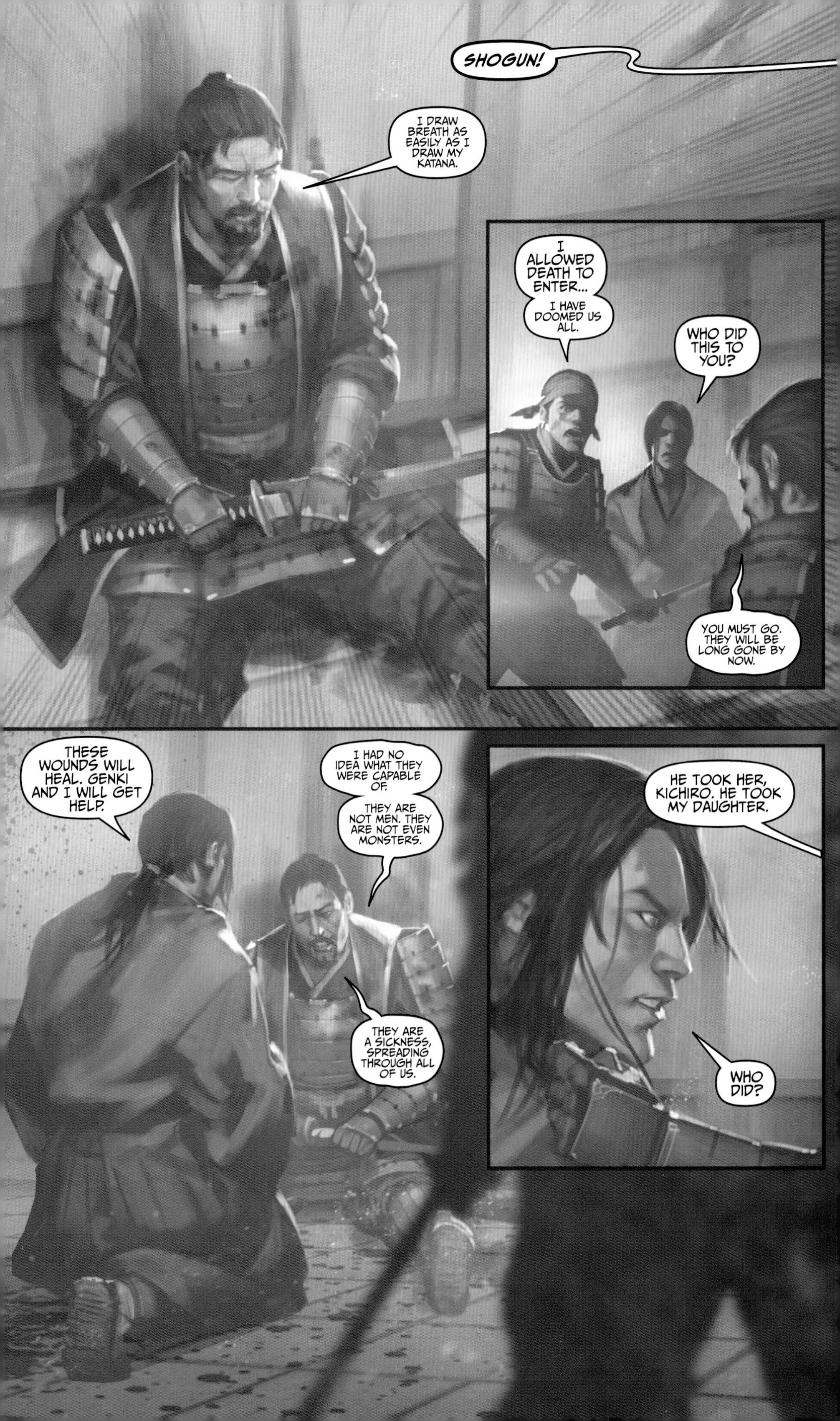
SHOGUN!
I DRAW BREATH AS EASILY AS I DRAW MY KATANA.
I ALLOWED DEATH TO ENTER...
I HAVE DOOMED US ALL.
WHO DID THIS TO YOU?
YOU MUST GO. THEY WILL BE LONG GONE BY NOW.
THESE WOUNDS WILL HEAL. GENKI AND I WILL GET HELP.
I HAD NO IDEA WHAT THEY WERE CAPABLE OF.
THEY ARE NOT MEN. THEY ARE NOT EVEN MONSTERS.
THEY ARE A SICKNESS, SPREADING THROUGH ALL OF US.
HE TOOK HER, KICHIRO. HE TOOK MY DAUGHTER.
WHO DID?

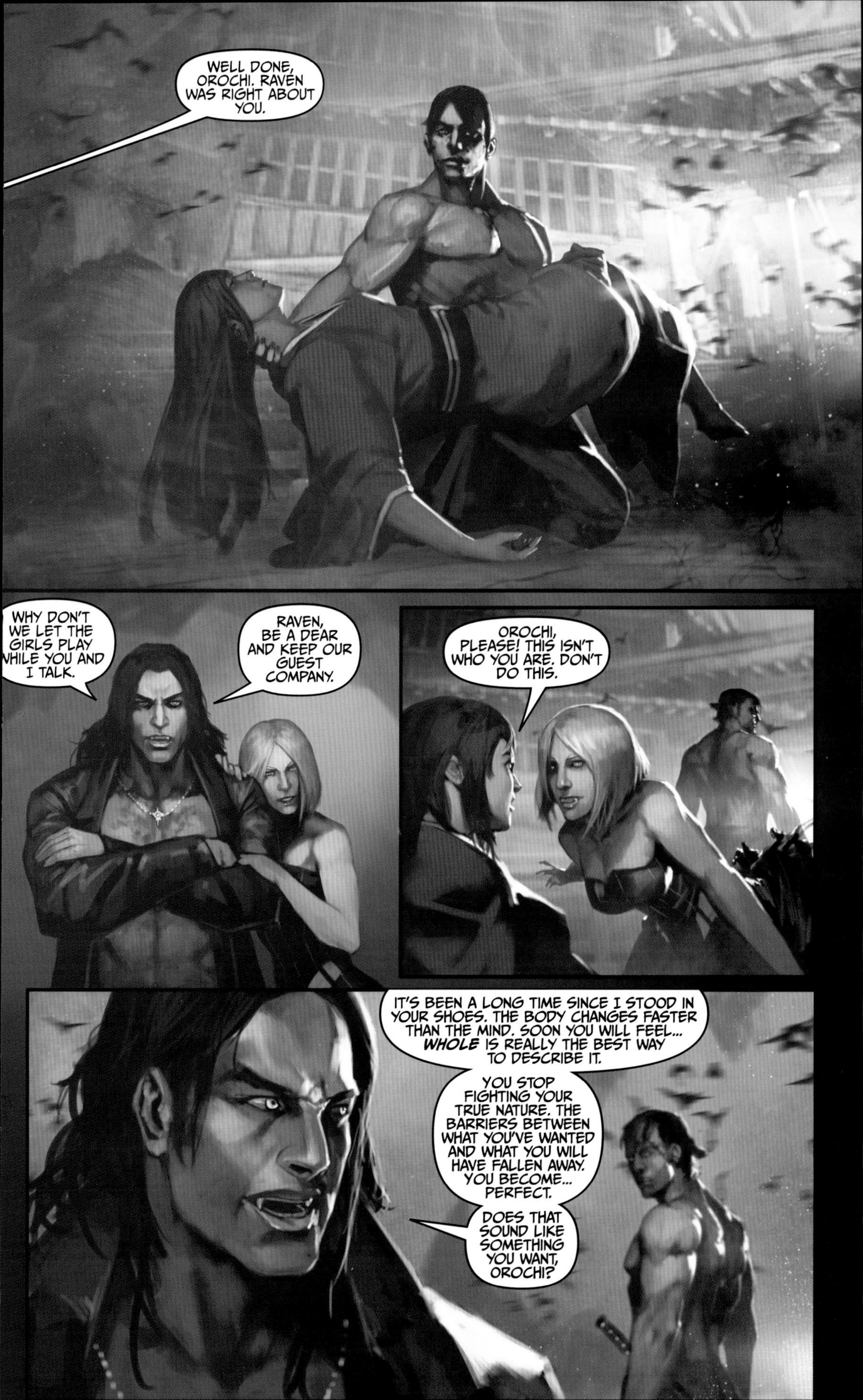
WELL DONE, OROCHI. RAVEN WAS RIGHT ABOUT YOU.
WHY DON'T WE LET THE GIRLS PLAY WHILE YOU AND I TALK.
RAVEN, BE A DEAR AND KEEP OUR GUEST COMPANY.
OROCHI, PLEASE! THIS ISN'T WHO YOU ARE. DON'T DO THIS.
IT'S BEEN A LONG TIME SINCE I STOOD IN YOUR SHOES. THE BODY CHANGES FASTER THAN THE MIND. SOON YOU WILL FEEL... *WHOLE* IS REALLY THE BEST WAY TO DESCRIBE IT.
YOU STOP FIGHTING YOUR TRUE NATURE. THE BARRIERS BETWEEN WHAT YOU'VE WANTED AND WHAT YOU WILL HAVE FALLEN AWAY. YOU BECOME... PERFECT.
DOES THAT SOUND LIKE SOMETHING YOU WANT, OROCHI?

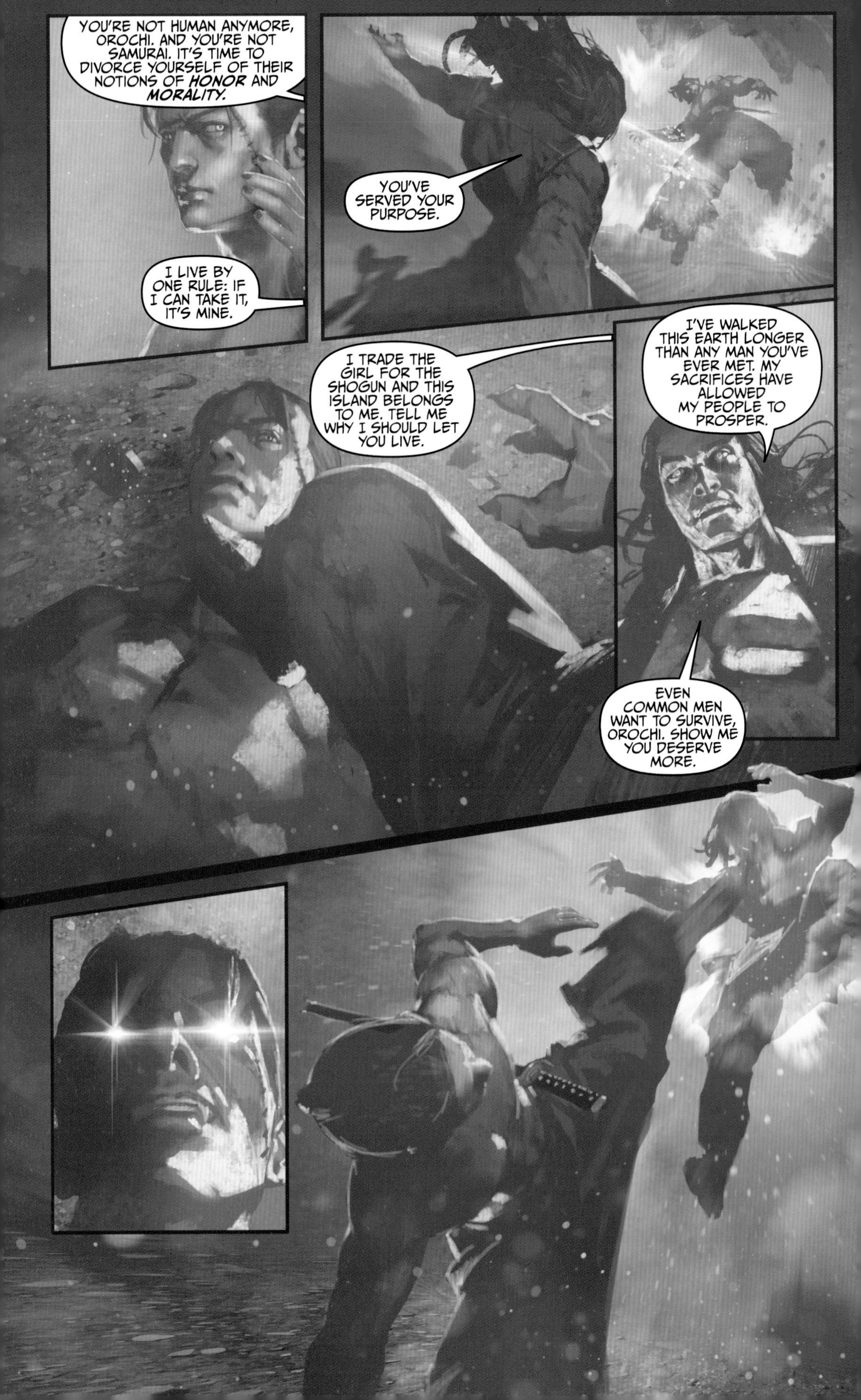
YOU'RE NOT HUMAN ANYMORE, OROCHI. AND YOU'RE NOT SAMURAI. IT'S TIME TO DIVORCE YOURSELF OF THEIR NOTIONS OF *HONOR* AND *MORALITY.*
I LIVE BY ONE RULE: IF I CAN TAKE IT, IT'S MINE.
YOU'VE SERVED YOUR PURPOSE.
I TRADE THE GIRL FOR THE SHOGUN AND THIS ISLAND BELONGS TO ME. TELL ME WHY I SHOULD LET YOU LIVE.
I'VE WALKED THIS EARTH LONGER THAN ANY MAN YOU'VE EVER MET. MY SACRIFICES HAVE ALLOWED MY PEOPLE TO PROSPER.
EVEN COMMON MEN WANT TO SURVIVE, OROCHI. SHOW ME YOU DESERVE MORE.

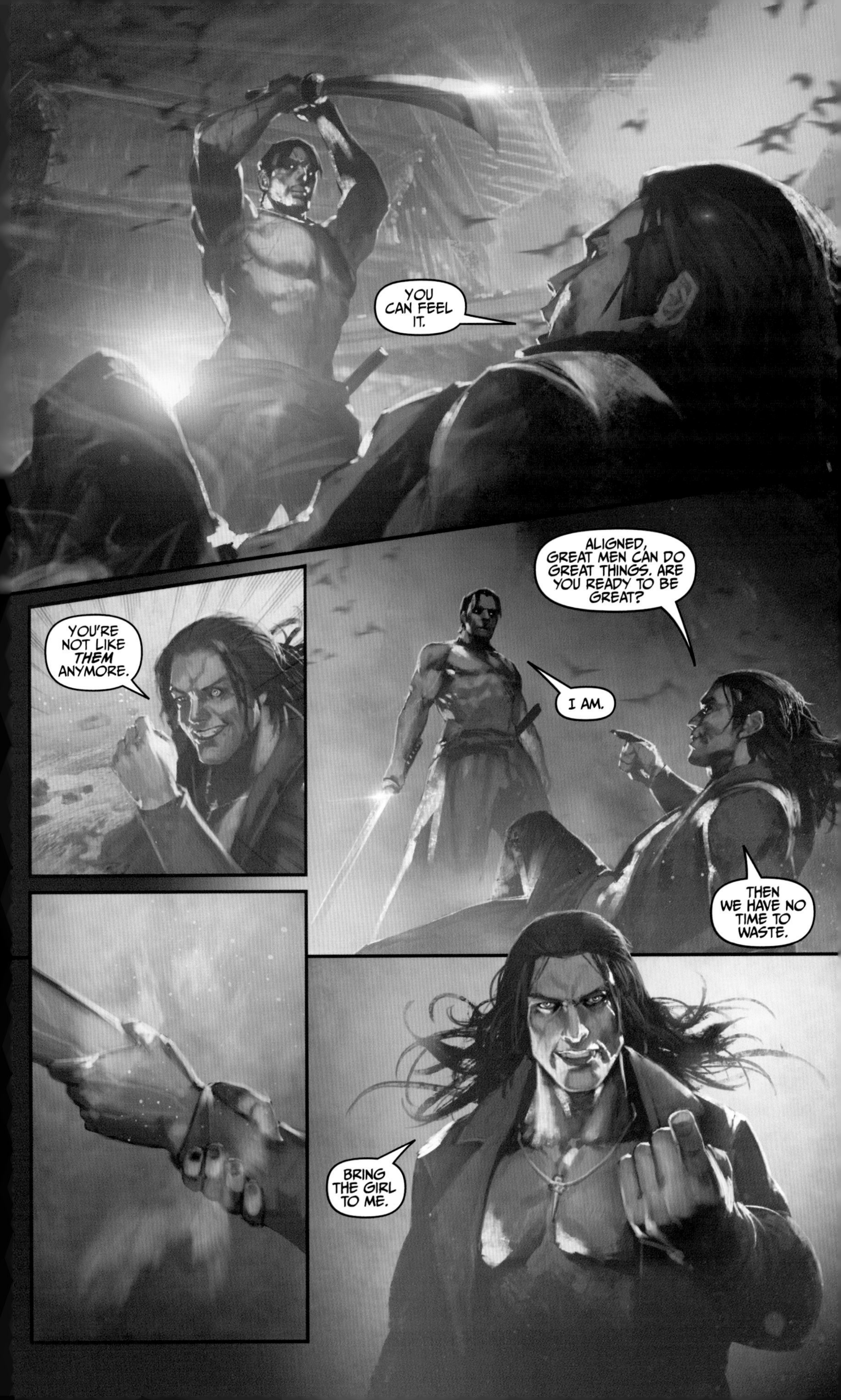
YOU CAN FEEL IT.
YOU'RE NOT LIKE *THEM* ANYMORE.
ALIGNED, GREAT MEN CAN DO GREAT THINGS. ARE YOU READY TO BE GREAT?
I AM.
THEN WE HAVE NO TIME TO WASTE.
BRING THE GIRL TO ME.

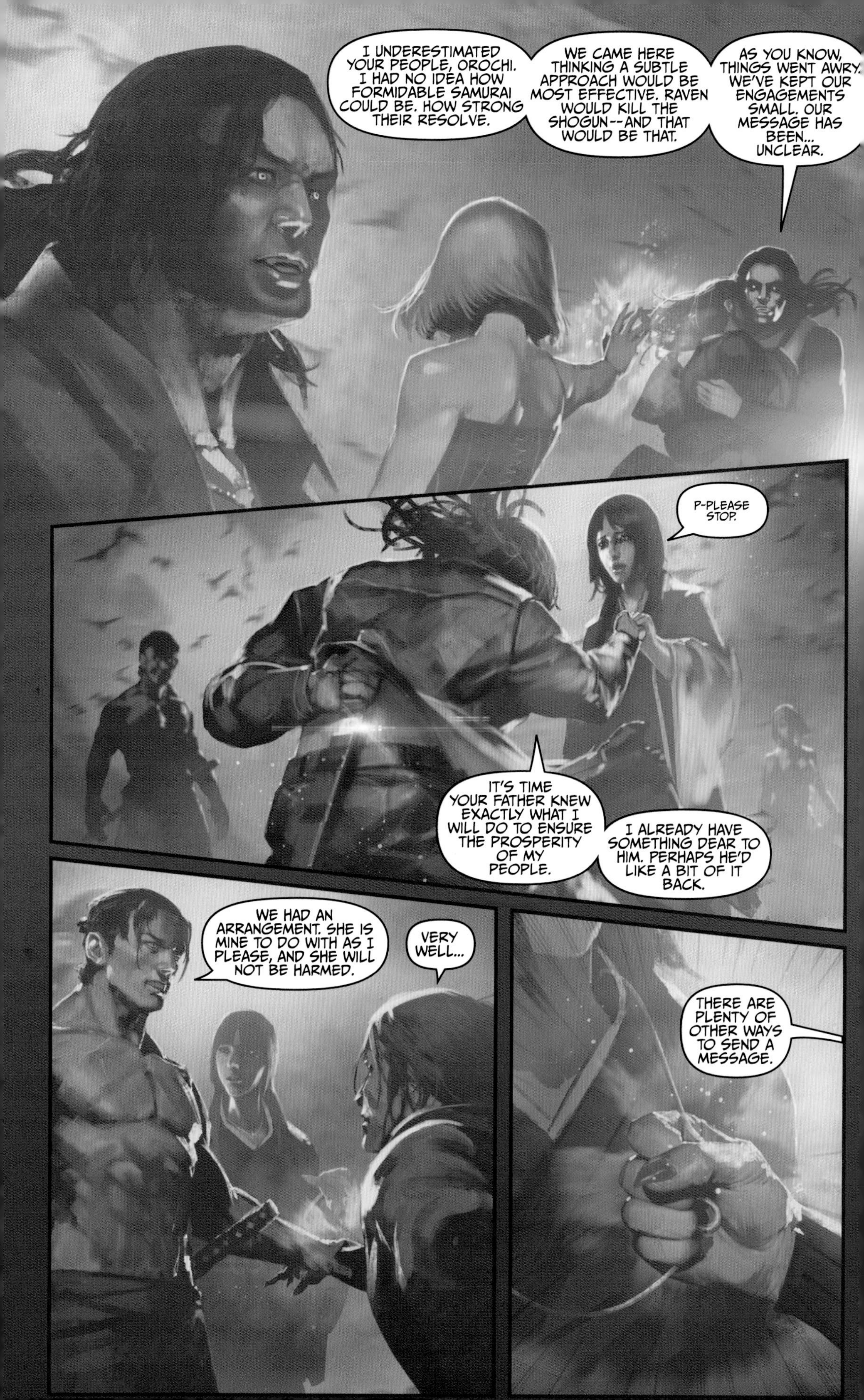
I UNDERESTIMATED YOUR PEOPLE, OROCHI. I HAD NO IDEA HOW FORMIDABLE SAMURAI COULD BE. HOW STRONG THEIR RESOLVE.
WE CAME HERE THINKING A SUBTLE APPROACH WOULD BE MOST EFFECTIVE. RAVEN WOULD KILL THE SHOGUN--AND THAT WOULD BE THAT.
AS YOU KNOW, THINGS WENT AWRY. WE'VE KEPT OUR ENGAGEMENTS SMALL. OUR MESSAGE HAS BEEN... UNCLEAR.
P-PLEASE STOP.
IT'S TIME YOUR FATHER KNEW EXACTLY WHAT I WILL DO TO ENSURE THE PROSPERITY OF MY PEOPLE.
I ALREADY HAVE SOMETHING DEAR TO HIM. PERHAPS HE'D LIKE A BIT OF IT BACK.
WE HAD AN ARRANGEMENT. SHE IS MINE TO DO WITH AS I PLEASE, AND SHE WILL NOT BE HARMED.
VERY WELL...
THERE ARE PLENTY OF OTHER WAYS TO SEND A MESSAGE.

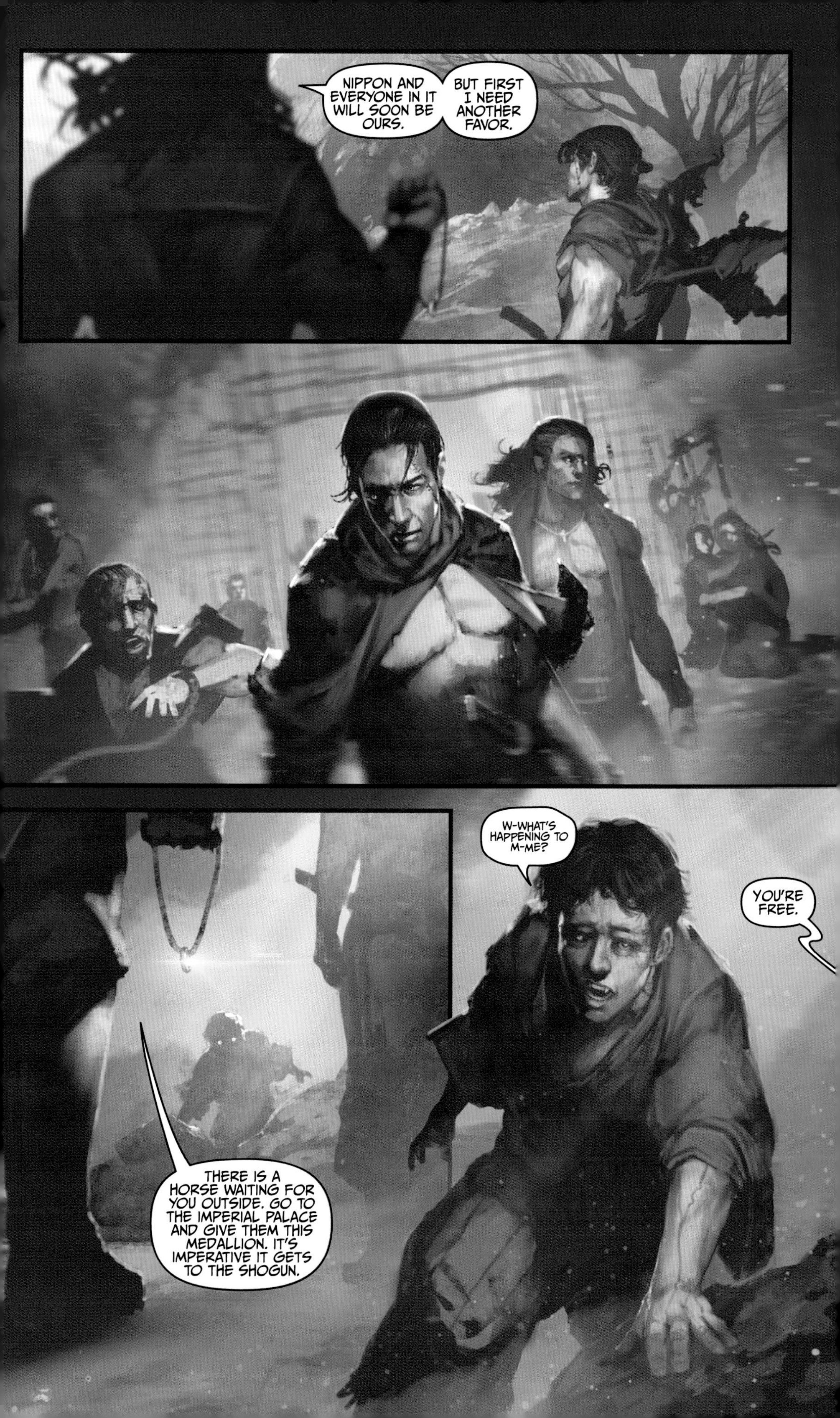
NIPPON AND EVERYONE IN IT WILL SOON BE OURS.
BUT FIRST I NEED ANOTHER FAVOR.
W-WHAT'S HAPPENING TO M-ME?
YOU'RE FREE.
THERE IS A HORSE WAITING FOR YOU OUTSIDE. GO TO THE IMPERIAL PALACE AND GIVE THEM THIS MEDALLION. IT'S IMPERATIVE IT GETS TO THE SHOGUN.

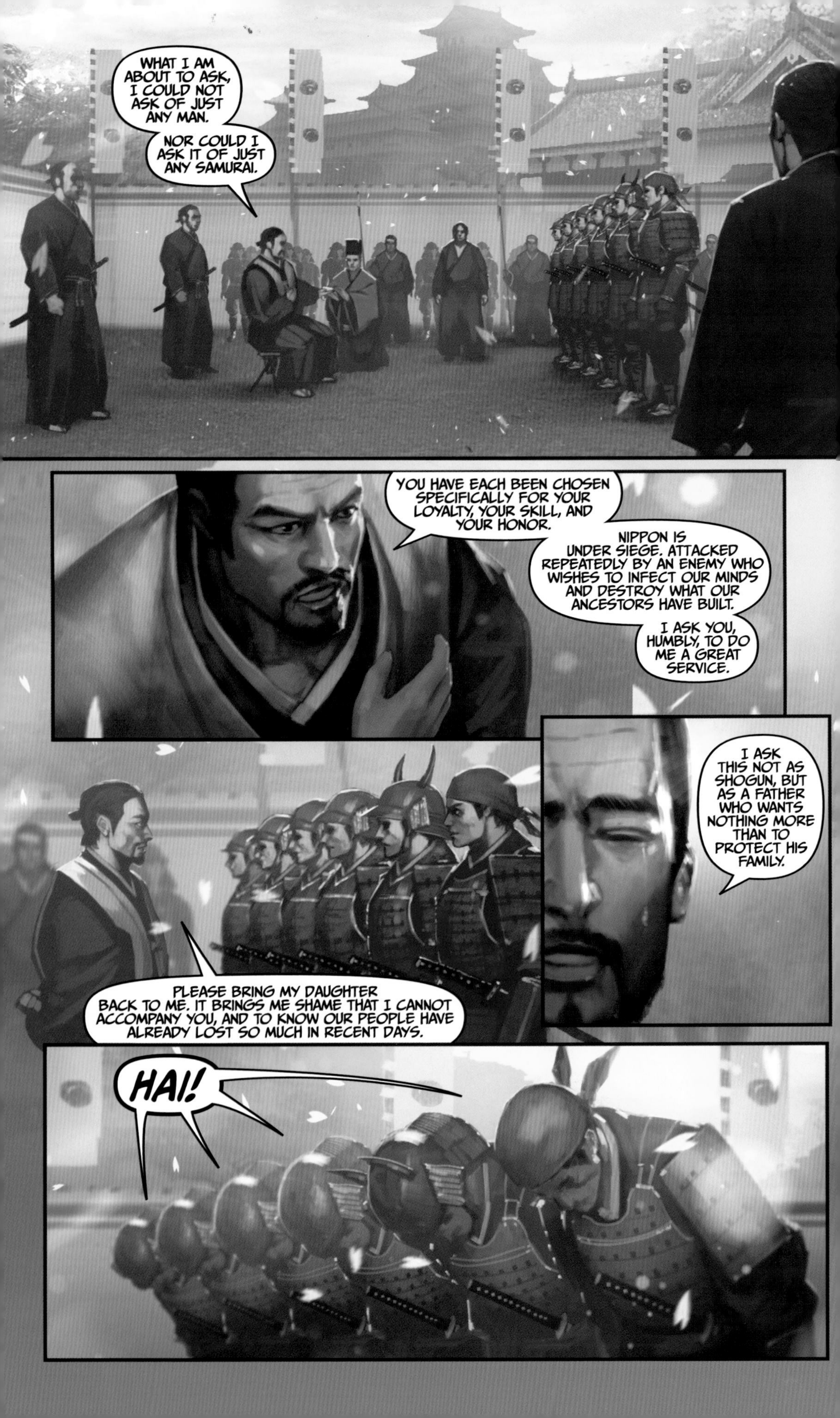
WHAT I AM ABOUT TO ASK, I COULD NOT ASK OF JUST ANY MAN.
NOR COULD I ASK IT OF JUST ANY SAMURAI.
YOU HAVE EACH BEEN CHOSEN SPECIFICALLY FOR YOUR LOYALTY, YOUR SKILL, AND YOUR HONOR.
NIPPON IS UNDER SIEGE. ATTACKED REPEATEDLY BY AN ENEMY WHO WISHES TO INFECT OUR MINDS AND DESTROY WHAT OUR ANCESTORS HAVE BUILT.
I ASK YOU, HUMBLY, TO DO ME A GREAT SERVICE.
I ASK THIS NOT AS SHOGUN, BUT AS A FATHER WHO WANTS NOTHING MORE THAN TO PROTECT HIS FAMILY.
PLEASE BRING MY DAUGHTER BACK TO ME. IT BRINGS ME SHAME THAT I CANNOT ACCOMPANY YOU, AND TO KNOW OUR PEOPLE HAVE ALREADY LOST SO MUCH IN RECENT DAYS.
HAI!

YOU HONOR ME.

I AM IN YOUR DEBT.

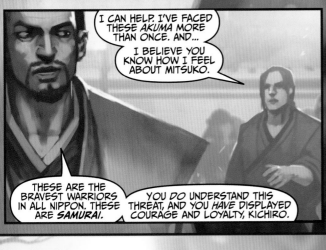

I CAN HELP. I'VE FACED THESE *AKUMA* MORE THAN ONCE. AND...

I BELIEVE YOU KNOW HOW I FEEL ABOUT MITSUKO.

THESE ARE THE BRAVEST WARRIORS IN ALL NIPPON. THESE ARE *SAMURAI*.

YOU *DO* UNDERSTAND THIS THREAT, AND YOU *HAVE* DISPLAYED COURAGE AND LOYALTY, KICHIRO.

YET YOU ARE NOT SAMURAI.

I SEE NO REASON WHY YOU CANNOT BE.

IT TOOK SOME TIME FOR THE SHOGUN'S WORDS TO MAKE SENSE.

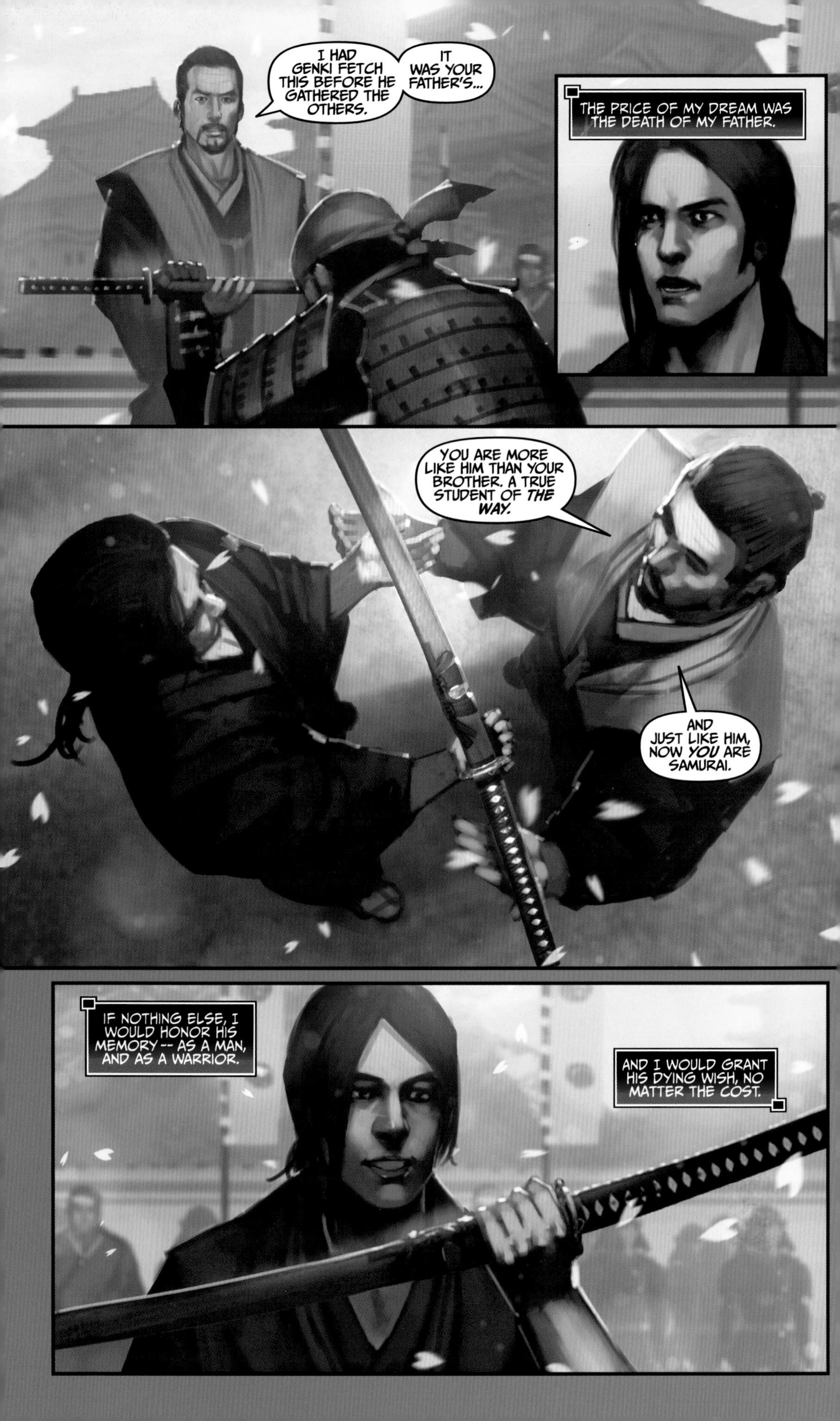
I HAD GENKI FETCH THIS BEFORE HE GATHERED THE OTHERS.
IT WAS YOUR FATHER'S...
THE PRICE OF MY DREAM WAS THE DEATH OF MY FATHER.
YOU ARE MORE LIKE HIM THAN YOUR BROTHER. A TRUE STUDENT OF *THE WAY.*
AND JUST LIKE HIM, NOW *YOU* ARE SAMURAI.
IF NOTHING ELSE, I WOULD HONOR HIS MEMORY -- AS A MAN, AND AS A WARRIOR.
AND I WOULD GRANT HIS DYING WISH, NO MATTER THE COST.

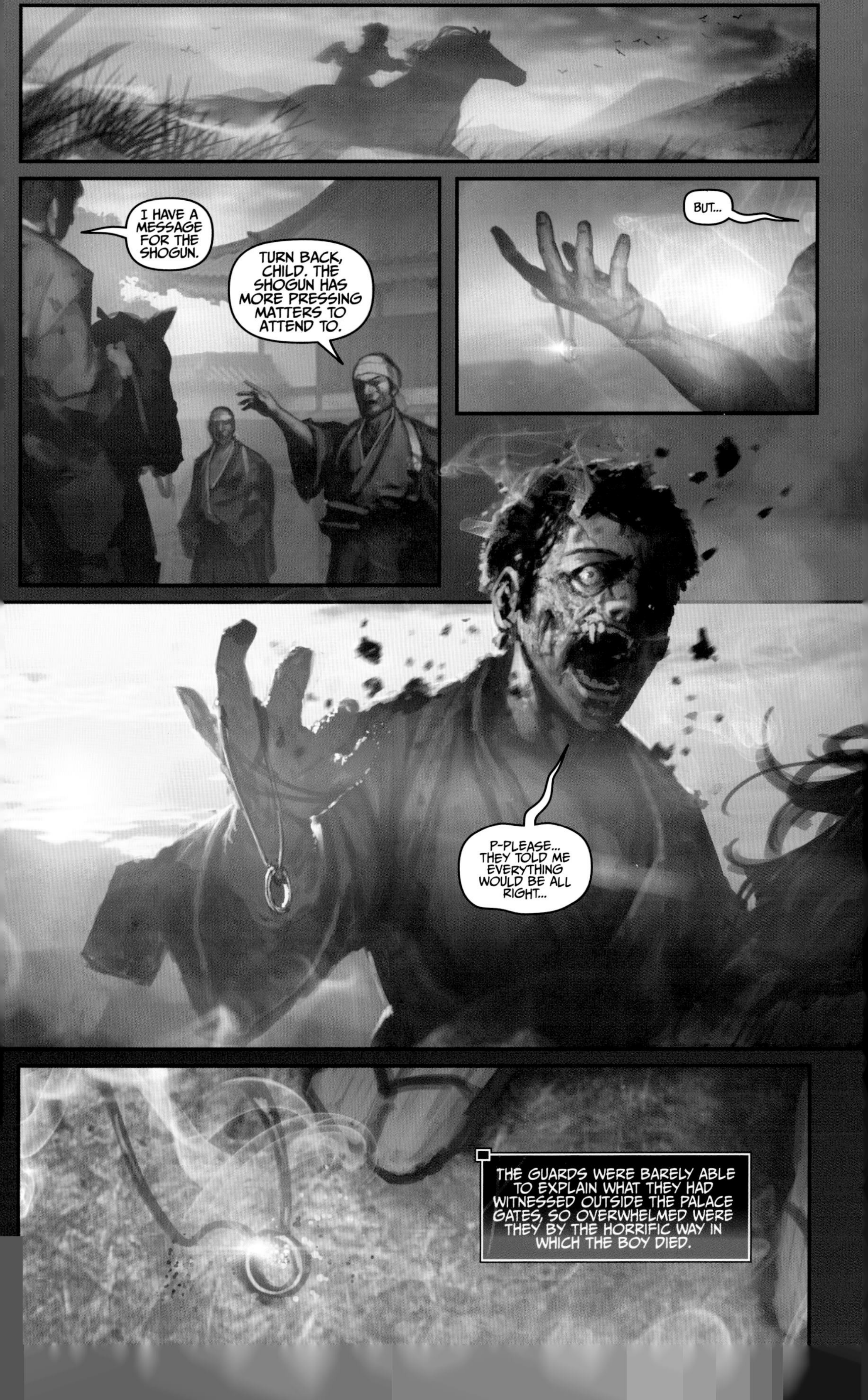
I HAVE A MESSAGE FOR THE SHOGUN.
TURN BACK, CHILD. THE SHOGUN HAS MORE PRESSING MATTERS TO ATTEND TO.
BUT...
P-PLEASE... THEY TOLD ME EVERYTHING WOULD BE ALL RIGHT...
THE GUARDS WERE BARELY ABLE TO EXPLAIN WHAT THEY HAD WITNESSED OUTSIDE THE PALACE GATES, SO OVERWHELMED WERE THEY BY THE HORRIFIC WAY IN WHICH THE BOY DIED.

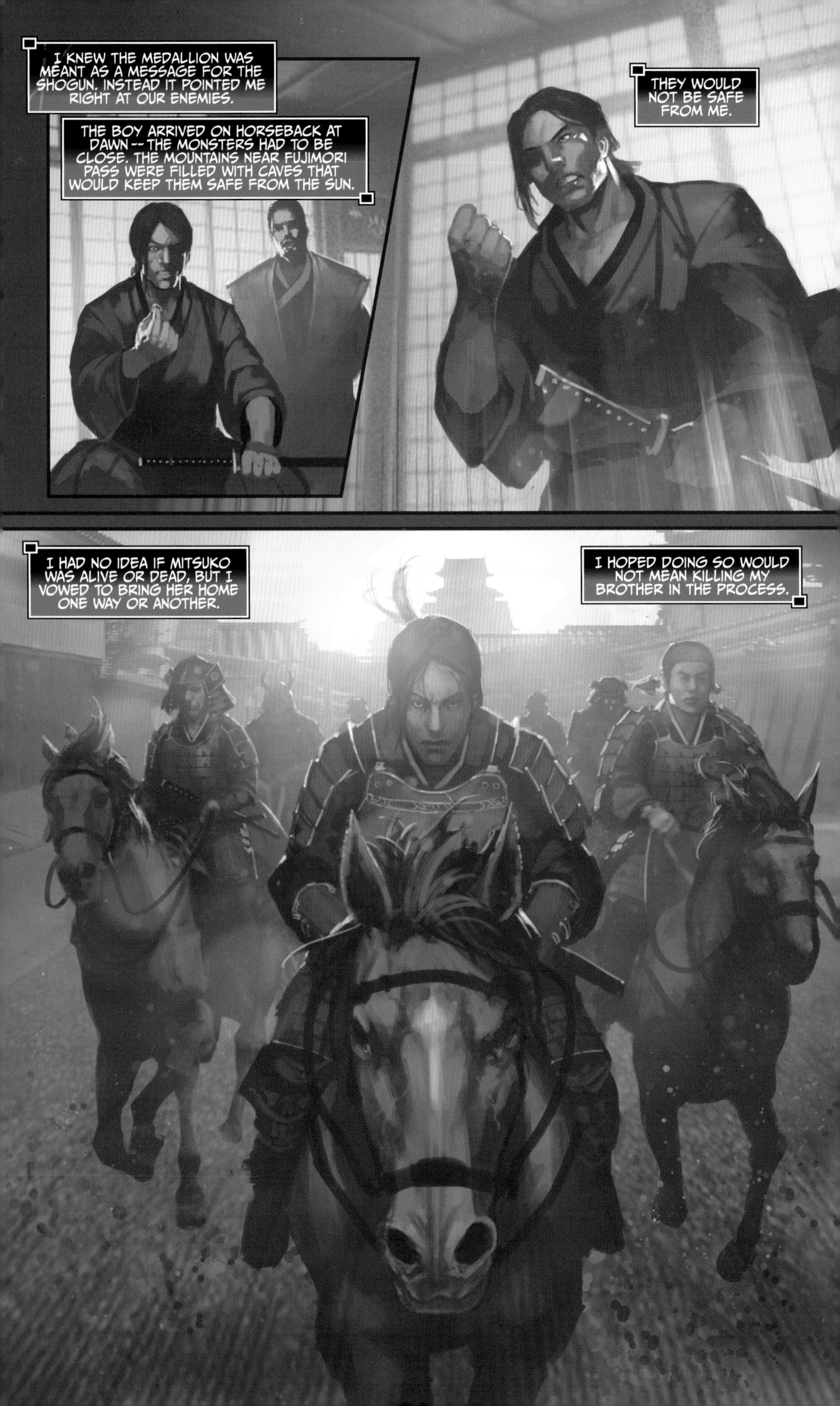
I KNEW THE MEDALLION WAS MEANT AS A MESSAGE FOR THE SHOGUN. INSTEAD IT POINTED ME RIGHT AT OUR ENEMIES.
THE BOY ARRIVED ON HORSEBACK AT DAWN -- THE MONSTERS HAD TO BE CLOSE. THE MOUNTAINS NEAR FUJIMORI PASS WERE FILLED WITH CAVES THAT WOULD KEEP THEM SAFE FROM THE SUN.
THEY WOULD NOT BE SAFE FROM ME.
I HAD NO IDEA IF MITSUKO WAS ALIVE OR DEAD, BUT I VOWED TO BRING HER HOME ONE WAY OR ANOTHER.
I HOPED DOING SO WOULD NOT MEAN KILLING MY BROTHER IN THE PROCESS.

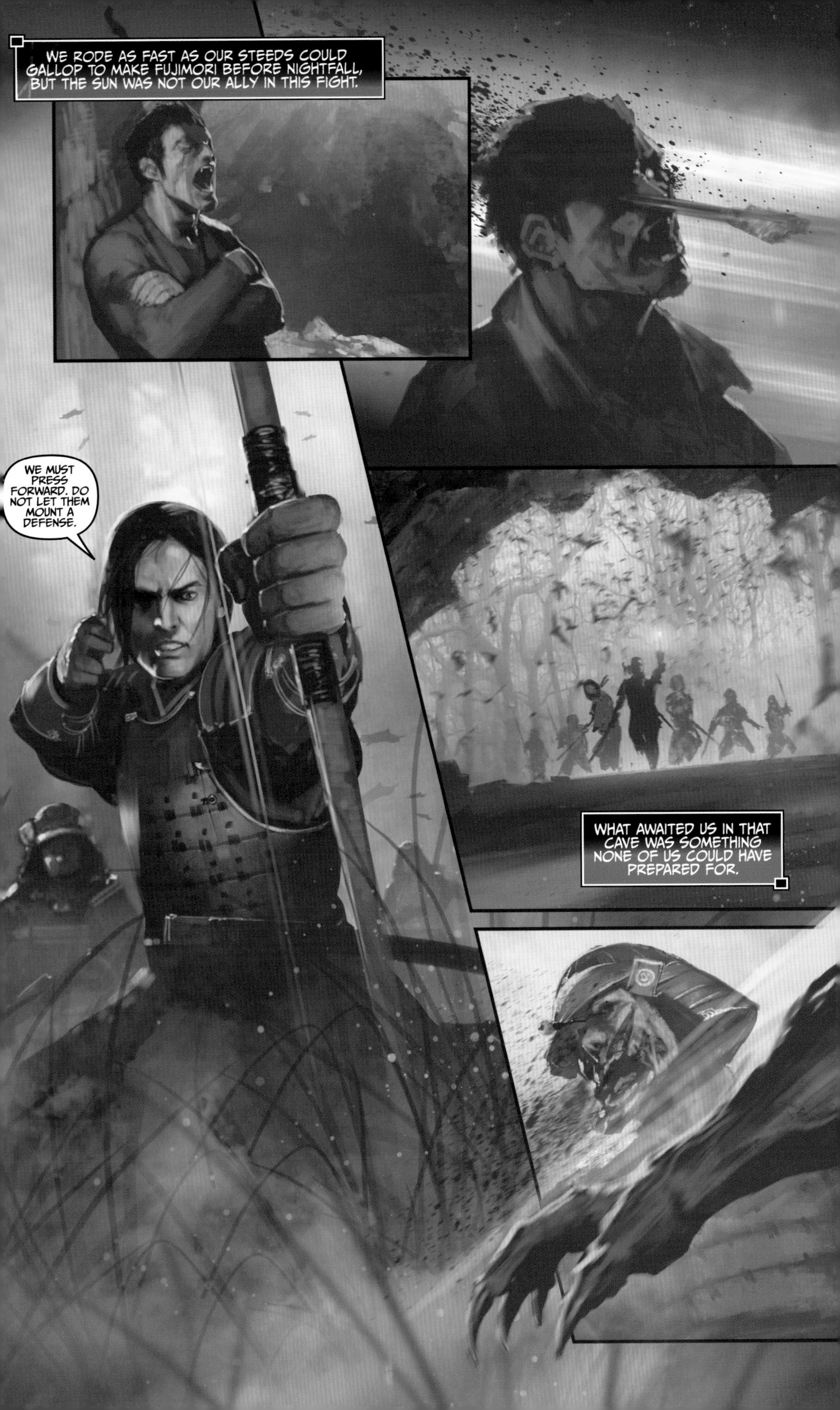
WE RODE AS FAST AS OUR STEEDS COULD GALLOP TO MAKE FUJIMORI BEFORE NIGHTFALL, BUT THE SUN WAS NOT OUR ALLY IN THIS FIGHT.
WE MUST PRESS FORWARD. DO NOT LET THEM MOUNT A DEFENSE.
WHAT AWAITED US IN THAT CAVE WAS SOMETHING NONE OF US COULD HAVE PREPARED FOR.

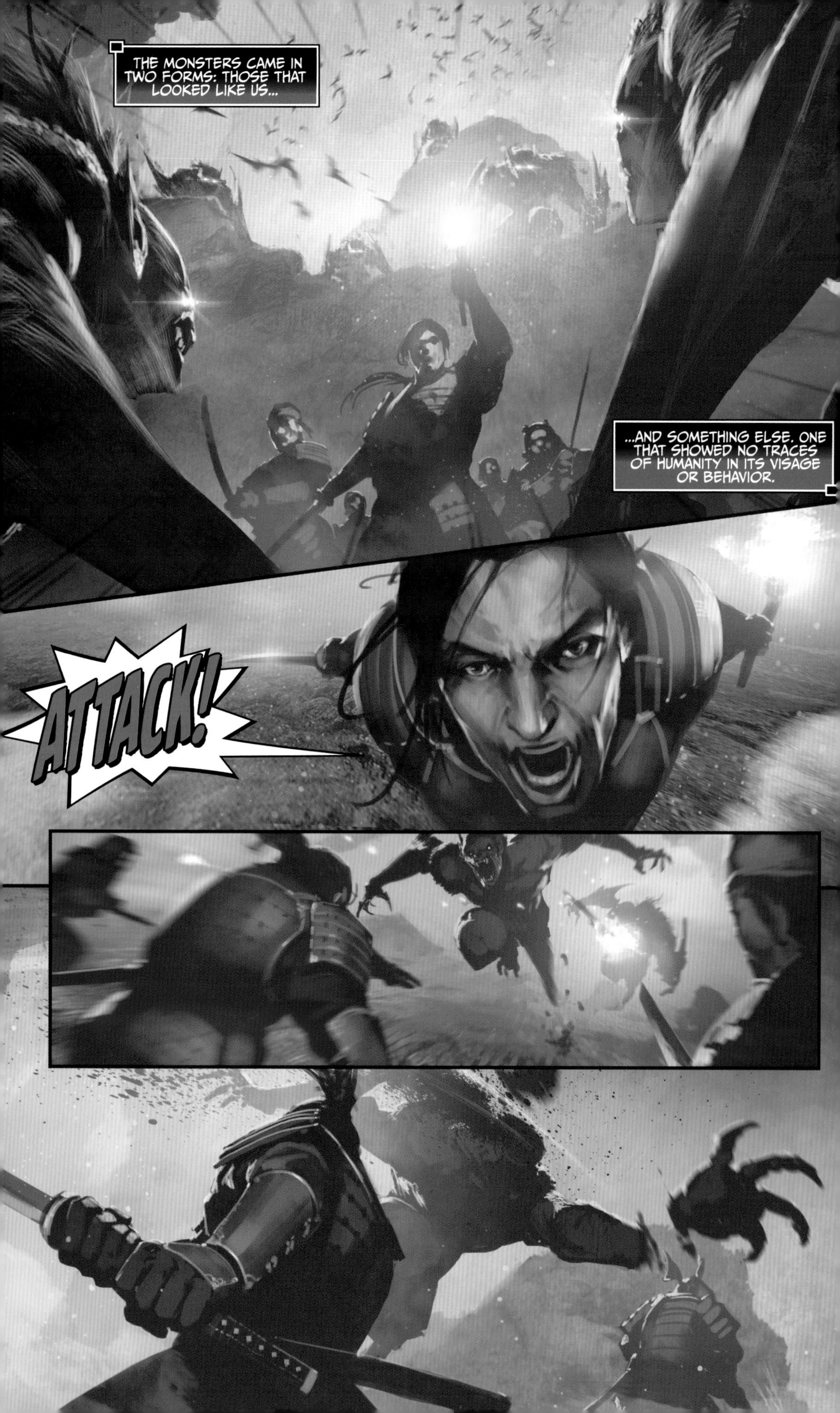
THE MONSTERS CAME IN TWO FORMS: THOSE THAT LOOKED LIKE US...
...AND SOMETHING ELSE. ONE THAT SHOWED NO TRACES OF HUMANITY IN ITS VISAGE OR BEHAVIOR.
ATTACK!

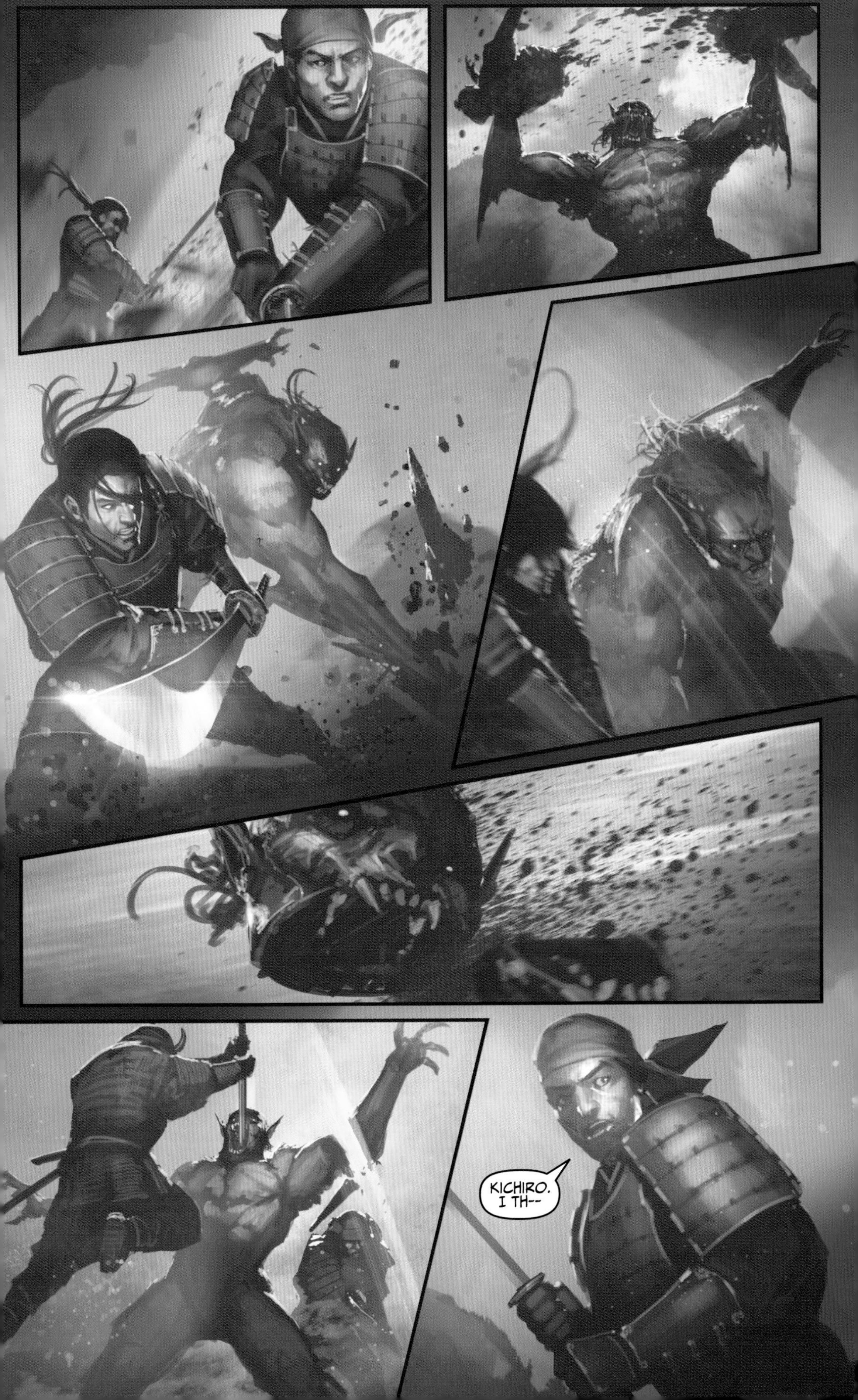
KICHIRO. I TH--

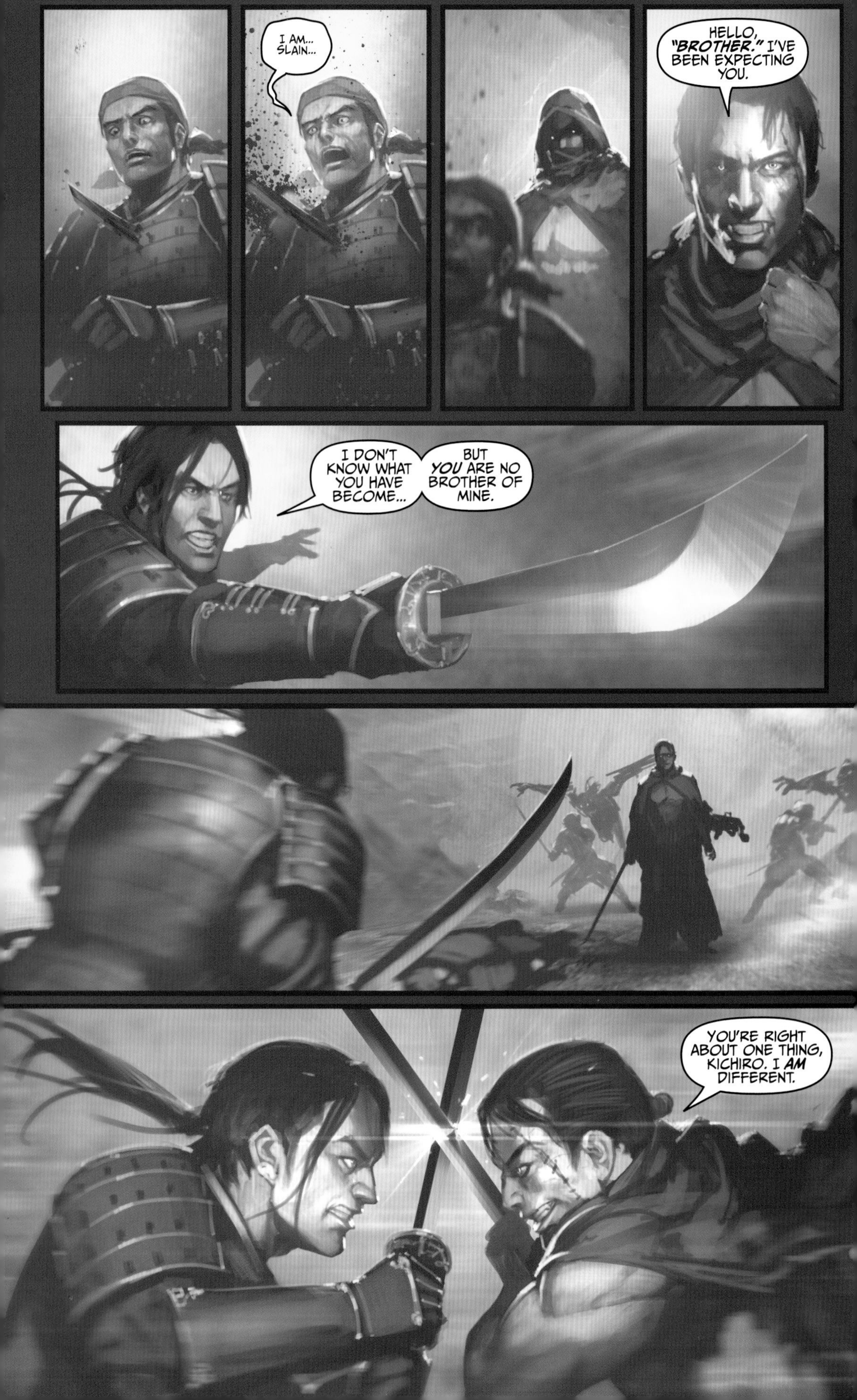
I AM... SLAIN...
HELLO, "***BROTHER.***" I'VE BEEN EXPECTING YOU.
I DON'T KNOW WHAT YOU HAVE BECOME...
BUT ***YOU*** ARE NO BROTHER OF MINE.
YOU'RE RIGHT ABOUT ONE THING, KICHIRO. I ***AM*** DIFFERENT.

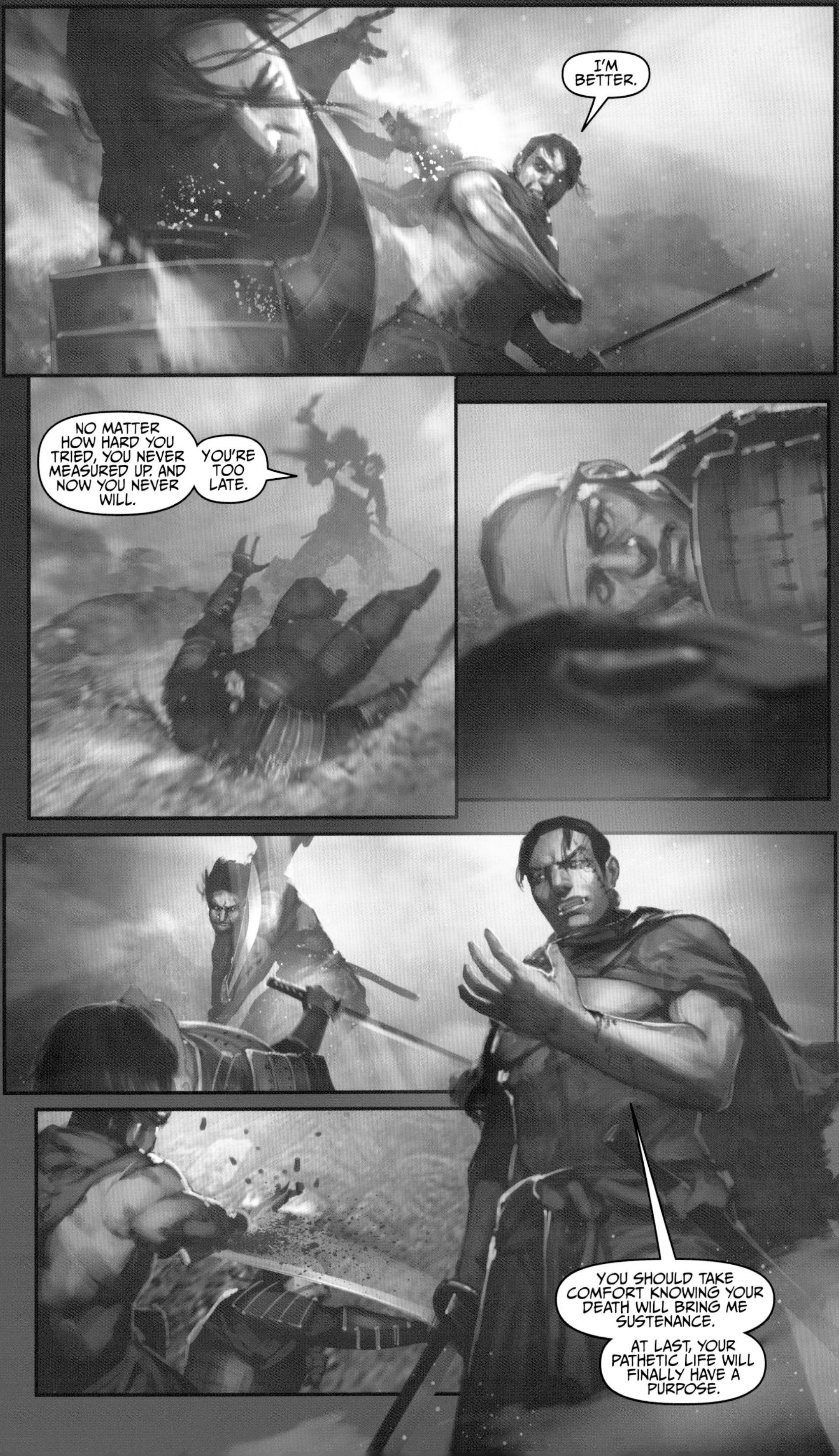
I'M BETTER.
NO MATTER HOW HARD YOU TRIED, YOU NEVER MEASURED UP. AND NOW YOU NEVER WILL.
YOU'RE TOO LATE.
YOU SHOULD TAKE COMFORT KNOWING YOUR DEATH WILL BRING ME SUSTENANCE.
AT LAST, YOUR PATHETIC LIFE WILL FINALLY HAVE A PURPOSE.

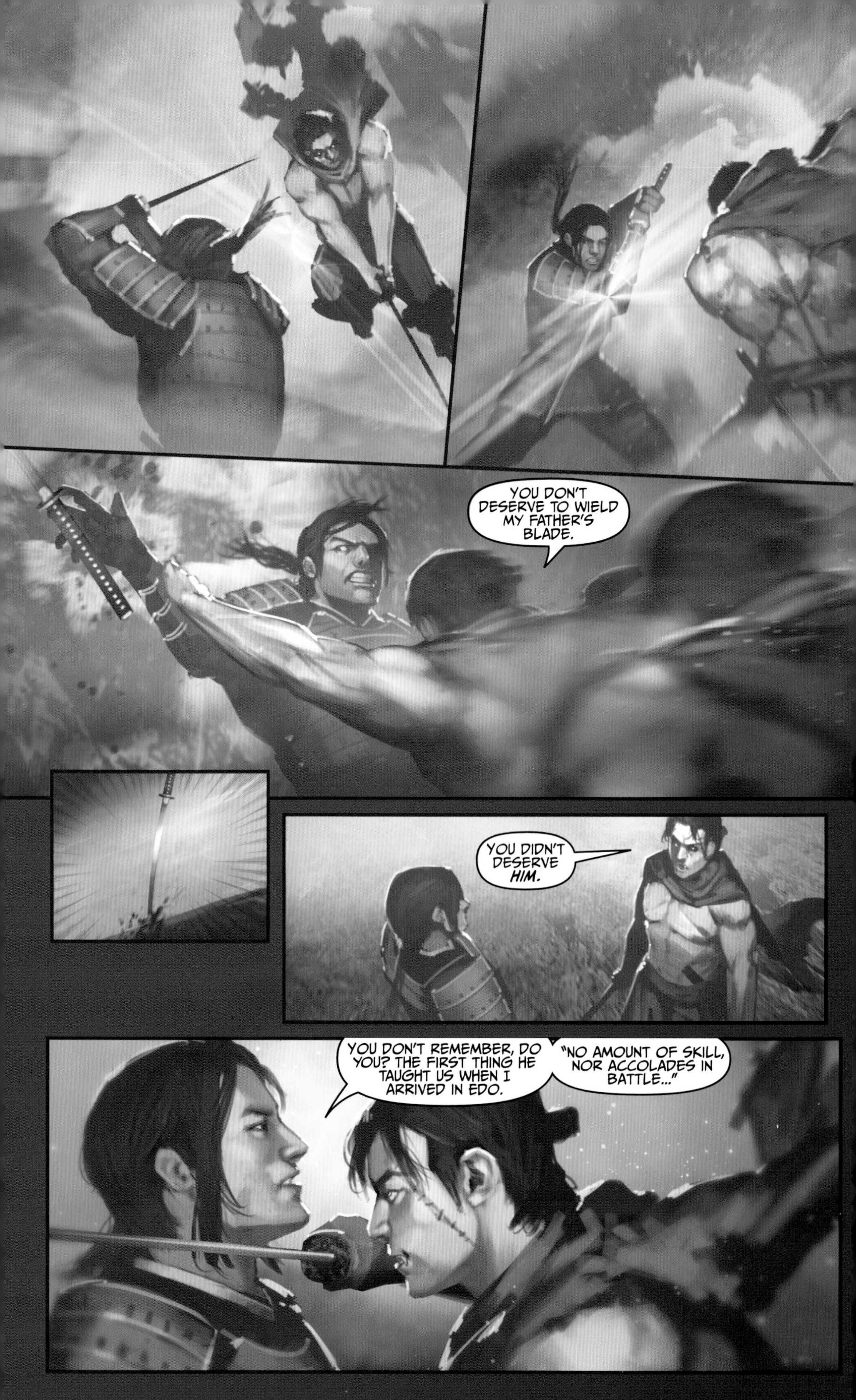
YOU DON'T DESERVE TO WIELD MY FATHER'S BLADE.
YOU DIDN'T DESERVE *HIM.*
YOU DON'T REMEMBER, DO YOU? THE FIRST THING HE TAUGHT US WHEN I ARRIVED IN EDO.
"NO AMOUNT OF SKILL, NOR ACCOLADES IN BATTLE..."

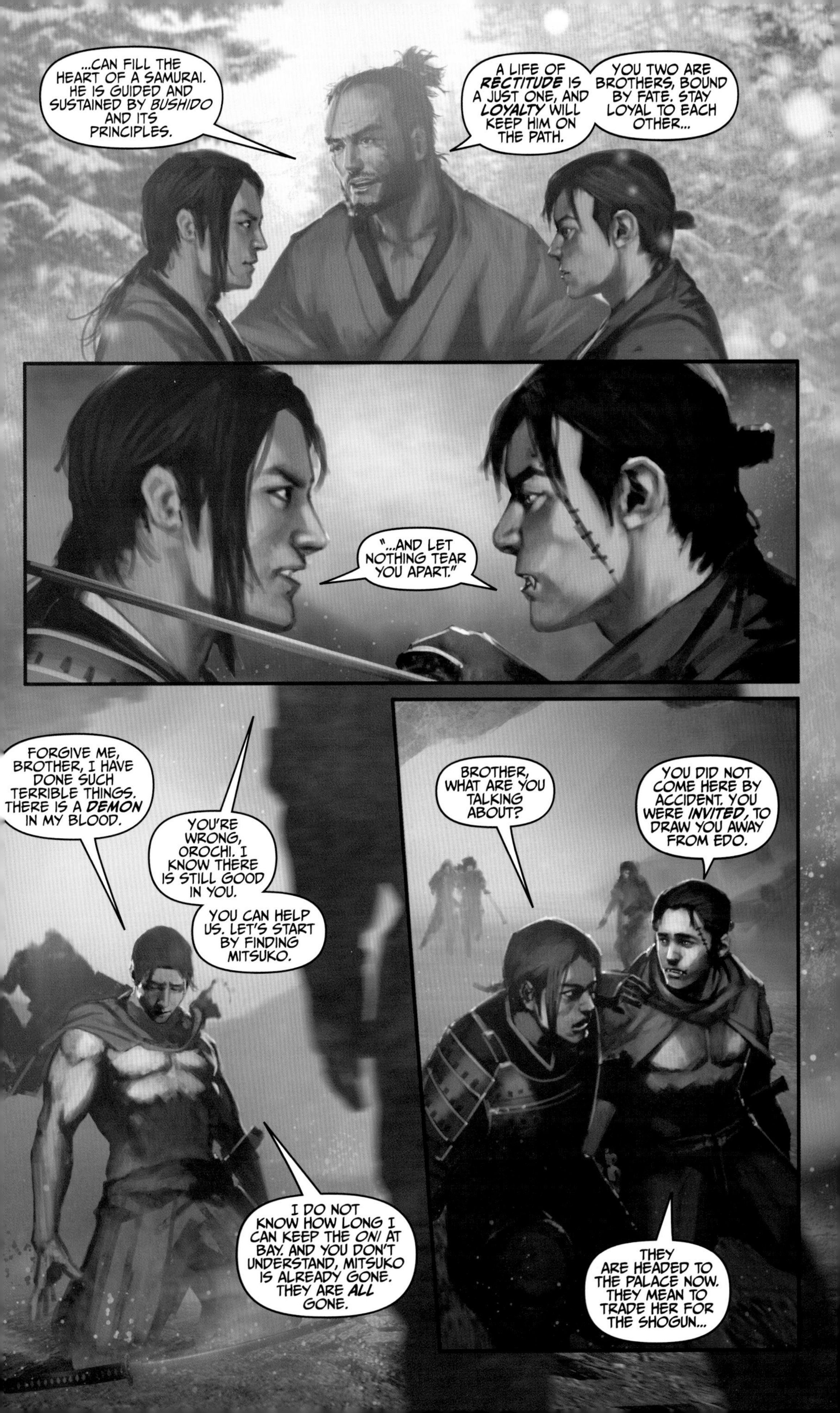
...CAN FILL THE HEART OF A SAMURAI. HE IS GUIDED AND SUSTAINED BY *BUSHIDO* AND ITS PRINCIPLES.
A LIFE OF ***RECTITUDE*** IS A JUST ONE, AND ***LOYALTY*** WILL KEEP HIM ON THE PATH.
YOU TWO ARE BROTHERS, BOUND BY FATE. STAY LOYAL TO EACH OTHER...
"...AND LET NOTHING TEAR YOU APART."
FORGIVE ME, BROTHER, I HAVE DONE SUCH TERRIBLE THINGS. THERE IS A ***DEMON*** IN MY BLOOD.
YOU'RE WRONG, OROCHI. I KNOW THERE IS STILL GOOD IN YOU.
YOU CAN HELP US. LET'S START BY FINDING MITSUKO.
I DO NOT KNOW HOW LONG I CAN KEEP THE *ONI* AT BAY. AND YOU DON'T UNDERSTAND, MITSUKO IS ALREADY GONE. THEY ARE ***ALL*** GONE.
BROTHER, WHAT ARE YOU TALKING ABOUT?
YOU DID NOT COME HERE BY ACCIDENT. YOU WERE ***INVITED***, TO DRAW YOU AWAY FROM EDO.
THEY ARE HEADED TO THE PALACE NOW. THEY MEAN TO TRADE HER FOR THE SHOGUN...

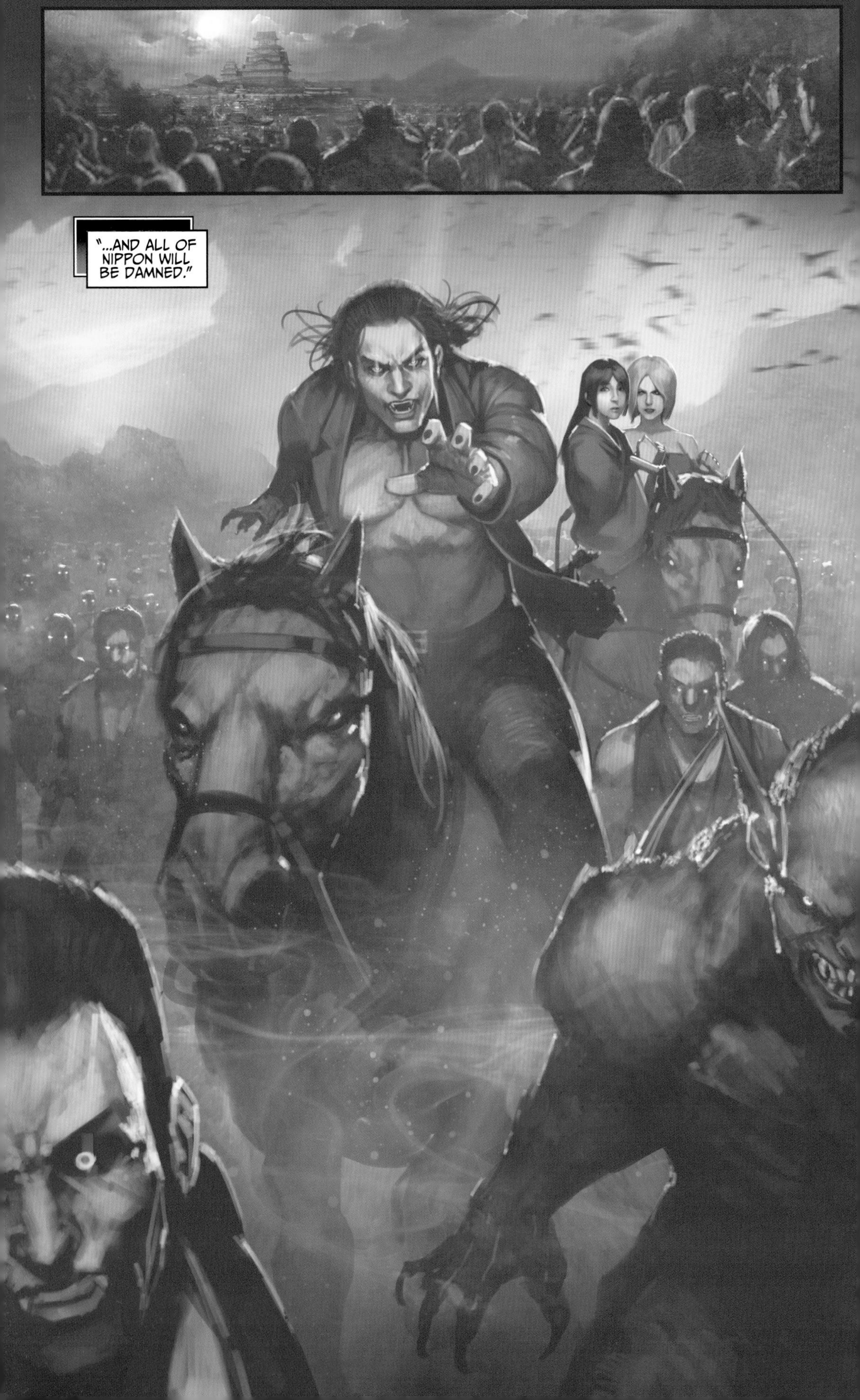
"...AND ALL OF NIPPON WILL BE DAMNED."

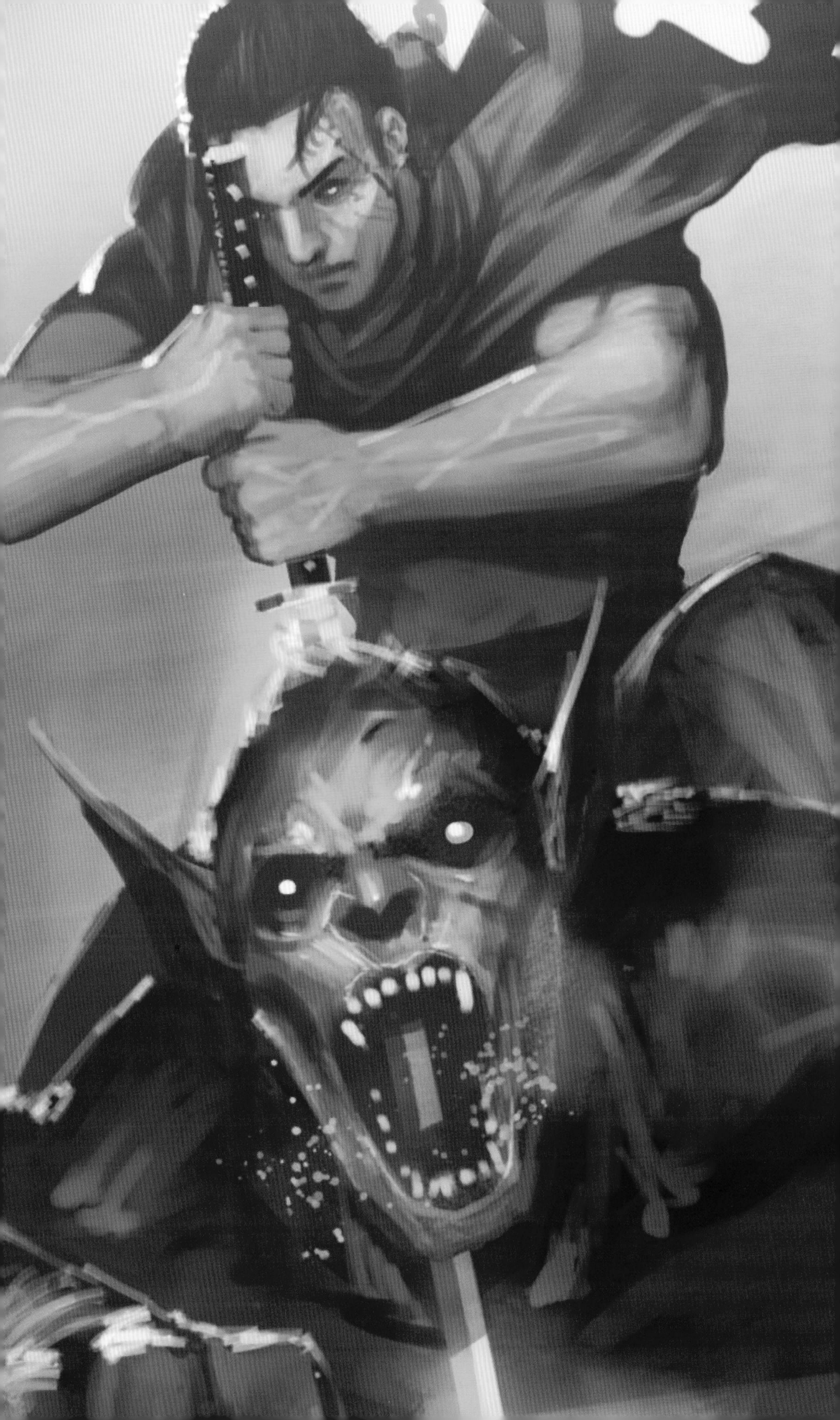

Chapter Five

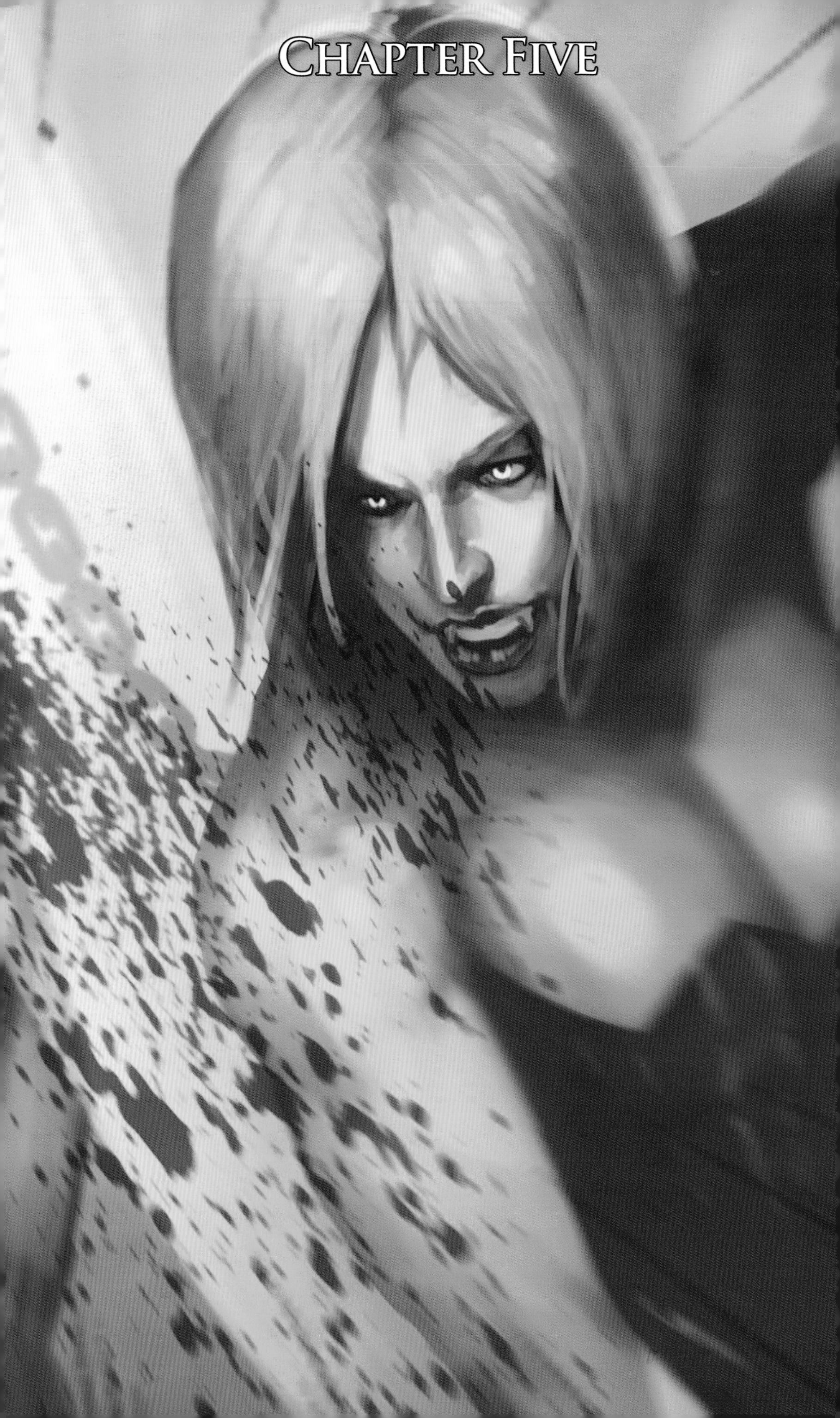

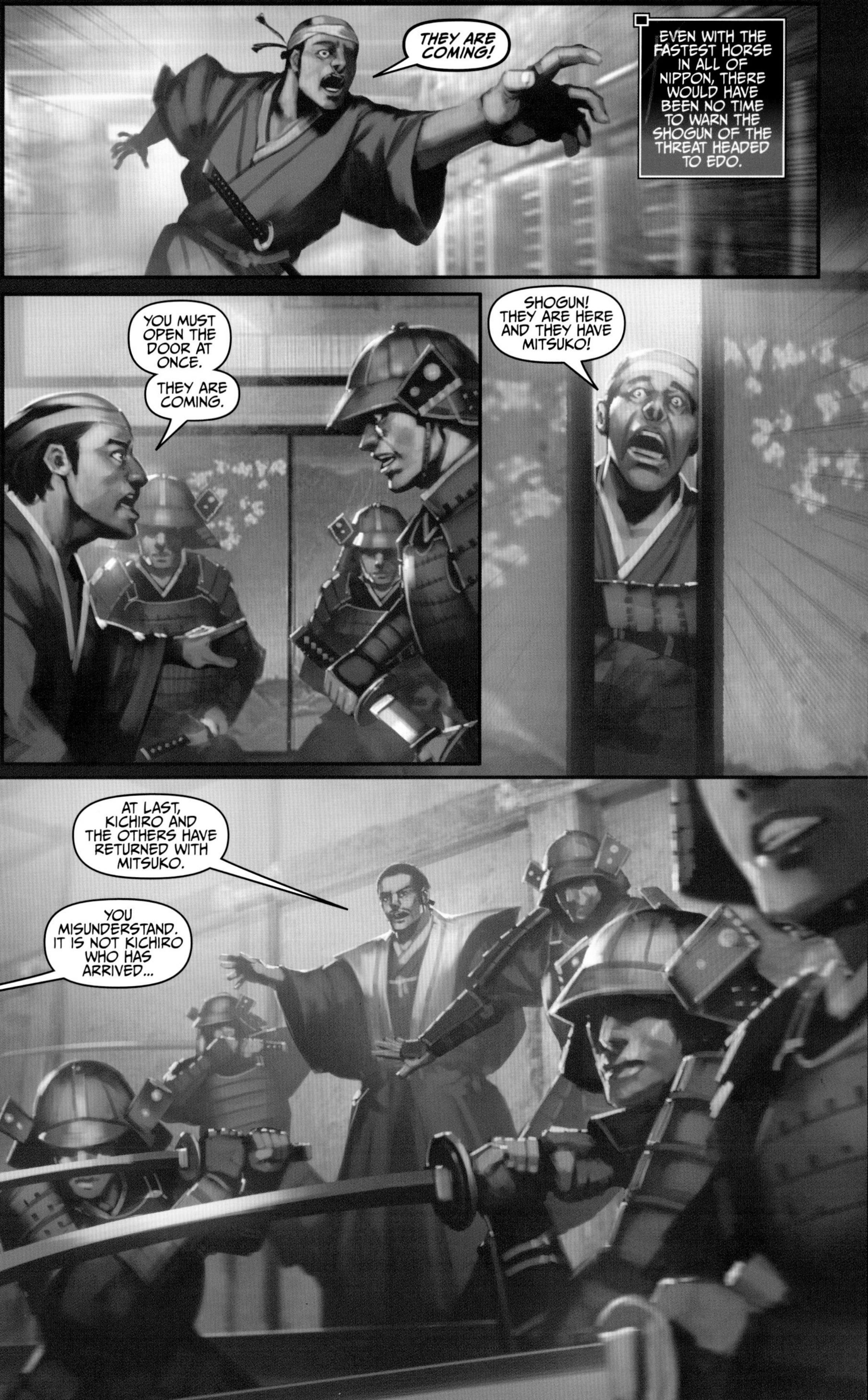
THEY ARE COMING!
EVEN WITH THE FASTEST HORSE IN ALL OF NIPPON, THERE WOULD HAVE BEEN NO TIME TO WARN THE SHOGUN OF THE THREAT HEADED TO EDO.
YOU MUST OPEN THE DOOR AT ONCE.
THEY ARE COMING.
SHOGUN! THEY ARE HERE AND THEY HAVE MITSUKO!
AT LAST, KICHIRO AND THE OTHERS HAVE RETURNED WITH MITSUKO.
YOU MISUNDERSTAND. IT IS NOT KICHIRO WHO HAS ARRIVED...

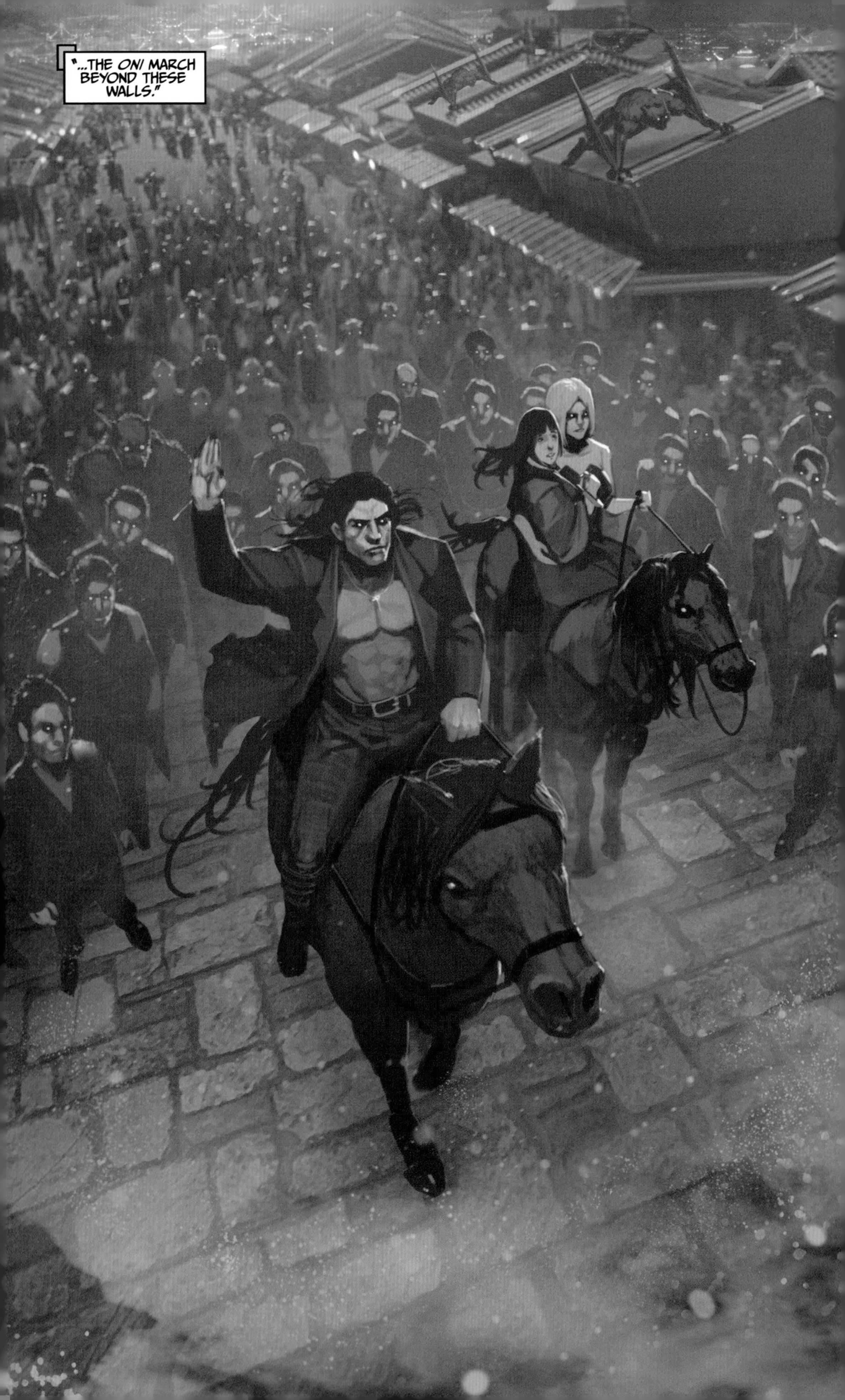
"...THE ONI MARCH BEYOND THESE WALLS."

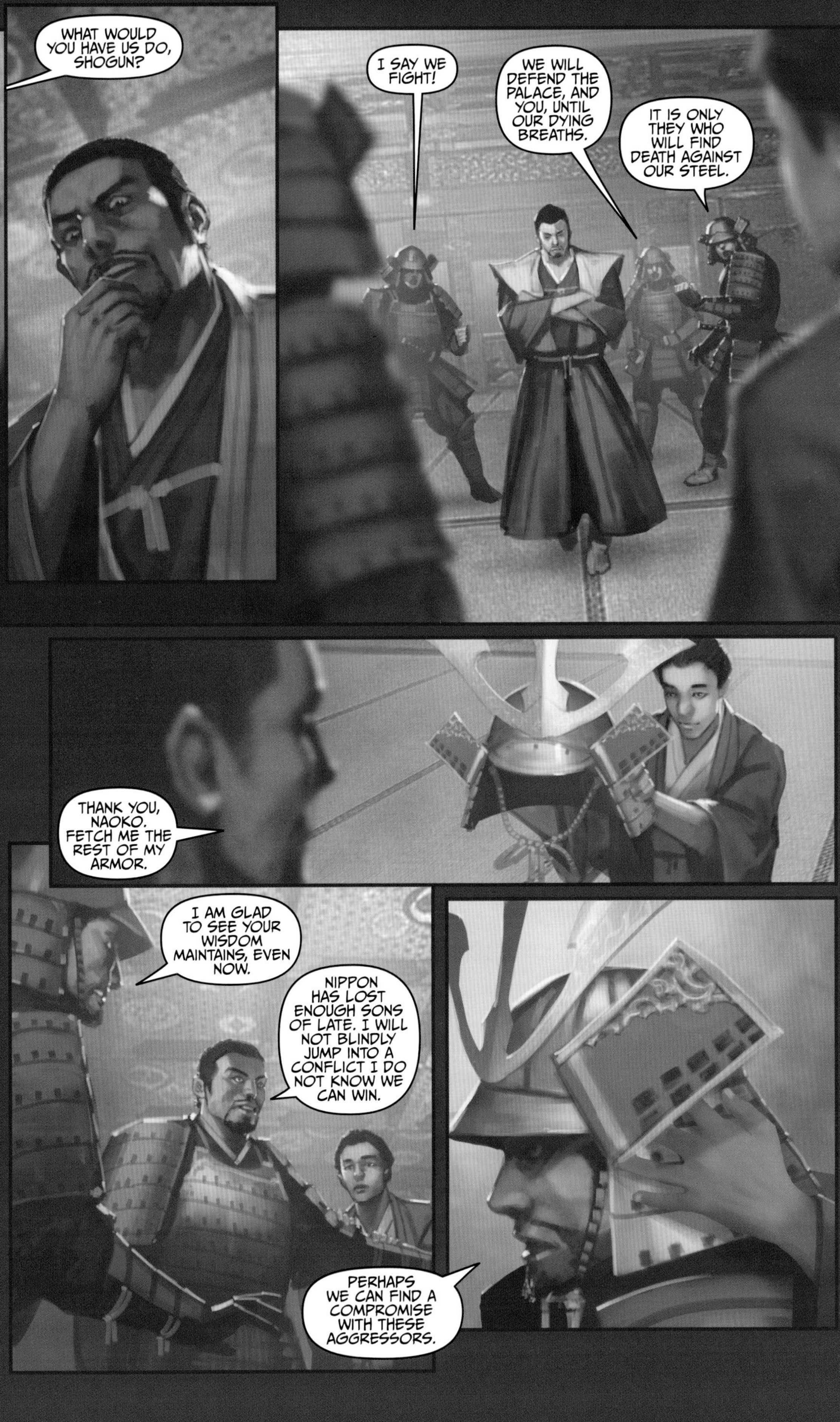
WHAT WOULD YOU HAVE US DO, SHOGUN?
I SAY WE FIGHT!
WE WILL DEFEND THE PALACE, AND YOU, UNTIL OUR DYING BREATHS.
IT IS ONLY THEY WHO WILL FIND DEATH AGAINST OUR STEEL.
THANK YOU, NAOKO. FETCH ME THE REST OF MY ARMOR.
I AM GLAD TO SEE YOUR WISDOM MAINTAINS, EVEN NOW.
NIPPON HAS LOST ENOUGH SONS OF LATE. I WILL NOT BLINDLY JUMP INTO A CONFLICT I DO NOT KNOW WE CAN WIN.
PERHAPS WE CAN FIND A COMPROMISE WITH THESE AGGRESSORS.